The Best of All Possible Worlds

The Best of All Possible Worlds

A STORY OF PHILOSOPHERS, GOD, AND EVIL

Steven Nadler

Farrar, Straus and Giroux

New York

Farrar, Straus and Giroux
18 West 18th Street, New York 10011

Distributed in Canada by Douglas & McIntyre Ltd.
Printed in the United States of America
First edition, 2008

Library of Congress Cataloging-in-Publication Data
Nadler, Steven M., 1958–
    The best of all possible worlds : a story of philosophers, God, and evil /
Steven Nadler. — 1st ed.
        p.   cm.
    Includes bibliographical references and index.
    ISBN-13: 978-0-374-22998-6 (hardcover : alk. paper)
    ISBN-10: 0-374-22998-8 (hardcover : alk. paper)
    1. Philosophy, Modern—17th century.   2. Good and evil.   3. God.
4. Leibniz, Gottfried Wilhelm, Freiherr von, 1646–1716.   5. Malebranche,
Nicolas, 1638–1715.   6. Arnauld, Antoine, 1612–1694.   I. Title.

B801.N33 2008
190.9'032—dc22

                                                                2008029143

Designed by Michelle McMillian

www.fsgbooks.com

1   3   5   7   9   10   8   6   4   2

Frontispiece: *Satan in Paradise, a scene from Milton's* Paradise Lost,
engraving by Gustave Dore, 1870

FOR RED,

TEACHER AND FRIEND

Contents

	Preface	*ix*
1.	Leibniz in Paris	3
2.	Philosophy on the Left Bank	23
3.	Le Grand Arnauld	52
4.	Theodicy	78
5.	The Kingdoms of Nature and Grace	108
6.	"Touch the Mountains and They Smoke"	141
7.	The Eternal Truths	184
8.	The Specter of Spinoza	217
	Epilogue	241
	Notes	*255*
	Bibliography	*281*
	Acknowledgments	*287*
	Index	*289*

Preface

The history of philosophy is punctuated by momentous and deservedly famous episodes. The trial and death of Socrates; Plato's coronation of the philosopher-kings in the *Republic*; Augustine's spiritual (and sexual) turmoil and subsequent epiphany, so eloquently captured in his *Confessions*; Aquinas's encyclopedic reconciliation of faith and reason in the *Summa Theologiae*; Descartes's formulation of the *cogito ergo sum* argument; and Kant's grand project of establishing once and for all the proper domain of metaphysics in the *Critique of Pure Reason*—to his mind, the philosophical equivalent of the Copernican revolution in astronomy—constitute only a few of philosophy's greatest hits.

This book is not about any such marquee event. It tells a story that involves neither global paradigm shifts nor revolutionary philosophical insights. It is not concerned with any discoveries that transformed the world, inventions that saved civilization, or confrontations that changed history. It is a relatively intimate and quiet story about three philosophers, onetime friends who, for a brief period, were together in Paris in the 1670s but soon went their separate ways, personally and philosophically. Much of the action takes place not in the academy or the salon, early modern French society's counterparts to the ancient Greek agora, but in books, articles, reviews, and letters. Sometimes, the conversation is direct and highly public; just as often, it is a virtual dialogue that must be reconstructed from private writings, marginalia, and viva voce comments that exist for us only because someone saw fit to record them.

It is a rich and fascinating moment in the history of ideas, one that involves perennial questions of philosophy about the world, human nature, morality, freedom, rationality, and, above all, God. Of the principal actors, only the brilliant philosopher, scientist, and mathematician Gottfried Wilhelm Leibniz is likely to be familiar to most readers today. But to their contemporaries, the Catholic priests Antoine Arnauld and Nicolas Malebranche were intellectual celebrities of the first order. These were the greatest philosophical and theological minds of their time, and their opinions and disputes were well known to much of the learned world of the seventeenth century.

The three thinkers differed vastly in personality and temperament, and so their relationships were full of drama. As their philosophical divergences became more obvious (and more irreconcilable) over the years, the grand debate in which they engaged—the subject of this book—grew in intensity, with insults and abuse (and an occasional apology) hurled across great distances both geographic and religious. There is much passion behind the philosophy, primarily because in this period, philosophical disagreements rarely failed to have theological, moral, political, and even salvational implications. These philosophers believed that the truths with which they were contending had ramifications not just for this world but for the hereafter as well.

In the seventeenth century, the problem of evil mattered. Philosophers and theologians wrestled with the question of how to reconcile the obvious fact that the world is full of sin and suffering with what for them was the nonnegotiable belief that the universe was created by an infinitely good, wise, all-powerful, and all-knowing God. But the problem of evil was only one battle in a much larger conflict. Behind it lay the even greater and more important challenge of getting the conception of God right: How does God act? With what faculties and capacities is He endowed? To what extent is His behavior, like ours, amenable to rational understanding? Can His ways be explained and justified? In this story, not just the problem of evil but practically every issue of metaphysics, natural philosophy (natural science), epistemology, ethics, and politics intersects with the fundamental question of how to represent the nature of God and of His agency. An early modern thinker's conception of God was of great consequence for his views on the origins and nature of the universe, the possibility of human knowledge, the objectivity of moral and aesthetic values, and the principles of justice.

Leibniz and Malebranche, adopting a traditional view, believed that God is, in many respects, very much like us: guided in His choices by rational deliberation and acting for the sake of what He (infallibly) believes to be good. Arnauld, taking a more radical course—one traced by his philosophical mentor, Descartes—argued that such anthropomorphism in the depiction of divine agency is dangerous to true Christian faith; God, he insisted, is not a rational "person," and no comparison can be drawn between the way God acts and the way we act. The God of Leibniz and Malebranche is endowed with practical reason; the God of Arnauld transcends reason altogether. One camp saw the universe as the product of wisdom and as embodying eternal, objective values of goodness and beauty; the other regarded all of creation, including every truth and every normative value, ultimately as the effect of an arbitrary, all-powerful will. Great stakes indeed.

This was the philosophical debate occupying center stage in the final quarter of the seventeenth century, a debate whose vehemence was fueled by religious differences, ecclesiastic rivalries, political developments, and even personal passions. Leibniz, Arnauld, and Malebranche are long dead, and their intellectual world has disappeared with the early modern social, religious, and political landscape that served as its backdrop. But the philosophical questions they confronted—Why is there something rather than nothing? Why is the world as it is, not just physically but morally as well? Why do bad things happen to good people? How can we make sense of suffering and human evil that often seem beyond comprehension?—puzzle us still.

The Best of All
Possible Worlds

Leibniz in Paris

In the early spring of 1672, a German secret agent arrived in Paris. He carried with him a plan that he and his patrons believed could pave the way to peace among nations and eventually return to Europe the religious unity that had been lost with the Protestant Reformation.

It was a grandiose project based on visionary hopes. Although the visit had been approved, even encouraged, by the French, the envoy was uncertain as to what kind of reception to expect. He was new to the diplomatic game and unfamiliar with the ministers with whom he hoped to meet. He must also have been forewarned by his superiors about the pitfalls of making alliances in the volatile political environment of the seventeenth century, and especially with as unpredictable and opportunistic a partner as France. What might be agreed to one day could easily be the forgotten victim of new alliances the next. With the possibility of difficult and protracted negotiations ahead, an extended stay in the city was arranged, and the agent settled into an apartment on the Left Bank. There was some urgency to his mission, however, as the great powers were once again on the brink of war.

For eighty years, from France's decades of civil turmoil in the sixteenth century through the falling out of the German states between 1618 and 1648—the so-called Thirty Years War—the continent had been wracked by incessant conflict. There were various causes for these hostilities, including domestic political crises; class struggle; territorial disputes; the clash between centralized power and local independence within the Holy Roman Empire (a vast domain extending west to east from France to Poland, and north to south from the Low Countries to the Italian states); and long-standing feuds involving the Empire, France, Spain, Denmark, Sweden, England, the Netherlands, and others. As mercenary armies marched across frontiers and waged their battles with little regard for collateral damage, civilian populations were decimated, crops were ravaged, and the social and economic upheaval made life utterly miserable. The medieval Western world of many small kingdoms, however competitive, violent, and unstable a place it may have been, had given way to the uncertainties of post-feudal society and to the more complicated and destructive rivalries within and among great nation-states.

Gone, too, was the general uniformity of faith that—despite schisms and heresies, as well as the occasional threat of unbelief—had long comforted medieval Europe in the face of violence, pestilence, and other evils. The wars of the late sixteenth and early seventeenth centuries were also, especially in France and Germany, religious wars, the sad legacy of the Reformation. In France, the majority Catholics battled Calvinist Huguenots—a vicious conflict that was only superficially (and momentarily) quieted by the Edict of Nantes in 1598, which granted religious and political rights to the Protestants. In the lands of the Holy Roman Empire, the tenuous unity among the three hundred member-states was undone by fighting among Catholic,

Lutheran, and Calvinist forces. The German troubles were exacerbated by outside meddling: when one side seemed about to prevail, sympathetic factions from elsewhere came to the aid of the other. Thus, in the 1630s, just as Catholic Bavaria and its Counter-Reformation allies were about to overwhelm the Lutheran territories of the north, French, Danish, and Swedish forces intervened on behalf of the Protestants.

Finally, with the land of Europe laid to waste and the warring parties drained of their resources, some degree of order was restored in 1648 with the signing of the Peace of Westphalia. This broad series of agreements was supposed to bring an end to the warfare and introduce lasting peace and stability to the continent. The treaty redrew political boundaries and established new religious ones. The German lands were now individual sovereign states, with each to determine its own official religion. (The Peace also thereby signaled the formal dissolution of the Holy Roman Empire.)

The respite, however, was only temporary, and over the intervening years dynastic rivalry, expansionist desire, and, above all, economic competition fueled a number of relatively short-lived but highly consequential conflicts, particularly among France, Spain, England, and the Netherlands. With the new year of 1672, the one-hundredth anniversary of the beginning of the hostilities that ended with the Peace,[1] Europe seemed destined to endure yet another century of fighting.

As in 1572, everyone's attention was once again focused on a strategically important and highly lucrative corridor of territory bordering the North Sea: the Low Countries, what is now Belgium, Luxembourg, and the Netherlands. The first time around, the attack had been led by Spain, which was seeking to keep rebellious provinces in line. The Hapsburgs, occupying the Spanish throne, inherited these properties of the French dukes of Burgundy in the mid-sixteenth century. But distant Catholic rule did not sit well with the local Calvinist population that dominated in the seven northernmost provinces, and by the early 1570s the revolt was in full force. Spain responded with a considerable show of strength, and the war lasted eighty years (concluding with the Treaty of Münster, part of the terms of the Peace of Westphalia).

This time, it was France that had made the first move. As one of the superpowers of the period, the Bourbon monarchy represented an effective counterweight to its Iberian Hapsburg archenemy. The aggressive and ever-acquisitive Louis XIV had long been covetous of the southern Low Countries, the Catholic provinces that remained loyal to Spain and were now called the Spanish Netherlands; he wanted to see them restored to French rule. Louis finally invaded Flanders and the other southern provinces in 1667. Then, in alliance with the prince-bishop of Cologne, the Elector of Münster, and the crown of England, the French king turned his sights on what was now the Dutch Republic, the Protestant provinces of the northern Netherlands that, having won their independence from Spain, were currently enjoying their Golden Age.

There were long-standing political and economic grievances between France and the United Provinces, including clashes over trade, territory, and alliances. It was also a classic confrontation between old and new, between Catholic and Protestant, and between royal absolutism and republicanism. While occasionally willing to side with Holland when it suited its geopolitical purposes—for example, in the Second Anglo-Dutch War, in 1665—the long-established French monarchy had little tolerance for the upstart Calvinist republic. It even actively sought to undermine the quasi-democratic federation of equal and independent provinces and replace it with a centralized government ruled by a kinglike figure, one who would serve France as a reliable and like-minded ally in the turbulent political mix of the period. As tensions increased, a number of attempts at a negotiated settlement between the two powers failed. Not one to wait for a diplomatic solution when a military one was at hand, Louis declared war on the Dutch in January 1672.

By the time the German emissary set off for Paris in late March on behalf of his employer, Johann Philipp von Schönborn, the Elector of Mainz, the French army had already crossed the Dutch border. Johann Philipp and other German princes, whose lands were still recovering from the devastation of the Thirty Years War, were worried that they might be next on Louis's agenda. The Elector took the advice of his minister of state, Baron Johann Christian von Boineberg, and sent his young privy counselor to France to see if the Sun King's attention could be turned to other, perhaps more enticing projects.

It was no ordinary diplomat whom the Elector and the baron entrusted with this delicate foreign mission. While inexperienced in foreign affairs and physically and socially awkward, he was gifted in many ways. The twenty-six-year-old man on his way to the French capital was a philosopher-scientist-mathematician of great promise, an individual destined to become a major player in Europe's intellectual life in the seventeenth century. He was, in fact, one of the great geniuses of all time.

Gottfried Wilhelm Leibniz was born on July 1, 1646, in the Lutheran town of Leipzig, part of Saxony. His father, Friedrich, was vice chairman of the philosophy faculty and a professor of moral philosophy at the University of Leipzig. His mother, Catharina Schmuck, was Friedrich's third wife.[2]

Leibniz studied liberal arts at the University of Leipzig and earned his bachelor's degree in 1663 with a dissertation titled *A Metaphysical Disputation on the Principle of Individuation*. Despite his talents for abstract philosophical thinking, he decided on a career in law. After a summer studying mathematics at the University of Jena, he returned to Leipzig to pursue his degrees in jurisprudence. Although Leibniz received the bachelor's degree, the university refused to grant him a doctoral degree, which was required for admission to the university's faculty. The problem had nothing to do with the merit of Leibniz's work but everything to do with professional rivalries and probably some personal grievances against him. Academia in Leipzig was a highly competitive enterprise, and it seems that more senior candidates for the doctorate conspired to marginalize younger, albeit equally deserving candidates, including Leibniz. There is some reason to believe, moreover, that the wife of the dean of the law faculty took a dislike to Leibniz and influenced her husband against him.[3] Leibniz was deeply stung, but possessed of a restless energy, he did not dwell on the affair. He saw that his future lay elsewhere and simply took his dissertation and moved to the University of Altdorf, where he was awarded a doctorate in jurisprudence in 1666.

By this time, Leibniz realized that he was, after all, not so interested in a university career in a law faculty. He believed that he could pursue his political, legal, and scientific schemes more effectively outside a formal academic setting. He thus turned down the offer of a professorship at the University of Nuremberg and, through the patronage of Baron von Boineberg (whose acquaintance he probably made through an alchemical society to which they both belonged), soon entered the service of Boineberg's once and future employer, the Elector of Mainz. By 1668, Leibniz, while not yet a resident at the court, was already laboring on revisions to Mainz's legal code. In 1670, he and Boineberg moved to Mainz, where Leibniz took up an appointment as the powerful Elector's privy counselor of justice and served on the state's high court of appeals. During this period, he also put in time as Boineberg's personal secretary, librarian, and policy adviser, undertaking for the baron a variety of legal, political, diplomatic, and literary projects. These included cataloguing Boineberg's library and composing arguments to help settle the question (satisfactory to the interests of the Elector and his allies) of succession to the Polish throne, which had recently become vacant after King Johann Casmir's abdication.

It is not enough to say that Leibniz was a man of many interests. He was always thinking and acting well beyond the official jurisprudential and political duties of his position, and his extraordinary intellect knew practically no bounds. He lived by Terence's famous saying *humani nil a me alienum puto* ("I consider nothing pertaining to human affairs outside my domain"). Leibniz was a true polymath, and by the end of his long life he had made substantial and lasting contributions to the fields of philosophy (including metaphysics, logic, ethics, and epistemology), law, politics, mathematics, natural science, linguistics, theology, history, Bible criticism, and even engineering and technology. Both an accomplished scholar and a highly original thinker in his own right, he was a *devoté* of the new but not without a profound respect for the old. He sought, for example, to reconcile the progressive scientific ideas of his contemporaries (such as Galileo, Descartes, and Huygens) with the ancient metaphysical insights of Plato and Aristotle.

During his years in Mainz, Leibniz began work on what he called his "universal characteristic," a so-called "alphabet of human thought." This was a profoundly ambitious scheme for reducing all ideas and reasoning to a single, perspicuous symbolic system. Later in life, he referred to this project as his "universal symbolism . . . in which all truths of reason would be reduced to a kind of calculus."[4] The all-encompassing language and method would eliminate the many sources of confusion and error that he believed derive from our imprecise everyday language, and thus would allow us to achieve the highest degree of certainty in thinking and efficiency in philosophical communication. In this period, Leibniz also started developing his ideas in physics. In 1671, he published his *New Physical Hypothesis*. This treatise is composed of two essays, the "Abstract Theory of Motion" (which he dedicated to the Académie des Sciences, in Paris) and the "Concrete Theory of Motion" (dedicated to the Royal Society, in London). In these and other scientific and metaphysical writings, Leibniz addresses a wide variety of questions, including the nature of matter, mind, and motion; the fundamental principles governing the collision of bodies; and—something that would occupy him throughout his career—the problem of the continuum, or the generation of a continuous quantity from discontinuous units (such as a line from points, continuous motion from discrete movements, and time from moments). He also wrote on jurisprudential and religious themes (including the immortality of the soul and the resurrection of the body) and on political matters. He even published (anonymously) a satire on Louis XIV and his militaristic ambitions, *The Most Christian Mars*, in which he mockingly "justifies" the French king's aggressive behavior toward his European neighbors by explaining that since the Flemish, Dutch, and German lands lay between France and "the Turks," Louis has first to pass through the lands of these "poor Christians" before attacking the enemy to the east.[5]

Leibniz began by far the greatest and most ambitious of his projects in this period, one that would assume immense significance and consume much energy throughout his life: his self-appointed mission to heal the schism at the heart of Western Christianity. He believed that the issues that divided Catholics and Protestants in Europe at the time were not so insuperable that some common ground could not be found. Much of the problem, he insisted, lay not in basic dogma but in the particular, nonessential beliefs and customs that had developed within each tradition. "Most of the objections that can be made against Rome regard the practice of the people rather than the dogmas," he wrote in 1682.[6] If only one could discover and properly interpret the core beliefs that unite all Christians—and distill them from the layers of ecclesiastic organization, ceremonial observance, and sectarian understanding within which they had become encrusted—there would be a possibility of reuniting the faithful within a single church. Leibniz would begin his reasoning with the Catholics and Lutherans in the German lands, but his hopes extended to a reconciliation throughout all of European Christendom.

It is probably no accident that many of Leibniz's patrons were former Protestants who had converted to Catholicism: Johann Philipp; Baron von Boineberg; the duke of Hanover, Johann Friedrich von

Braunschweig–Lüneburg, whom Leibniz would serve after his Paris sojourn; and Ernst von Hessen-Rheinfels, who in the 1680s played essentially the same role in Leibniz's life as Boineberg does in the pre-Paris period. While Leibniz himself remained a Lutheran throughout his life (although it is unclear how deeply he held his religious beliefs), his discussions and plans with these Catholic authority figures stimulated and sustained his commitment to a grand ecumenical project.

Leibniz believed that with little difficulty, Lutherans could approve the substance of much of what had been proclaimed by the Catholic Church's Council of Trent. Meeting from 1545 to 1563, and acting in response to the threat posed by the Protestant Reformation, this ecumenical body was charged with specifying those doctrines of salvation, sacramental theology, and canon law that constitute the core and non-negotiable principles of Christianity; it also sought to standardize the practice of the Latin Mass, into whose celebration many modifications had been introduced over time. If there were any controversial or ambiguous claims about grace, penitence, justification, or other mysteries arising from the council's deliberations, Leibniz insisted, they could easily be reinterpreted in a way consistent with both Catholic dogma and the principles of the Confession of Augsburg of 1530, which established the articles of faith for Lutherans.

It was an extremely optimistic, even utopian perspective to take. The divide between Roman Catholicism and Lutheranism seemed unbridgeable on many central points. Where the Catholics allowed for salvation through good works, the Lutherans insisted on justification through faith alone. Moreover, Lutherans believed that a human being was completely passive under the influence of grace, while the Council of Trent explicitly condemned this opinion. But Leibniz was nothing if not an optimist. Thus, in the late 1660s and early 1670s, while still at the court in Mainz, and at the urging of the Catholic Boineberg, he began composing a number of theological and religious works devoted not just to refuting atheists and materialists but also to showing that there is room for essential doctrinal agreement between Catholics and Protestants. He hoped to win approval from the Pope for his philosophically informed but (from Rome's point of view) rather unorthodox interpretations of various Christian dogma, especially those concerning the Eucharist. In writings later collected as the *Catholic Demonstrations*, Leibniz argued for the existence of God and for the immateriality and, consequently, the immortality of the soul. He then showed how the miraculous transubstantiation of the wine and bread into the blood and body of Christ at the moment of consecration could be understood in a way that was both acceptable to Protestants (who rejected transubstantiation, the standard Catholic idea that the substance of the bread is destroyed or removed and replaced with the substance of Christ's body during the Eucharist, albeit underneath the freestanding sensory appearance of bread) and consistent with the Council of Trent's demand that there be a "real presence" of Christ in the host.[7]

Throughout Leibniz's career, much of what he says about God, freedom, grace, and evil—including his claim that ours is the best of all possible worlds—relates to this grand unification project. His choice of correspondents, the content and tenor of his writings, even his residence and travels were often dictated by the interfaith dialogue he sought to initiate and the religious reconciliation he hoped eventually to accomplish.

Mainz was a small town. Despite the presence of the court of the Elector, it was not cosmopolitan enough for a man of Leibniz's ambitions. His gaze, like that of many intellectuals of the time, was directed to the cultural and intellectual capital of Europe: Paris.

Leibniz followed events on the French intellectual scene closely. He sought correspondents in Paris who could enlighten him on current events, recent publications, and the activities of philosophical and scientific societies. Above all, he had a keen interest in what was happening at the Académie des Sciences. He aspired one day to belong to this young but august body, and the dedication of his "Abstract Theory of Motion" to the Académie was no doubt a ploy to gain its favor. To Leibniz, Paris was "the most knowledgeable and powerful city in the universe."[8] If there was to be any hope of advancing his scientific, mathematical, and philosophical interests, not to mention realizing his dream of ecumenical unity, he would have to find a way to get there.

The opportunity finally arrived with the French invasion of the Netherlands. Even before the attack on the Dutch Republic, Leibniz had been pondering how the German states should deal with the growing French threat. He believed that the best defense would be to send Louis XIV's army on a detour. This would require convincing the king that his real interests lay elsewhere, away from the German lands and from Christian territory altogether.

What Leibniz had in mind was a new crusade against the infidel. This time, however, the target would be not Jerusalem but Egypt. A conquest of that ancient land would benefit not only France, Leibniz intended to argue, but all of Europe. It would bring intramural peace among the Western powers and allow the Christian states to band together and strengthen their defenses against the ever-present Muslim threat from the east, especially the Turks.

Boineberg was very enthusiastic about Leibniz's *Consilium Aegyptiacum*, and he was soon able to enlist the Elector's support for it. He had Leibniz draft a memorandum for the French king that outlined the plan and highlighted its advantages both for France itself—much more effectively than an open war, a successful Egyptian campaign would weaken the Dutch military and economy and render the French "masters of the seas"—and, more momentously, for "the well-being of all humankind."[9] It was a fantastical project—"a bit chimerical," as Boineberg puts it in his cover letter to the French king—but it was, Boineberg thought, the Electorate's best hope.

The French foreign minister, Simon Arnauld de Pomponne, was initially intrigued by the proposition, although he thought that its execution would demand more detail. He discussed the matter with the king, and in a letter of February 1672 he encouraged Boineberg or a representative to come to Paris to present the plan formally.

Boineberg knew that the mission had to be a secret one, lest the Dutch get word of it. He also suggested to Pomponne that it would be best if the author of the project himself came to lead the discussions with the French. Thus, in March 1672, Leibniz was on his way to Paris. In his bag was his "Plan for a New Holy War."

The Paris that greeted Leibniz was not yet Baron von Hausmann's city of grand boulevards. But neither was it any longer the walled medieval town that it had been up through the sixteenth century. In fact, just a few years before Leibniz's French sojourn, the king and his powerful finance minister, Jean-Baptiste Colbert, had decided to remake the city into a modern metropolis. They began by tearing down the medieval ramparts that encased the northern and southern sections of the city—then, as now, divided into Left and Right banks by the River Seine—and replacing them with tree-lined thoroughfares. This allowed the city to flow seamlessly into the *faubourgs*, or outlying residential areas. They also initiated a campaign of monumental architecture in the classical style: grand public buildings, triumphal arches, commemorative statues, and open public squares. The landmark structures of the Collège des Quatre-Nations, Les Invalides, the Observatoire, and the Gobelins all date from this period.[10] In all, Louis and his minister spent over twenty million *livres* on architecture and landscaping for Paris, much of it on the Louvre and the adjacent Tuilleries, despite the fact that the king himself did not much care for the city and far preferred his new and still-expanding home at Versailles. (He decamped from the Louvre, the royal palace adjacent to the river on the Right Bank, in February of 1670, never again to spend another night there; by 1683, the entire court had moved to Versailles, at a great inconvenience to those who still had to carry out their business in Paris, more than ten miles away.) The result of all this construction was a much more open and navigable city, less dense in its housing and less congested on its byways than the medieval version.

This was the time when Paris became known as the City of Lights, mainly because of the great increase in the number of streetlamps keeping the city illuminated at night. This modern feature—along with broader streets and renovated bridges—allowed for safer passage of the city's thousands of horse-drawn carriages, a relatively recent addition to its transportation system. These luxurious vehicles took their fashionable owners to the city's cultural riches—to the theater at the Palais Royale, where one could enjoy the latest comedy by Molière or tragedy by Racine, or to the recently built opera house, where one could hear the premiere of a new work by Jean-Baptiste Lully, the king's official *compositeur de la musique instrumentale*. Colbert's Paris was an elegant, technologically progressive, cosmopolitan, and aristocratic place. It was also, like any city of its size at that time, poor, dirty, malodorous, and often dangerous.

The royal administration was not only concerned with giving the city a new façade. Following the model of earlier governments, and especially that of Cardinal Richelieu, Colbert and his team also sought to renovate the soul of the city and refine its creative and intellectual life. While Richelieu established the Académie Française in 1635, and the young Louis XIV (at the urging of Charles Le Brun, the official court painter) founded the Académie Royale de Peinture et de Sculpture in 1648, Colbert gave the king's moral and financial support to the Académie des Sciences, officially founded in 1666, as well as to an Académie des Inscriptions et Belles-Lettres (1663) and an Académie Royale d'Architecture (1671). With these institutions in place, Paris quickly became the place to be for anybody in the arts, letters, or sciences.

Leibniz landed in this remade Paris, Europe's undisputed arbiter of culture, ideas, and taste, on March 31, 1672. He had in hand a letter of introduction from Boineberg to Arnauld de Pomponne. Boineberg praised Leibniz's "fine qualities," and described him as "a man who, while his appearance may not suggest it, can very well carry out what he promises."[11] Boineberg admired his protégé—he later referred to Leibniz as "an inexhaustible treasury of all the most wonderful sciences that a solid mind is capable of mastering"[12]—but as Boineberg's letter suggests, Leibniz did not look the part of a diplomat. He was short and gangly, with a prominent nose overshadowing a thin mouth. His large head was made to seem even larger by an oversize wig, and his gait was anything but graceful. He was impatient with formal etiquette and uncomfortable with the banalities demanded by polite company. By his own admission, he did "not make a very good first impression." Despite all this, he was quite a sociable man who enjoyed good conversation and entertainments—something his success as a courtier would depend on, no matter how ill-suited he may have appeared for the job.

After announcing his presence to Pomponne and thereby discharging himself of his first official order of business, Leibniz wasted no time as he waited for a response from the French court. He was finally in Paris and took full advantage of all the city had to offer. Where he lived upon his first arriving is unknown. It may have been in a community of expatriate Germans in the Hôtel des Romains on the rue Ste.-Marguerite. But by May 1673, he was settled in lodgings in the St.-Germain neighborhood on the Left Bank (what is today the Sixth Arrondissement), on the rue Garancière, just behind the church of St.-Sulpice and around the corner from the Luxembourg Palace. The location was perfect. It was a short walk to the academic world of university faculties and the nearby *collèges*, the Quartier Latin (so called because of the language of instruction), and not far from the French administrative and diplomatic heart on the Île de la Cité and at the Louvre. It also offered convenient access to Paris's cultural offerings.

Leibniz often went to the theater, once catching a performance of one of Corneille's works, and was a great admirer of opera as well.

Upon his arrival, he immediately started taking French lessons. While working in Mainz for the Elector, he must have had some familiarity with French, if only a basic reading knowledge. But he needed to be fluent and idiomatic in the language that was becoming, along with Latin, the lingua franca of the international Republic of Letters. (By the end of his stay, Leibniz said that he had come to "speak in Parisian."[13]) He also studied Greek, with Pierre-Daniel Huet, at that time an assistant tutor to the Dauphin, later the bishop of Arranches and a major figure on the French philosophical and theological scene.

Leibniz also made the rounds of Paris's scientific and philosophical community and sought out the savants who could be of service to his intellectual plans. "Paris is a place where it is difficult to distinguish oneself," he wrote. "One finds here the most expert men of our time, in every kind of science, and it would take a lot of work and a bit of fortitude to make a name for oneself here."[14] The city, he says in a letter to his friend Louis Ferrand soon after his arrival, "is paved with so many learned people," and he regretted the amount of time he had to spend on his official business. "I am reduced to a voluntary hermetic existence, speaking practically to no one aside from two laborers, in the midst of so many great men."[15] Still, life in Paris was not all diplomatic drudgery for Leibniz: when not engaged in what he called *mon affaire*, he attended meetings of the Académie des Sciences in the king's library and mingled with its international cohort of mathematicians, physicists, and astronomers, including Giovanni Cassini, the discoverer of Jupiter's spot and of the gap in Saturn's rings; Otto de Guericke, a fellow alumnus of the University of Leipzig; the Danish astronomer Olaus Roemer; and Claude Perrault, a French doctor and physicist.

In terms of his own development, the most important acquaintance that Leibniz made in Paris was the Dutch scientist and mathematician Christiaan Huygens. Huygens had been in Paris since 1666, brought there by Colbert himself to create the Académie des Sciences. Leibniz had extraordinary natural mathematical talent but was still a relative novice in the discipline. Neglecting for a time his other interests, especially those for which he needed more advanced mathematical training, he worked closely with Huygens, supplementing those lessons by reading the mathematical papers of Blaise Pascal, and quickly gained a solid reputation as a mathematician. "I am attending here neither to jurisprudence, nor to belles lettres, nor to controversies (things that principally occupied me in Germany), and instead I have begun basic studies to understand mathematics, in which I have had the good fortune to discover thoroughly unfamiliar truths, as letters from the most skilled mathematicians of our time will attest."[16] Good fortune indeed: by the end of Leibniz's four-year stay in Paris, he had invented the calculus.

Leibniz hardly ignored his other philosophical and scientific concerns while in Paris. His writings from this period cover a range of issues in metaphysics, physics, logic, and philosophical theology, many of which continue the lines of thought he had been pursuing while still in Mainz. In his papers between 1672 and 1676, there is more work on the problem of the continuum in a variety of domains, as well as essays on the cohesion of bodies, the nature of the soul, the cause of motion, the relationship between mind and body, and "the existence of a most perfect being." Since 1669, Leibniz had also been concerned with a reconciliation between the new mathematical science of nature—devoted to clearly formulated, quantifiable mechanistic explanations of phenomena—and some of the metaphysical principles of the ancients, especially the dynamic role that, in the Aristotelian philosophy, immaterial entities (such as minds or souls) play in the world of bodies.[17] Moreover, this period marked the beginning of his long-term concern with the problem of evil and his idea that ours is the best of all possible worlds. Nonetheless—and this is an indication of Leibniz's prodigious intellectual energy—as much attention as all of these other questions received, they often took a backseat at this time to his mathematical education.

During his Paris period, Leibniz also made a short voyage to England, in early 1673. There he attended meetings of the Royal Society and made the acquaintance of England's own leading scientists, including Henry Oldenburg, Robert Boyle, and the irascible Robert Hooke—but not, notably, Isaac Newton, with whom Leibniz would soon engage in a priority dispute over the invention of the calculus. Oldenburg, the Society's corresponding secretary, arranged for Leibniz to give a demonstration of the arithmetical calculating machine that he had been working on in Paris. The event was not entirely successful, as Leibniz had some trouble getting the machine to work properly, but that did not prevent the Society from unanimously electing him a fellow in April of that year.

He did not have as much luck with his French scientific colleagues. Despite Leibniz's growing reputation and the evident admiration for him among many of his peers—"Never has a foreigner . . . had a more favorable reception from the people of merit," he wrote in 1672[18]—there was solid resistance to admitting this young German to the king's official body of learned gentlemen. In 1675, Leibniz's nomination for membership to the Académie des Sciences was rejected. The fact that he was not a Catholic did not help his cause. Leibniz, however, believed that his nationality was the true reason for his rejection. He suspected that some of the academicians felt that there were already enough foreign members in the organization. He also blamed the matter on personal animus, as he had the disappointment he experienced at the University of Leipzig; in this case, it was envy over his talents and accomplishments. He did not receive the honor until 1700.

This slight did little to deflate Leibniz's high opinion of himself. While he was capable of self-deprecation before his social superiors, particularly those with whom he wished to ingratiate himself (often for the purpose of financial gain), he was also given, on occasion, to exaggeration. In a letter of 1675, with only a handful of publications to his name, he nonetheless describes "the renown that I have acquired in the courts of Princes and among a good part of the learned and illustrious of Europe."[19] Leibniz had a robust sense of his own innate talents and a clear idea of what he could, if properly supported, contribute to the good of humankind. Fortunately, his grandiose self-assessment turned out to be correct.

In the end, the Egyptian plan never got very far. It is unclear whether the French king ever gave it a formal hearing; Leibniz certainly never had the chance to present it to Louis directly, and may never even have seen the foreign minister, Pomponne, with whom he had some difficulty arranging a meeting. Besides, with France already in control of a large portion of Dutch territory, an important element of the project was moot (although Leibniz continued to revise the plan to keep it up with current events). Moreover, despite his initial interest in the project, Pomponne soon dismissed the whole idea as ridiculous and anachronistic. As early as June 1672, he declared that "holy wars . . . have been out of fashion since Saint Louis."[20] (Louis IX had died in 1270.)

Leibniz was sorely disappointed. While the Egyptian project was a convenient excuse for an extended stay in Paris, he took it very seriously; it was something he had long worked on and in which he had placed great hope. Still, there were other business matters to attend to. One of Boineberg's other motives in sending his secretary to France was to have Leibniz take care of some of his financial interests there, including the collection of back rents he was owed on several properties. And in November 1672, Boineberg's son, Philipp Wilhelm, arrived in Paris to be tutored by Leibniz. It was not an easy job—Leibniz set up a very demanding daily schedule, but the young man had other things on his mind besides book learning—and Leibniz would soon chafe under these duties.

Then, in December of that year, devastating news arrived. Baron von Boineberg was dead from a stroke. Leibniz was deeply affected by the loss. He called Boineberg "one of the great men of the century," and regarded him not only as his employer but also as a close friend.[21] Boineberg's death was followed just a few months later by the death of their mutual employer, Johann Philipp. With his two patrons gone, Leibniz now was in danger of being cast adrift. While these deaths meant there was less pressure to return soon to Mainz, they also represented the possibility of losing the moral and financial support that would allow him to remain in Paris. Fortunately, the new Elector, Lothar Friedrich von Metternich, saw the advantage of having an agent in the French capital, and he agreed to allow Leibniz to continue on as a kind of cultural attaché who would report back on scientific and artistic matters.[22]

Leibniz loved Paris. He had arrived with enormous expectations, and the city exceeded all of them. It was an exciting environment for him, both intellectually and socially, and his experience there played a crucial role in his philosophical development and in his reputation in the world of ideas. He also enjoyed himself immensely in the French capital and was reluctant to leave. Always seeking to improve his financial condition, Leibniz nevertheless turned down a number of potentially lucrative offers while in Paris—including the positions of secretary to the chief minister of the king of Denmark and counselor to Johann Friedrich, duke of Hanover. Although he had been dismissed as Philipp Wilhelm's tutor by the Boineberg family in September 1674 and his relationship with the family had slowly deteriorated after the baron's death, Leibniz had means enough to linger in Paris for over a year. Eventually, however, he had to face economic reality. In late 1675, in need of a secure position with a guaranteed salary, he agreed at last to serve Johann Friedrich as counselor and director of the ducal library in Hanover. He was supposed to be on duty by January 1676, but succeeded in putting off his departure from Paris—and in testing the duke's patience—for months. Finally, in October, he saw that he could delay no more and took his leave of Paris, never to return.

I t is unclear how much of Leibniz's mature philosophy, as appears in his writings from the late 1680s on, was developed during his Paris years.[23] It is certain that a number of central elements of his later thought—metaphysical theses about minds, bodies, and nature; theological theses about God; and moral theses about happiness and human well-being—were already in place at the time. Leibniz may not yet have arrived at his famous "monadology" or mysterious "preestablished harmony"; he was still seeking the ultimate metaphysical truth about the world, unsure about what was really real in things and their relationships. But he had already come to the firm conclusion that, despite the evil and sin that we see around us, regardless of how much suffering and imperfection we encounter, this world of ours is, among all the possible worlds that God could have created, the absolute best—and that God created it for just that reason. It was also in Paris that Leibniz was able, for the first time, to test this cornerstone of his philosophical legacy, for he encountered there a number of philosophers deeply involved in thinking about these very same issues. Some of them challenged his way of thinking about God and evil, and others provided him with tools for precisely formulating his ideas.

2

Philosophy on the Left Bank

A t the end of the rue St.-Jacques, past the Sorbonne and through the intersection with the Boulevard St.-Germain, just where the street reaches the Seine, there is a small bridge. The bridge is called the Petit Pont, and it connects the Left Bank with the Île de la Cité. On the island just on the other side of the bridge is the gothic cathedral of Nôtre Dame and its large plaza.

It is a nondescript bridge, nothing like the magnificent Pont Neuf that runs all the way across the narrower west end of the island and over to the Right Bank. It is, though, probably the oldest bridge in Paris. It was originally constructed of wood sometime during the Roman occupation of Gaul, and it has been rebuilt many times. Not until 1186 was it transformed into a stone structure; the last reconstruction was in 1853. The bridge is just over thirty meters long, crossing the narrowest channel of the river in the city.

Despite its modest appearance, the Petit Pont holds an exalted place in the intellectual history of Paris. Before the founding of the University of Paris in 1215, before the endowment of the *collèges*, just as the cathedral schools were becoming great centers of learning, it was on this bridge that philosophy first found a home in the city. Here Peter Abelard and other masters associated with the school of Nôtre Dame, as well as itinerant logicians and metaphysicians, held forth *en pleine air*, lecturing students and overseeing disputations. These were highly public, often raucous exercises, and anyone was free to listen or engage the master in argument. There was even a quasi-formal school of philosophy associated with the bridge, led by Adam of Balsham, an Englishman also known as Adam Parvipontanus, or Adam du Petit Pont.

Over four centuries later, the Petit Pont was a ten-minute walk from Leibniz's lodgings behind the church of St.-Sulpice. He would have traversed it many times in his relentless quest to meet with Arnauld de Pomponne and other ministers to convince them of the virtues of the Egyptian plan. By 1672, however, philosophy in Paris had long been an indoor activity, practiced mainly in the arts and theology faculties of the university, as well as in the liberal arts curricula of the *collèges de pleine exercise*, preparatory schools for university often associated with one religious order or another (such as the Jesuits). In the official degree-granting institutions and their associated schools, philosophy was exclusively a clerical affair; the learned doctors and masters of the faculties had to have taken ecclesiastic vows.

It was also, for the most part, an Aristotelian affair. Teaching in logic, natural philosophy (including physics), moral philosophy, and metaphysics, all part of the arts curriculum, was based on textbooks by latter-day commentators and expositors of Aristotle's thought. Even in the higher faculties of theology and medicine, the curriculum was set by the principles of the peripatetic philosophy. Aristotle taught that nature is governed by four types of causality (material, efficient, formal, and final) and is grounded in four primary qualities (wet, dry, hot, and cold) whose various combinations gave rise to the four elements (earth, air, fire, and water); the cosmos is a system of concentric spheres, each inhabited by the fixed stars or a heavenly body, with the earth at the center of the innermost sphere; reasoning follows the syllogistic and modal canons of Aristotle's organon; and achieving happiness or human flourishing is a matter of following the mean and acquiring the proper moral and intellectual virtues.

Although the general Aristotelian content of the curriculum had been set for centuries by intellectual and religious tradition—and the great medieval Scholastic theologians, such as Thomas Aquinas, were mostly Aristotelians—it was now, in seventeenth-century France, also mandated by law. In 1624, the Parlement of Paris had issued a decree requiring that teaching in the university be based exclusively on the works of Aristotle. In 1671, this writ was renewed and made the law of the land by order of the king. Thus, one year before Leibniz's arrival in his city, the archbishop of Paris, François de Harlay, issued the following proclamation:

> The king, having learned that certain opinions that the faculty of theology had once censored, and the Parlement had prohibited from teaching and from publishing, are now being disseminated, not only in the university, but also in the rest of this city and in certain parts of the kingdom . . . and wishing to prevent the course of this opinion that could bring some confusion in the explanation of our mysteries, pushed by his zeal and his ordinary piety, has commanded me to tell you of his intentions. The King exhorts you, sirs, to make it so that no other doctrine than the one brought forth by the rules and statutes of the university is taught in the universities and put into theses, and leaves you to your prudent and wise conduct to take the necessary path for this.[1]

The archbishop, the king, the university rectors, and many others were particularly worried about the increasing influence among professors in the arts and theology faculties of a philosophy of more recent vintage than the Aristotelian variety. To control it was not just a matter of exercising discipline within the academy. Although the founder of this school of thought had been dead for more than twenty years by the time of the later prohibition, his ideas were spreading with a religious fervor among the educated class in Paris and beyond.

On Saturday, June 24, 1667, the intellectual community of Paris, along with many ecclesiastics and aristocrats and a large crowd of curious onlookers, gathered in the church of Ste. Geneviève du Mont. The occasion was the return to France of the remains of the philosopher and scientist René Descartes, who had died in 1650. Descartes had lived in the Netherlands for most of his adult life, although his final months were spent in Sweden, where he went, reluctantly, to provide philosophy lessons to Queen Christina. Unprepared for the harsh winter—Sweden was, he said, a land "where men's thoughts freeze like the water"—and forced to rise at the ungodly hour of four o'clock in the morning, the fifty-three-year-old Descartes died of pneumonia on a frigid day in February. Now, seventeen years later, with his remains finally back in his native country, Descartes's friends and admirers intended to commemorate the occasion with a ceremony in one of France's most revered sites, close by the university and named for the patron saint of Paris. (The church was torn down in the eighteenth century; the Panthéon now stands in its place.)

The event, with great pomp and circumstance, was to begin with a mass, followed by an oration prepared by one of Descartes's closest friends, Claude Clerselier, and delivered by Father L'Allemant, chancellor of the University of Paris. No sooner had the proceedings begun, however, than they were interrupted by the authorities. The king, concerned about the effect that such open glorification of the philosopher would have, declared at the last minute that there should be no public eulogies for Descartes. The rest of the interment ceremony continued as planned, but Descartes's praises were not to be sung on this day.[2]

The king also had Descartes's philosophy in mind when, four years later, he issued the edict forbidding the teaching of any philosophy other than Aristotle's. The new system of Cartesianism represented, in the opinion of the court, the Church, and university officials, the greatest threat to the intellectual status quo. Descartes's scientific program and its metaphysical and epistemological foundations were slowly but surely making converts among the professors; it had already infiltrated learned society at large, where in private gatherings and public addresses its principles were studied, tested, and promoted. Much more was at stake than Aristotle's status as "the philosopher." As the proclamation's reference to "our mysteries" indicates, the authorities believed that nothing less than the fundamental dogmas of the Catholic faith were at risk from the Cartesian contagion.

In his *Discourse on Method* (1637), *Meditations on First Philosophy* (1641), and *Principles of Philosophy* (1644)—the latter designed as a textbook suitable for replacing the Scholastic compendia currently used in the schools—Descartes explicitly rejects the basic principles of Aristotelian philosophy. The Aristotelian Scholastics described a hylomorphic world picture—one in which individual things, or substances, are composite entities constituted by matter and forms. Matter is responsible for the numerical individuality of a thing, its concrete "this-ness" or place in space and time. The forms inhering in a thing's matter include a "substantial" form, which accounts for its essential properties and designates it as belonging to a certain natural kind, and "accidental" forms, which account for the nonessential properties that differentiate individuals within the same kind. Thus, the difference between a horse and a cow lies in the fact that two parcels of matter are informed by different substantial forms. The difference between one horse and another horse is that the two individual horses, while they both possess the same substantial form (the horse form), possess different accidental forms (for example, one has the form whiteness, the other has the form brownness). In a human being, the body has its own substantial form, making it a human body (as opposed to a horse body). But there is also the human soul, which is the substantial form that transforms a human body into a living, intelligent human being.

The metaphysics of substantial and accidental forms also plays an important role in Aristotelian natural science. Medieval and early modern Scholastics employed these forms, sometimes called "real qualities," to explain the phenomena of nature, including the generation, alteration, and corruption of individual substances and the dynamic behavior of bodies. An individual thing of a certain kind comes into being, changes, and goes out of being because its matter receives or loses the relevant forms. And because matter by itself is purely passive, all activity in natural things, especially their efficient causal powers, derives from the forms and qualities inhering in the matter.

This model of explanation can be illustrated by three cases of natural phenomena that have special importance for early modern science: color, gravity, and magnetism. A swan is white because the quality whiteness is present in it; and wine and gold have their respective visible colors because the requisite real qualities of wine and gold are present in them. True color, then, unlike merely apparent color, is neither a property of light nor an effect in the sense organs or mind of the perceiver, but a certain quality that a body must possess in order to be colored. In the case of gravity, heavy bodies fall and light bodies (for example, fire) naturally rise upward because of the presence of heaviness (*gravitas*) and lightness (*levitas*). These qualities are the primary efficient causes of the motions of bodies toward or away from the center of the world. As for magnetism, a lodestone has its capacity to attract iron because it possesses the "attractive quality" or "magnetic virtue," often explicitly referred to by Scholastic thinkers as an occult quality.[3]

By the mid- to late seventeenth century, explanations in terms of Aristotelian forms and qualities had become the object of both literary satire and philosophical critique. Molière effectively ridicules the theory's empty pretenses in *Le Malade imaginaire* (1673). Asked during his disputation why opium puts one to sleep, the play's university candidate responds "because there is a dormitive virtue in it, the nature of which is to dull the senses." The chorus of examiners enthusiastically applauds and welcomes him into "our learned body."[4]

Progressive philosophers and scientists of the seventeenth century accused the partisans of Aristotelian natural philosophy of accounting for phenomena with circular pseudo-explanations. The Scientific Revolution was based on a radical change in the conception of the elements, organization, and dynamic principles of the cosmos. The sun, not the earth, was said to be the center of all things (although for a long time it was prudent to hedge this claim as a mere "hypothesis" or, to use Descartes's term, "fable"), with the planets following elliptical orbits around the sun. Matter was a uniformly extended substance present throughout the terrestrial and celestial realms, which did away with the heavenly "fifth essence" of medieval thinkers. The phenomena of the heavens were thus essentially no different from the phenomena we see around us on earth: the same thing that caused Newton's apple to fall caused the planets to stay in their orbits around the sun. And the forces acting on bodies were described by laws that could be formulated in mathematical terms. Early in the century, Galileo investigated the acceleration of falling bodies and showed that the distance traveled increased as the square of the time elapsed; later, Newton used geometry to derive Kepler's laws of planetary motion from the inverse square law of gravitation (which says that the attractive force exerted between two bodies is inversely proportionate to the square of the distance between them).

The new science also represented a methodological reorientation, a reform of the conceptual tools of scientific explanation. In formulating and testing explanations and predictions, the scientist's fundamental responsibility was not to the authority of some ancient philosopher or religious orthodoxy, but to the critically controlled collection of data and the experimental verification of hypotheses—in short, to the rational and empirical pursuit of truth. Moreover, there were procedural and substantive constraints on the formulation of those hypotheses. Galileo, Descartes, the English chemist Robert Boyle, and the French atomist Pierre Gassendi, among others, were committed to providing clear, nontrivial, and testable explanations of phenomena in terms that were transparent and relatively simple. Such explanations needed truly to *explain*, to show in a perspicuous manner how things came about. The mysterious qualities of the Aristotelians, these thinkers insisted, did nothing of the sort. Descartes, expressing a sentiment shared by his colleagues, argued that the "qualities or forms that certain philosophers suppose to inhere in things" do not at all make clear how the phenomenon to be explained is produced.

> They have all put forward as principles things of which they did not profess perfect knowledge. For example, there is not one of them, so far as I know, who has not supposed there to be weight in terrestrial bodies. Yet although experience shows us very clearly that the bodies we call "heavy" descend toward the center of the earth, we do not for all that have any knowledge of the nature of what is called gravity, that is to say, the cause or principle that makes bodies descend in this way.[5]

It may be true, but it is certainly not very helpful, to claim that a body is heavy and falls to the center of the earth because it possesses the form or quality "heaviness." The principle that is being offered as an explanation itself stands in need of explanation.

Descartes and other partisans of the so-called mechanical philosophy sought to replace such opaque accounts of natural phenomena with explanations that appealed to only two items, both a veritable part of everyday experience: matter and motion. Color, for example, is explained by the way in which the material texture of a body reflecting light affects the spin and direction of moving particles of light, which in turn affect the tiny bodies composing the sense organs with which they come into contact. Gravity is simply the result of the pushing of bodies against one another, with certain visible bodies being propelled downward by the motion of other, much smaller and less visible bodies moving in the opposite direction.[6]

For a Cartesian scientist, what makes these mechanistic models of scientific explanation possible is a fundamental dualist principle at the heart of Descartes's metaphysics.[7] The mind and the body, Descartes argues, are radically distinct and mutually exclusive things. These two substances have absolutely nothing in common, neither their underlying essences nor their "modes" or properties. Mind, or mental substance, is nothing but pure thought, an immaterial thing whose sole activity is thinking; its properties include only individual thoughts—that is, ideas (including sensations, concepts, and mental images) and acts of volition. Body, or material substance, is nothing but extension, or three-dimensional space. For a Cartesian, a body has only purely geometric properties—size, shape, and divisibility—along with mobility and impenetrability.[8] Bodies, therefore, cannot have characteristics proper to minds, such as thoughts or feelings, not even accidentally. They certainly cannot contain immaterial, soul-like forms or qualities that cause certain physical behaviors by endowing a body with a kind of mental activity (such as "seeking" its natural resting place). Only a human being, who, alone in nature, is a union of the two substances, is animate in the sense of having both a body and a mind, or soul (*anima*). The attributes and behaviors of all other bodies—even those of nonhuman animals—must be explained as an engineer might explain the workings of a machine. Whatever cannot be reduced to a function of the shape, size, motion, and impenetrability of material parts cannot belong to a body. By thus emptying the corporeal world of everything spiritual and ridding matter of what he saw as the magical, agent-like forms and qualities of Aristotelian philosophy, Descartes ensured that all the phenomena of physical nature, no matter how complex, would have a purely mechanistic—and, ultimately, mathematical—

explanation. Everything in the natural world could be reduced to pieces of matter moving around and colliding with—and moving, dividing, adhering to and separating from—other pieces of matter.

Catholic theologians immediately understood the ramifications of this metaphysics of nature for their most cherished dogma. They worried about what mind-body dualism meant for the eternal fate of the soul, despite Descartes's insistence that there was no better way to secure the soul's immortality; and they worried about what such a materialistic picture of nature meant for the operation of divine providence in the world. What troubled Descartes's theological opponents above all else, however, were the implications his physics seemed to have for the miracle of the Eucharist. They did not see how Descartes's system could explain the real presence of Christ in the host at the moment of consecration. Indeed, they believed that Descartes's conception of bodily substance rendered transubstantiation impossible. According to the Aristotelian explanation long favored by the Church, the substance of the bread is literally replaced by the substance of the body of Christ, while the real accidents of the bread (its color, shape, taste, and aroma) miraculously remain without their natural underlying support (the matter and substantial form of the bread); this is why the host still looks and tastes and smells like bread even after the priest has consecrated it. But Descartes has eliminated such real accidents. The properties of any body are just modifications of its extension—its shape, size, and corpuscular texture—and are thus inseparable from it. If you take away the substance (extension) of the bread, then you necessarily take away its accidents, too.

Descartes himself, shy of engaging in theological disputes, was only reluctantly drawn into discussions about how his metaphysics was consistent with the Catholic dogma of the Eucharist.[9] He defended his conception of body by showing that he, no less than the Aristotelians, could account for the real presence of Christ in the host. He argued that since the body of Christ took on exactly the same extended features of the bread it replaced, it would affect the sense organs in precisely the same way the bread did, and thus would have all the sensory *appearances* of the bread.[10] He was wisely cautious, however, and wanted to make sure that in these replies to his critics he said nothing that would cause him trouble with ecclesiastic authorities. To his friend the priest Marin Mersenne—who was preparing Descartes's *Meditations* for publication along with the objections that Descartes had had him solicit from various philosophers and theologians and with Descartes's replies to those objections—he wrote, "I am not yet sending you the last sheet of my reply to M. Arnauld, where I give an explanation of transubstantiation according to my principles, because I want first to read the Councils on this topic."[11]

Descartes's concern was justified. In 1663, his works were placed by the Catholic Church's Sacred Congregation for the Doctrine of the Faith on the Index Liborum Prohibitorum, or List of Prohibited Books, with the proviso that they be proscribed *donec corrigantur*, "until corrected." The Vatican authorities made no explicit mention of what needed correcting, and with Descartes already dead for thirteen years, there was little chance that any correcting would be done. Most scholars agree, however, that what gave the censors the greatest offense were Descartes's attempts to explain the Eucharist according to the principles of his mechanical philosophy.[12]

France, however, tended to resent ultramontane meddling in its affairs. Even the French clergy often took umbrage with Rome's centralized and authoritarian approach to disciplinary and doctrinal matters. The Sacred Congregation's prohibition did not have the force of law in the realm of Louis XIV, and had little effect on what did or did not get read and discussed among the literate elite of Paris.

Paris in 1672 was full of Cartesians. They dominated conversations in the fashionable salons of the aristocracy, lectured to learned societies, and performed experiments in private academies. There were Cartesians in the gatherings held regularly in the apartments of Madame de Sévigné—just as there had been in the circle that used to meet in the *hôtel* of the late Marquise de Sablé, where one of the more popular topics of conversation was the compatibility of Cartesianism with Eucharistic transubstantiation. And there were Cartesians teaching physics and metaphysics in some of the independent *collèges*.[13] Most worrisome of all to the philosophy's religious opponents were the Cartesians in the abbeys and priories that housed the regular clergy. The Benedictines, the Oratorians, and even the Jesuits harbored individuals with Cartesian sympathies, while the austere Jansenists at Port-Royal de Paris earned (quite undeservedly) a reputation for being "as devoted to Cartesianism as they are to Christianity."[14] Nevertheless, Cartesians were still a persecuted minority in the university faculties. The University of Paris, especially, was not a friendly environment for Descartes's ideas. But this was more than made up for by Descartes's enduring grip in nonacademic settings. As the great nineteenth-century historian of Cartesianism, Francisque Bouillier, notes of this period, "for more than a half-century, in France there did not appear a single book of philosophy, there was not a single philosophical discussion, that did not have Descartes as an object, whether it was for or against his system."[15]

Leibniz was well aware of all this Cartesian activity in the city and he sought out venues where he could engage Descartes's partisans. Unfortunately, he was too late for the weekly meetings presided over at the home of Jacques Rohault, the premier Cartesian physicist of the period. These *mercredis*, so called because they were held on Wednesdays, came to an end with Rohault's death in 1671 and were not revived until 1680, by Rohault's student and one of the leading Cartesians of the last quarter of the century, Pierre Sylvain Régis. And while Leibniz would have heard much talk about the new philosophy among the members of the Académie des Sciences, little of it would have been positive. One of the founding members of the Académie was Gilles Personne de Roberval, one of Descartes's most implacable foes—it was his place that Leibniz hoped to occupy after 1675, when

Roberval died—and this royal institution was still rejecting Cartesian candidates for membership in the 1670s.

On the other hand, the residence of the Duc de Liancourt, a sumptuous *hôtel* on the rue de Seine with which Leibniz was familiar, functioned as a home to an active Cartesian circle, as did the Hôtel des Muses, where from 1671 to 1674 the Dutch radical Frans van den Enden conducted a literary and political salon at which Leibniz was occasionally present.[16] Van den Enden had been a Latin teacher to the young Baruch Spinoza when he was living in Amsterdam in the early 1650s, and was responsible for introducing the future philosopher to the works of Descartes and other progressive thinkers. Within just a few years of opening his Parisian establishment, however, Van den Enden was caught up in a plot to overthrow the king and establish a republican form of government in France. Because he was a foreigner and, more important, not of noble lineage, he was not granted the courtesy of beheading given to his French coconspirators but was hanged for his crime.

Leibniz took full advantage of his time in Paris to acquire as much information as he could on Descartes's life and thought. He visited Clerselier to gain access to Descartes's letters and manuscripts, which Clerselier had in his keeping, and spent many hours copying (and thus preserving for posterity) a good number of them. At this point in his life, however, Leibniz was highly eclectic, and his omnivorous mind was open to a plurality of philosophical orientations. He may have been fascinated by Cartesianism, but he also fell in with a number of opponents of the new philosophy. His Greek tutor, Huet, elected in 1674 to the Académie des Sciences, later composed one of the more severe contemporary philosophical critiques of Descartes, the *Censure of Cartesian Philosophy*. A skeptic himself, Huet regarded Descartes as a dogmatist whose fallacious reasoning in the *cogito ergo sum* argument and his "viciously circular" proof of God's existence undermined the entire project of the *Meditations*. Although as a young man Huet had been a great admirer of "the dazzling wonders brought forth" by the

Cartesian philosophy, his disenchantment with the system dates from the time of his lessons with Leibniz, "when age, study and reflection yielded maturity of mind."[17] No doubt the talk between Huet and his pupil strayed occasionally beyond the finer points of Attic grammar.

Also during this period, Leibniz made the acquaintance of Simon Foucher, canon of Sainte-Chapel in Dijon but now residing in Paris, where he was a chaplain to a house of religious men on the rue St.-Denis. Although Foucher had been a regular attendee at Rohault's "Wednesdays," he came out in 1675 as another insightful, skeptical critic of Cartesianism with the publication of his *Critique of the Search After Truth*, a metaphysical and epistemological attack on Cartesian mind-body dualism.[18] Foucher and Leibniz met frequently in Paris, and their subsequent relationship by correspondence over the years was important for Leibniz's philosophical development. By the 1690s, however, their friendship was strained, as Foucher's critical skills were turned against Leibniz's own anti-Cartesian system.

Descartes himself had a rather limited mind," Leibniz wrote just a few years after his departure from Paris. "He excelled all people in speculation, but he discovered nothing useful for the portion of life that falls under the senses, and nothing useful in the practice of the arts. His meditations were either too abstract, as in his metaphysics and his geometry, or too much subject to the imagination, as in his principles of natural philosophy."[19] Whatever other criticisms Leibniz had of Cartesian philosophy—and there were many—this complaint that it was useless and that "while there have been many beautiful discoveries since Descartes . . . not one of them has come from a true Cartesian" was his most profound.[20] Leibniz thought that the most noble task of philosophy was to advance our knowledge and improve our lives.

Much of his own philosophy, especially in metaphysics and natural philosophy, is motivated by the humanist desire to demonstrate that even the most modern and progressive thinkers should not hesitate to make use of the discoveries of the ancients. Leibniz thought that in physics itself—in the specific hypotheses that scientists frame to explain things—the new mechanicism was the only approach to take. Specific scientific explanations of natural phenomena should appeal only to matter and to the laws of motion. However, Leibniz also insisted that the Cartesian version of the mechanical philosophy was based on an inadequate conception of matter, and so would never lead to the discovery of the true laws governing events in nature. Only a proper—Leibnizian—account of the metaphysical foundations of physical science would be capable of providing an understanding of the nature of bodily substances and of their relationships.

What mechanistically minded thinkers need for a correct notion of matter and a coherent account of substance, Leibniz claims, is a return to some of the elements of Aristotelian philosophy.

> Although all the particular phenomena of nature can be explained mathematically or mechanically by those who understand them, nevertheless the general principles of corporeal nature and of mechanics itself are more metaphysical than geometrical, and belong to some indivisible forms or natures as the causes of appearances, rather than to corporeal mass or extension. This is a reflection capable of reconciling the mechanical philosophy of the moderns with the caution of some intelligent and well-intentioned persons who fear, with some reason, that we are withdrawing too far from immaterial beings, to the disadvantage of piety.[21]

Leibniz was never himself a Cartesian. Writing before his Paris sojourn, in a 1669 letter to his former teacher Jacob Thomasius, he says, "I am anything but a Cartesian . . . I do not hesitate to say that I approve of more things in Aristotle's books on physics than in the meditations of Descartes; so far am I from being a Cartesian."[22] Even in Paris, and despite making the rounds of Cartesian society and acquiring a deep familiarity with its principles and personalities, it would be too much to say even that he flirted with becoming a member of "the Cartesian sect." While Leibniz had at one early point in his career "freed myself from the yoke of Aristotle,"[23] as he put it later in life, he quickly came to see that the mathematically spare picture of body propounded by Descartes needed to be supplemented by what he called "metaphysical entities." What he had in mind were the soul-like forms of the Scholastics.

Contrary to Descartes, Leibniz argues, physical bodies cannot be merely geometric beings, pure spatial extension in three dimensions. He had already arrived at this realization in Paris. "In the body there is something necessary besides extension," he wrote to Henry Oldenburg in December 1675. "The distinction between mind and matter is therefore not yet clear from the distinction between thought and extension."[24] If bodies were just bare spatial extension, then the phenomena of nature and the laws governing them would be very different from what they in fact are. Extension, because it is purely passive—subject only to modifications in shape, size, and motion understood kinetically—is incapable of grounding any of the dynamic features of bodies (such as elasticity). There is no room for any forces in Cartesian bodies, since the activity of such forces could not be explained in terms of extension and its modifications.[25] If Descartes were right, the smallest body would, upon impact with another body at rest, no matter how large, move the latter without the slightest loss in its own speed. Leibniz showed that Descartes's mistaken conception of matter had led him to fail to see that there is a distinction between force proper and mere quantity of motion, and that the true measure of force is the product of a body's mass and the square of its velocity, not the product of mass and speed.[26]

Moreover, if bodies were but parcels of extension, then there would be nothing substantial or real about them. Extension is by its nature divisible ad infinitum; any quantity of extension, no matter how small, can always be further divided—such is the nature of space. Purely geometrical bodies, then, would be only accidental collections of divisible, extended parts, each of which was itself only an accidental collection of divisible, extended parts, and so on. Such bodies would lack any real unity, a condition that Leibniz deems essential for being a true substance. "Since we can always go on in this way [of division], we would never reach anything about which we could say, here is truly a being."[27]

To account for the true behavior of bodies in nature, including their dynamic properties, and to ground the substantial reality of material things in an indivisible (because immaterial) active principle that unites its plurality of parts into an organic whole, Leibniz insists that there has to be in corporeal substances something besides extension, something "metaphysical" and not just geometrical. "This force is something different from size, shape, and motion, and one can therefore judge that not everything conceived in body consists solely in extension and in its modifications, as our moderns have persuaded themselves. Thus we are once again obliged to reestablish some beings or forms they have banished."[28] While Leibniz, unlike the Aristotelians, is careful to note that these forms should play no role in the explanations of phenomena offered within the confines of natural science, they are metaphysically necessary to understand *why* those explanations (and especially the laws that appear in them) are such as they are. "I believe that anyone who will meditate about the nature of substance . . . will find that the nature of body does not consist merely in extension, that is, in size, shape, and motion, but that we must necessarily recognize in body something related to souls, something we commonly call substantial form."[29]

> However, it is useless to mention the unity, notion, or substantial form of bodies when we are concerned with explaining the particular phenomena of nature . . . These

things are still important and worthy of consideration in their place. All the phenomena of bodies can be explained mechanically, that is, by the corpuscular philosophy, following certain principles of mechanics posited without troubling oneself over whether there are souls or not. But in the final analysis of the principles of physics and even of mechanics, we find that these principles cannot be explained by the modifications of extension alone, and that the nature of force already requires something else.[30]

Leibniz did have great respect for Cartesian accomplishments, despite his many unkind words. ("I have recognized that those who are completely Cartesian . . . merely undertake the job of interpreting or commenting upon their master, as the Scholastics did with Aristotle."[31]) His mature metaphysics, however, was built in conscious opposition to the Cartesian model. We live, he claims, in a world populated by bodily substances and their conglomerations. Each such substance is constituted by matter and form, with the matter providing the substance with its passive capacities and the form contributing the active forces. We are ourselves such substances, with the human soul functioning as the substantial form giving organic unity, life, and intelligence to the human being.

In keeping with the traditional philosophical understanding of substance deriving from Aristotle, according to which a substantial being is that which exists by itself and not in another thing, Leibniz maintains that an essential feature of substances is ontological self-sufficiency, or independence. He takes this condition to an extreme by arguing that a true substance needs nothing else to exist (other than God's concurrence) and depends on nothing but its own intrinsic active resources—its form—for its states of being. "This hypothesis is entirely possible. For why should God be unable to give substance, from the beginning, a nature or an internal force that can produce in it, in an orderly way . . . everything that will happen to it, that is, all appearances or expressions it will have, without the help of any created being?"[32]

Thus, Leibniz denies that there is any real causal interaction between substances, since that would amount to the states or properties of one substance being dependent upon the states or properties of another substance. The substantial beings making up Leibniz's world are absolutely independent entities, each one generating its own series of actions and states according to its own internal laws. These substances may *appear* to be causally interacting with one another, but that is because their self-generated active and passive states exhibit a lawlike correspondence, or "grand concomitance," among themselves—much as separate clocks, set to the same starting time and wound up, will each ring the hour independently of the other but in complete synchronicity.[33] The mind and the body that compose a human being, for example, are two distinct substances. When someone wills himself to raise his arm, the arm rises—not because the volition causes the arm to rise, but because the motions in the body follow from the body's own laws, at just the moment when the volition occurs in the mind according to the mind's laws. "Everything must arise for [a substance] from its own depths, through a perfect spontaneity relative to itself, and yet with a perfect conformity relative to external things." Every substance will be "as if in a world apart," but "there will be a perfect agreement among all these substances, producing the same effect that would be noticed if they communicated" through ordinary causal relationships.[34] This "hypothesis of concomitance," later called by Leibniz "preestablished harmony," is instituted by God in his choice to create this world.

Such is Leibniz's philosophical system of nature as he developed it in the decade after leaving Paris. A number of tensions and instabilities in the system led Leibniz eventually to decide that matter is itself merely phenomenal, not at all real, and that the universe is, in fact, composed at the most elementary level solely of individual, immaterial, mindlike atoms.[35] These spiritual "monads" are the basic meta-physical building blocks of all things, including what we apprehend as matter. In such an idealist picture, everything that is not itself a monad is only a function of perceptions or ideas belonging to monads. Even in that late period and throughout the early eighteenth century, how-ever, and having developed a philosophy so alien to what ordinary ex-perience seems to tell us about the nature of things, Leibniz continued to measure himself against what had long been and was still in France the dominant philosophical paradigm: Cartesianism.[36]

In the second half of the seventeenth century, there was no greater representative of Cartesian philosophy than a mild-mannered Orato-rian priest living across the river from Leibniz's apartments.

Nicolas Malebranche was born in Paris on August 6, 1638. He was one of the many children of Nicolas Malebranche, a royal secretary, and his wife, Catherine de Lauzon. Because of a malformation of the spine that plagued him all his life, young Nicolas was kept at home for his education and did not enter college for his studies in liberal arts until he was sixteen. He was deeply dissatisfied with the Aristotelian education he received there. "Verbal questions, frivolous subtleties, pitiable vulgarities, perpetual equivocations, no spirit, no taste, no Christianity," he is said to have complained.[37] Malebranche was no more pleased with his three years studying theology in the Scholastic mode at the Sorbonne. He decided not to take a position he had been offered as a canon at the Cathedral of Nôtre Dame de Paris. Instead, he entered the relatively new Congregation of the Oratory, where he was ordained a priest in 1664.

The Oratory had been founded in 1611 by Cardinal Pierre de Bérulle. It was a non-teaching order, dedicated (like so many of the orders established in the late medieval and early modern period) to a renewal of ecclesiastic life and a spiritual purification of the priest-hood. Bérulle himself had a deep veneration for St. Augustine, and in framing the guiding principles of the order was inspired by the life and ideas of the Bishop of Hippo. He is also reported to have been a good friend of Descartes's. Although the Oratory was, on the whole, anti-Cartesian, most likely for political reasons, there were members of the order who were strongly sympathetic to the new philosophy.

Malebranche himself did not actually read any of Descartes's works until just after taking his vows. He was strolling down the rue St.-Jacques one day in 1664 when he happened upon a copy of Descartes's *Treatise of Man*, a posthumously published work of mechanistic physiology, in a bookstall. The event was life-changing. According to Father Yves André, his earliest biographer, who heard the story from Malebranche himself, "the joy of becoming acquainted with so many new discoveries caused him such violent palpitations of the heart that he had to put the book down immediately and stop his reading in order to compose himself."[38] Malebranche devoted the next ten years of his life to studying mathematics and philosophy, especially of the Cartesian variety. He was particularly taken by Descartes's critique of the Aristotelian thought that Malebranche had earlier found so stultifying and sterile.

When Leibniz first settled into his Paris lodgings in 1672, Malebranche was a nobody. There was no reason why an ambitious German intellectual seeking to ingratiate himself with the cream of Parisian philosophical and scientific society would seek out an unknown Oratorian who had not yet written anything. All this changed dramatically in the spring of 1674 when Malebranche published the first volume of what would be his philosophical masterpiece, *The Search After Truth*, followed a year later by a second volume. Overnight, Malebranche became the new sensation on the French (and, soon after, the broader European) philosophical scene.

The *Search* is a monumental work that covers a wide range of topics in metaphysics, the theory of knowledge, moral philosophy, natural philosophy, and philosophical theology. In this and in subsequent writings, Malebranche, a far more religious man than Descartes or

Leibniz, offers to his readers a pious Augustinianism modified by the recent "discoveries" of the late author of the *Meditations on First Philosophy*. His overall project is to demonstrate the absolute dependence of creatures in all domains on God. This includes the radical ontological dependence that all things have on God's omnipotent power and the epistemological dependence that human beings as knowers have on God's intellect and wisdom. Malebranche argues, recalling Augustine's theory of divine illumination, that the ideas or concepts that we apprehend in our cognition of eternal truths (mathematical, metaphysical, and moral), that inform our perceptual acquaintance with things in the external world, and that we employ in ordinary abstract reasoning do not actually belong to us. Rather, they are God's ideas, present in His eternal Intellect but revealed to us for our own enlightenment. Our minds are created, contingent, finite, and particular substances made in the image of God but essentially limited in their capacities and resources. They are incapable of having states or properties that are infinite, eternal, and general. But the moral, metaphysical, and mathematical ideas that we use in our reasoning *are*, Malebranche claims, infinite, eternal, universal, and necessary. This is precisely what affords us our ability to conceive of an infinite being (God Himself) and our knowledge of eternal, universal, and necessary truths (for example, that the square of the hypotenuse of a right triangle is equal to the sum of the squares of the other two sides). It is also what explains the fact that we all recognize ourselves as compelled to assent to the same truths. "Two times two is four among all peoples. Everyone understands the voice of truth that ordains that we not do unto others what we would not wish done unto ourselves."[39] These ideas cannot be particular, transient states or properties of our highly individual minds; their locus must be an infinite, unchanging, and eternal domain to which everyone has, in principle, equal access—namely, the divine understanding. We perceive such ideas—which include the concepts of geometrical objects as well as the general, non-sensory ideas of created bodies insofar as they are pure extension—"because it pleases God to exhibit them to us." Or, as Malebranche puts it in a phrase that he was fond of repeating, "we see all things in God . . . because God wills that what in Him represent[s] them should be revealed to us."[40]

Malebranche insists that this natural and perpetual union between finite minds and infinite understanding, called the Vision in God, "places created minds in a position of complete dependence on God—the most complete there can be." Similarly, his account of causation in the natural world places all creatures in a position of complete and direct dependence on God, not only for their creation but also for their continuing existence and even for all of their particular states of being—including the actions they seem to bring about and the changes they suffer. Minds and bodies in nature, Malebranche argues, are absolutely devoid of any causal powers. God is the only true causal agent. Bodies do not cause effects in other bodies or in minds, and minds do not cause effects in bodies or even within themselves. God is directly, immediately, and solely responsible for bringing about all phenomena. Natural events are nothing but "occasional or secondary" causes of effects. When a needle pricks one's skin, the physical event is merely an occasion for God to cause one to have the relevant mental state (pain); volition in the soul to raise one's arm or think of something is only an occasion for God to cause the arm to rise or the idea to be present to consciousness; and the impact of one billiard ball upon another is an occasion for God to move the second ball. In all these contexts, God's ubiquitous causal activity proceeds in accordance with the general laws of nature—except in the case of miracles, which answer to higher-order laws that are unknown to us. God ordinarily acts to bring about an effect only when the requisite material or psychic conditions obtain; He does not move a billiard ball unless it is struck by something. This is why it at least *appears* to us that bodies and minds in nature causally affect one another and why nature exhibits the lawlike regularity and correlation among events that it does.[41]

Part of Malebranche's argument for this unorthodox theory—also found among certain medieval thinkers[42]—derives from his Cartesian heritage. If a body is nothing but pure, passive extension, as Descartes insists, then it is incapable of having any active forces among its properties. Thus, one body cannot be the true cause of the motion of another body. Extended bodies can only receive motion; they cannot generate it, neither in themselves nor in other bodies. Nor, despite appearances, can a body be the true cause of any mental state—such as color sensations or pain—since that, too, would go well beyond the capacities of extension alone.

Moreover, Malebranche, following a well-established philosophical tradition extending back to Aristotle, believes that a causal relationship involves a kind of necessity. If two things or states of affairs are truly causally related, and not just an accidental sequence of events, then there is a necessary connection between them: if one happens, then the other *must* happen. "A true cause as I understand it is one such that the mind perceives a necessary connection between it and its effect."[43] However, Malebranche also believes that the necessity at the heart of causation is a strict logical necessity. If one thing is the true cause of another, then the one occurring without the other must be a logical contradiction—and thus absolutely inconceivable. But, he argues, we cannot find such logical necessity between any natural events, mental or physical. Even if every time a person wills himself to raise his arm, his arm rises, it is not logically inconceivable that he should will to raise his arm and it does not rise; such are the principled limitations faced by finite (that is, non-omnipotent) creatures. And it is logically possible, although highly unlikely, that one billiard ball should, upon being struck by another, do something other than move in the ordinary manner. On the part of God, however, it is absolutely inconceivable that He should will something to happen and that it not happen; this is just the meaning of omnipotence. If an omnipotent being wills x, then it follows with logical necessity that x

happens. "The mind perceives a necessary connection only between the will of an infinitely perfect being and its effects . . . it is a contradiction that [God] should will and that what He wills should not happen."[44] Thus, no finite mind or body is the true cause of any event. The necessity required for true causation exists only between God's volitions and what He wills, and the true cause of any event is therefore God's will.

Malebranche's most powerful argument derives from traditional philosophical and theological assumptions about God's relationship to creation. According to a long-standing principle, God does not just create the world and then let it run its course independently of any further divine action. "If the world subsists, it is because God continues to will its existence." This is true not only of the universe at large, but also of every single item in the universe. "Thus, the conservation of creatures is, on the part of God, nothing but their continued creation . . . Creation does not pass because the conservation of creatures is—on God's part—simply a continuous creation."[45] And when God conserves or re-creates a thing, it must be in some concrete mode of being or another. In conserving a body, for example, God does not do so abstractly, outside of all spatial relations to other bodies; rather, He must conserve that body in some particular place or situation. If God wills from one moment to the next that a body continue to exist in the same place relative to other bodies, then that body is at rest. On the other hand, if God wills that the body exist in a series of different but contiguous places relative to other bodies over the course of a sequence of moments, then the body is in motion.

> God can neither conceive nor consequently will that a body exist nowhere, nor that it does not stand in certain relations of distance to other bodies. Thus, God cannot will that this armchair exist, and by this volition create or conserve it, without situating it here, there or else-

> where . . . Thus, the motive force of a body is but the
> efficacy of the will of God, who conserves it successively
> in different places.[46]

The motion and rest of bodies is due entirely to God's ongoing causal power; created bodies have no causal efficacy of their own to move themselves or other bodies. The same is true of created minds, all of whose thoughts, sensations, and even volitions derive from God.

This "system of occasional causes," as Leibniz, who would become one of the doctrine's more persistent critics, called it (it is now referred to simply as "occasionalism"), seemed to him quite bizarre. The development of the system derives from some of the same scientific concerns that eventually led Leibniz himself to revive the substantial forms of the Scholastics. Although Malebranche, as a good Cartesian, believes that bodies are nothing but extension, he nonetheless, like Leibniz, recognizes that passive extension alone cannot account for the dynamic behavior of physical things, nor can it ground the laws of motion. Thus, some metaphysical element needs to be introduced. Malebranche opts to supplement the geometric conception of matter with the activity of divine will rather than investing bodies with an active, soul-like form, as Leibniz does. Force, for Malebranche, is not something *in* bodies, as it is for Leibniz, but rather the effect of God's own efficacy.

Despite Malebranche's extensive work in physics—he was elected to the Académie des Sciences in 1699, mainly for his study of the laws governing the distribution of motion in the collision of bodies, laws that Leibniz eventually convinced him were wrong—Malebranche's primary motivations were not scientific but apologetic. He was a priest, after all, and his doctrines were intended to turn us away from the adoration of creatures and toward God as the ultimate source of what is good, true, and real. Power is a divine thing, and "we therefore admit something divine in all the bodies around us when we posit forms, faculties, qualities, virtues, or real beings capable of producing certain effects through the force of their nature; and thus we insensibly adopt the opinion of the pagans."[47] This, Malebranche insists, is idolatry. We are to love and worship God alone as the one true cause. Once we realize that creatures are not the active source of good and evil, Malebranche hopes, we will give up this "most dangerous error of the philosophy of the ancients" and redirect our reverence from transitory goods to the eternal true cause.

The publication of the *Search* caused quite a stir in Parisian intellectual circles. Leibniz's friend Foucher, no fan of the Cartesians, was so provoked by what he read in Malebranche's first volume that he could not even wait until volume two appeared before publishing an attack on the work. (He claims to have been unaware that what he had was only the first part of a two-part treatise.) His critique of the *Search* was delivered to the printer's in December 1674, a mere six months after the appearance of the original. Malebranche was a highly sensitive man, who never took criticism well. But he was especially annoyed with Foucher, whom he accused of completely misunderstanding his views. "It seems to me that when one criticizes a book," he complains with uncharacteristic testiness in his response to Foucher, "one ought first to have read it."[48]

Leibniz read the book. Ever curious about what was new and noteworthy on the philosophical scene, he would have obtained a copy of Malebranche's work soon after learning that it had been published. The two men may have known each other by this time, either through the local network of salons and academies or through their many mutual acquaintances. Malebranche probably knew Leibniz's writings on motion. He seems not to have owned the two treatises composing the *New Physical Hypothesis*, but nonetheless may have read them when they were published in 1671. Or he would at least have learned about the work's contents, either from his English friends, including Oldenburg, who heard part of it presented to the Royal Society, or from the discussions that ensued in Paris after the other part was presented to the Académie des Sciences in 1672.[49] If Malebranche and Leibniz were not yet personally acquainted by the summer of 1674, then Leibniz must have sought out a meeting with the new author after reading his book, so much of which was devoted to issues dear to Leibniz. Perhaps he asked Foucher, whom he knew to be at the time writing his critique of Malebranche, to facilitate something. All three men were in Paris, and a rendezvous would not have been difficult to arrange, as long as Malebranche and Foucher were still on speaking terms.

What is certain is that sometime between mid-1675 and mid-1676—about a year after the publication of the first volume of the *Search*—Leibniz and Malebranche got together for a serious discussion.[50] They met in Malebranche's rooms at the Maison de l'Oratoire on the rue St.-Honoré (on the Right Bank, just on the other side of the Tuileries), surrounded by the books of Malebranche's well-stocked library and some apparatuses he used for scientific experiments. The two men had much in common. Like Leibniz, Malebranche was an accomplished mathematician and a budding physicist. But their discussion at this meeting was focused on matters metaphysical. Almost immediately after the meeting, Leibniz wrote to Malebranche. "After returning home, I meditated on what we talked about. It is very true, as you remarked, that one cannot sufficiently reflect on all these things in the heat of discussion."[51] In the letter, he brings up their "agitated" disagreement over the nature of matter, which Malebranche (faithful to Descartes) insisted is just extension. Leibniz took issue with this opinion, and especially with the argument that Malebranche offered for the Cartesian conclusion that a vacuum—or empty space, devoid of matter—is impossible (because any such space would have to have its own extension, and thus would itself be, by definition, a parcel of matter).[52]

This meeting with Malebranche was probably one of many while Leibniz was in Paris. It lies at the beginning of a long, cordial but philosophically contentious relationship between two of the great minds of the seventeenth century. The initial, apparently narrowly focused discussions on matter, space, and motion blossomed into a forty-year debate over the nature of the universe. Leibniz and Malebranche, encouraged and joined by others, argued about the laws of nature, the proper understanding of divine and human freedom, and, above all, whether or not ours is the best of all possible worlds. Many of these more profound questions must have been broached during the Paris conversations. They were of great interest and importance not only to Leibniz and Malebranche but also to a third person: a Jansenist priest renowned for his quick temper who was almost certainly present on some of these occasions.

3

Le Grand Arnauld

By September 1672, six months after arriving in Paris, Leibniz still had not been able to see Simon Arnauld de Pomponne. The king's secretary of state, having already decided that the Egyptian plan was a joke and not worth pursuing, had more important things to attend to. But Leibniz, probably unaware of the prevailing court view on the matter, was persistent in trying to secure a personal meeting. He finally enlisted the help of a mutual acquaintance, someone from whom a word of introduction might smooth the way. As Leibniz made yet another attempt on the ministry in the final days of that first Parisian summer, he carried with him the following letter to Pomponne:

> The person who brings you this packet is a German gentleman with an exceedingly impressive mind, and who is very skilled in all kinds of science. He has come to see me three or four times to talk philosophy. He has asked

me to give him a letter of recommendation to be able to talk to you on behalf of the minister of state of the Archbishop of Mainz, or some other prince of Germany—the person to whom he has spoken, not finding me at home when he last came, did not remember the name.[1]

The author of this note was Antoine Arnauld, brother of Robert Arnauld d'Andilly and uncle to the secretary of state. He was also known as "Le Grand Arnauld"—perhaps because he was the most illustrious and famous member of an illustrious and famous family, perhaps (according to one report from within the family) as an ironic comment on his diminutive stature.

Just a few years earlier, Leibniz would not have been able to secure such a letter from Arnauld. In fact, he would not have been able even to find Arnauld. This is because throughout the 1660s, Arnauld, while probably in Paris for the most part, was in hiding from his many and powerful enemies, some of whom would have liked to see him rotting in the Bastille.

Antoine Arnauld was born in 1612 to a notable, well-to-do, and very large family.[2] He was the twentieth and youngest child (the tenth to survive infancy) of Antoine Arnauld and his wife, Catherine Marion. Arnauld père, at one time an auditor of accounts for Henri IV, was a lawyer in Paris, often arguing before the Parlement of Paris. Among the cases he handled was the expulsion of the Jesuits from France, which earned the family the eternal enmity of that powerful religious order. While Arnauld, his parents, and his siblings were all unequivocally Catholic, the family history was not without a Huguenot strain. Arnauld's grandfather, also named Antoine Arnauld, converted to Protestantism at one point. He conveniently returned to the Church after the St. Bartholomew's Day massacre of 1572, an extraordinary months-long wave of violence in which Catholic mobs slaughtered French Huguenots by the thousands. Although some of

Arnauld's aunts and uncles remained in the Protestant fold, political ambition and economic reality generally trumped religious principle, and most of the extended clan was Catholic.

Throughout the seventeenth century, the Arnauld family was well known for the extreme—some might say ostentatious—piety of some of its members. Arnauld's sister Jeanne was the austere abbess of Saint-Cyr, while another sister, the charismatic Jacqueline, was appointed the abbess of Port-Royal in 1602, at the age of ten. Port-Royal was a convent in the lowlands of the Chevreuse Valley (not far from Versailles), and was originally governed by the Cistercian rule. When Jacqueline, now Mère Angélique, turned seventeen, she initiated a reform of the community under the guidance of Jean du Vergier de Hauranne, the abbot of Saint-Cyran, whom she brought in as Port-Royal's spiritual adviser and confessor. In 1624, Angélique moved the nuns in her charge to Paris, into quarters in the Faubourg St.-Jacques, called Port-Royal de Paris to distinguish it from the rural compound, thereafter called Port-Royal des Champs. Port-Royal des Champs continued to be used as a retreat from the city, and its connected outbuildings, called Port-Royal des Granges, housed a community of male *solitaires* who, while not under any formal religious vows, were dedicated to the life of the spirit and provided moral and material support for the nuns of the convent.[3]

Angélique's mentor, Saint-Cyran, was deeply devoted to the theological principles of his friend Cornelius Jansen, the bishop of Ypres (in the southern Low Countries) and a reformer within the Catholic Church. Like the Arnauld family, Jansen was an opponent of the Jesuits, whom he blamed for corrupting the faith and weakening its religious and moral foundations. In his monumental *Augustinus* (posthumously published in 1640), he argues for the restoration of St. Augustine and his more rigorous penitential and salvational doctrines to their rightful place of honor within the Church. Under Saint-Cyran's influence, Angélique transformed the Port-Royal community into an order inspired by Jansen's Augustinianism, which includes the belief in the essential corruption of human nature after the Fall and the utter inability of human beings to attain salvation through their own natural capacities, as well as a strict discipline with respect to the sacraments and other rites.

The issue that, above all, divided Jansenists from more mainstream Catholics in early modern France concerned the efficacy of divine grace. For centuries, Christian theologians had debated questions concerning the role that grace plays in a person's salvation: Is it possible for someone to do good works and achieve salvation without God's help? Is there anything one can do to earn that grace? And having received God's grace, is one thereby necessitated to do good works? By the seventeenth century, the standard Catholic position worked out by late medieval theologians such as Luis de Molina and adopted by many regular and secular clergy (including the Jesuits) was that minor good works, those that are meritorious and go some way toward earning one salvation, are possible without grace. Human nature after the Fall is not so corrupt that it is incapable of achieving, through its own natural faculties, some level of worthiness. Major good works, however, as well as perseverance in the face of temptation and the achievement of ultimate salvation, require grace. Every person, moreover, regardless of his or her merits, has in fact been granted what theologians called "sufficient grace"—that is, enough grace to allow for the performance of salvific works. But this is no guarantee that the person will make the proper use of such grace; everyone remains free to consent to or to resist God's divine aid. Grace, in other words, is not necessarily efficacious. It brings only the possibility of major good works, not the works themselves. And without the meritorious performance of those works made possible by grace, a person does not earn salvation.

In this way, the Catholic Church hoped to steer a steady doctrinal course between two alternative and unacceptable views. According to Protestantism, a human being is saved by grace and faith alone, independently of any good works, even those made possible by grace. Grace is given not to all but only to an elect few, with the actual distribution predetermined—or predestined—by God, regardless of the merits of individuals. There is no room within the Protestant framework for desert before or after grace; there is nothing one can do to earn grace or salvation, and one is not meritorious for having used grace properly. God has simply resolved to give the supreme gift of faith to some and to allow others to be damned, a resolution made independent of God's knowledge of the actions of those individuals. On the other hand, Pelagianism and semi-Pelagianism, long condemned as heresies by the Catholic Church (most famously by St. Augustine), were characterized by the idea that fallen human nature preserves a degree of freedom and power sufficient for good works and, through these, salvation. While God's grace may facilitate meritorious actions, it is not the only way to heaven; an individual can achieve blessedness through his own natural endeavors. For Pelagians, in other words, grace is useful but not necessary.

Jansen rejected both the Molinist view and the Pelagian view. Hewing to extreme Augustinian principles, he argued that fallen human nature is essentially and (outside of God's intervention) irredeemably corrupt; left to our own devices, we are incapable of performing any good acts. Living well without the aid of grace is not just difficult, as the Pelagians say, but impossible. Without divine grace, human beings will perform only sins. "Augustine teaches that man by his sin has fallen into the necessity of sinning."[4] God's supernatural help is absolutely required to free a person from servitude to concupiscence and for the performance of meritorious works. And this grace, as the term properly implies, is given in a completely gratuitous manner. One cannot earn grace, and God recognizes no deserts in the individuals to whom He grants it. Salvation is assigned by God through what Arnauld later calls "predestination without prescience," a selection without God either recognizing a person's merits or foreknowing what good deeds the person will do with the aid of grace. Even more troublesome to his Catholic critics, Jansen and his followers insisted on the absolute efficacy of God's grace. Grace is irresistible: we cannot freely choose not to make proper use of the gift God has provided. Unlike the standard Catholic view, for Jansenists an individual, if granted enough grace, must inevitably will to do good.

The doctrine of efficacious grace—and the stubbornness with which they clung to it—did not endear Jansenists to mainstream French theologians or ecclesiastic authorities, who came to see Jansenism as a variety of Protestantism (especially Calvinism) and Port-Royal as a bastion of religious subversion—more dangerous, even, than the Huguenots, since it pretended to be a part of the Catholic Church. The deterministic explanations of human wickedness and of the necessary efficacy of grace seemed to amount to a denial of human freedom and moral responsibility, and the principle of God's arbitrary election of the saved, independent of merit, reeked of strict predestination and seemed to undermine the Catholic notion of divine justice. The Jesuits, restored to France in 1603 after their brief exile, were further inflamed by the harsh Jansenist attack on Church discipline and especially Jesuit moral laxity. Saint-Cyran insisted that Catholic priests were abusing the holy sacraments by too frequently offering communion and by granting people absolution for their sins without engaging in a thorough examination of the motivation in their souls. The mathematician and philosopher Blaise Pascal, a Jansenist fellow traveler, composed his *Provincial Letters* as a satirical attack on Jesuit casuist practice. "Our Fathers," says one of the Jesuits in the work, "have dispensed men from the irksome obligation of actually loving God . . . This dispensation from the tiresome obligation of loving God is the privilege of the Evangelical over the Judaic law." The sacraments, Pascal concludes in perfect deadpan, are there to take the place of true contrition.[5] The Jansenists insisted that only a sincere and pure repentance should be able to earn one forgiveness for sins. Such contrition must come not from a fear of eternal punishment, but from a heartfelt conversion to faith—that is, it must come from a love not of self but of God.

The Jansenists, in short, were classic reformers, endowed with inflexible devotion to their ideals and moved by great zeal. Austere and rigorous both in their doctrines and in their lives, they found strength in the unshakable conviction that they alone were on God's true path. Like other such causes, the movement was also powerfully driven by personality. The pious community of nuns and *solitaires* may have found its intellectual inspiration and spiritual guide in Saint-Cyran, but it was the Arnauld family that made Port-Royal what it was by populating its abbey and associated societies and providing the necessary moral and financial support. Mère Angélique especially, until her youngest brother found his religious calling, provided the real leadership for the movement. By 1640, she had persuaded her mother, sisters, and nieces to give up their worldly concerns and take their vows as nuns at Port-Royal de Paris. Angélique was devoted, courageous, and inspiring, a paragon of religious virtue to her admirers. She was also imperious, demanding, and unforgiving and seems to have had a nasty temper. At one point, a friend, taken aback by her brusque and impatient manner, advised her to "be more gentle" in her dealings with others.[6]

These severe traits apparently ran in the family.

As a young man, Arnauld enjoyed the good life available to someone of his social standing. He partook of the material advantages that membership in a prosperous, well-connected family afforded him, including fine clothes and carriages, and he delighted in fashionable Parisian society. He initially planned on following in his father's footsteps into a career in law, and he showed little evidence of the exacting and austere piety that later led him to abandon the pursuit of ephemeral goods and devote himself to defending the Jansenist cause.

His worldly phase came to an end by the late 1630s. Arnauld was moved by the increasing religious devotion of his mother and sisters, and he was in frequent contact with Saint-Cyran, who had been seeking for some time to turn him from his profane ways. In 1639, finally persuaded of his true vocation, Arnauld decided to join the ranks of the *solitaires*. He completed his theological studies and received a doctorate from the Sorbonne—the theology faculty of the University of Paris—in 1641. Contrary to university tradition, he was not at that time admitted to membership in the Society of the Sorbonne, ordinarily granted to distinguished graduates. Arnauld's own thesis director, a Jesuit, was troubled by his student's Augustinian proclivities and, despite the unanimous support that Arnauld received from all the other professors, prevailed on Cardinal Richelieu—who had his own prejudices against anyone named Arnauld—to keep the new doctor from the status he deserved. Arnauld did not receive the honor until 1643, after the prime minister's death.

Now an ordained priest, Arnauld was ready to join the other members of his family at Port-Royal de Paris, where he became a confessor to the nuns. A man of fiery temperament and great intensity, he did nothing by half measures. He was completely overcome by the feelings of piety that had led him to withdraw from Parisian society and now sought only the solitude that would allow him to pursue devout reflection and attend to his own spiritual condition. Writing to his brother Robert in 1641, he says, "I am fully resolved to withdraw into this monastery [Port-Royal de Paris] as if into solitude and to henceforth flee the conversation of the world."[7] He rarely went out, not even to meetings at the Sorbonne, unless it was absolutely necessary. He looked upon the priestly benefices that he had been granted as a distraction and longed to be able to pass his pastoral duties on to someone else. According to Nicolas Fontaine, who knew Arnauld well and at the century's end composed the *Memoirs to Serve as the History of Port-Royal*, Arnauld "breathed nothing but penitence, spoke of nothing but penitence, and thought only of penitence."[8]

Circumstances eventually conspired against Arnauld's contemplative peace. The French Church regarded the Jansenist reformers with increasing concern and began to make life difficult for them. Despite the fact that there were some well-placed clerics sympathetic to the movement who could, for a time, give it a degree of protection—among them the Archbishop of Paris, who was an admirer of Mère Angélique—Saint-Cyran's enemies were powerful and numerous, and they took active measures to weaken, if not wholly dissolve, the community with which he was associated.

Saint-Cyran had been thrown into prison in May of 1638 on the orders of Richelieu, who argued that his views were heretical, although the cardinal also harbored some personal animosity against him.[9] One month later, the *solitaires* at Port-Royal de Paris were expelled from their residence on the grounds of their suspect morality—the order came from the archbishop, who could no longer ignore the urgings of the Jesuits—while those housed in the country at Port-Royal des Champs were subjected to intimidation by the king's officials. Things got even worse after 1640, with the appearance of Jansen's *Augustinus* and its subsequent condemnations. The police even tried to interrogate Mère Angélique, but the archbishop thought that they had crossed the line and intervened on her behalf.[10]

Once Saint-Cyran was released from prison after Richelieu's death, Arnauld felt that it was safe to take up his pen in support of the cause and to compose apologetic works on behalf of his spiritual adviser and Jansen, and to defend the theological and ethical doctrines for which Port-Royal stood. He was reluctant to give up his cherished but short-lived solitude, and he was well aware of the risks he was taking. Writing to Saint-Cyran, Arnauld says, "God has called on me to engage in a struggle that may cause me great harm, and maybe even death, and I understand what is expected of me in the defense of truth."[11] With the persecution of his family, friends, and colleagues, he felt that he had no other choice.

Arnauld was certainly well suited to the task. Port-Royal and Jansenism could not have asked for a more zealous and able champion. Arnauld had a powerful intellect, one of the most penetrating minds of his time. He was learned, quick-witted, analytically rigorous, and tenacious. Endowed with a famously combative personality, he never shied from debate, and excelled at intellectual jousting. He could also be severe, rude, quick to anger, uncompromising, and intolerant. Arnauld was an irascible man, impatient with those who were of slower minds than he and harsh to those who had the temerity to disagree with him. Like many brilliant people, he cared little for the courtesies of discourse and often alienated those who had considered themselves his friends. He was, above all else, an intense man of extraordinary passion. According to Fontaine, he "pursued things with all the force and vivacity of his fire . . . he was always led by the impetuosity of his zeal."[12] It is hard to imagine his ever being satisfied with the quiet, retiring life that he had originally pictured for himself.

The war against the Jansenists was waged on a number of fronts: theological, philosophical, and political, as their religious opponents had increasing success in persuading the secular authorities that the movement represented a threat not just to ordinary piety but also to the peace of the king's realm.

Arnauld entered the fray in 1643 with tremendous éclat when he published his *On Frequent Communion*, the most famous and incendiary of all his works. In this bold defense of the moral principles of Saint-Cyran and indictment of the Jesuits' indulgent penitential ethics, Arnauld argues that occasionally depriving oneself of holy communion until one is in a properly contrite state of mind is a more effective way to develop a sincere commitment to God and a more beneficial means of absolution than the weekly, even daily communion recommended by the Jesuits. This strict Jansenist position on sacramental discipline represents, to Arnauld's mind, the only viable Catholic position and the best bulwark against the Protestants' heretical devaluation of the sacraments.

Arnauld was under no illusions about the reaction his position would provoke. "It is far better to cause trouble and to shock the community than to abandon the truth," he writes in his preface to the work. In fact, the book immediately came under attack not only from the Jesuits and other clergy, as was to be expected, but also from the court of Louis XIII. It was feared that the austere position Arnauld defended was so demanding and difficult to fulfill that it excluded ordinary people—and even royalty—from redemption, and that it therefore would lead them to abandon the faith. The furor was so great that Arnauld was forced to go into hiding.

Rather than prudently waiting for things to quiet down, Arnauld immediately turned to the ever-dangerous question of grace. In his *Apology for M. Jansenius, Bishop of Ypres*, which appeared in 1644, he defends Jansenist doctrine as nothing but faithful Augustinianism and accuses his opponents of holding Pelagian views on freedom and salvation. Far from leading to moral negligence, Arnauld argues, Jansenist teachings on grace only emphasize our total dependence on our creator and alone encourage the proper glorification of God. Again, the French clergy reacted harshly, insisting that Augustine was not the only Church father who spoke with authority on these issues.

The intellectual and doctrinal disputes around Saint-Cyran's ideas and Arnauld's writings were the source of only a part of the Jansenist troubles in these years. The Port-Royal cause took a more concrete turn for the worse during the difficult period known as the Fronde, which lasted from 1648 to 1653. This was a series of social and political rebellions by segments of the nobility, in which they fought with the king over such issues as prerogative, finances, and foreign policy. The populace was deeply and often violently divided during these conflicts, and while Cardinal Mazarin (ruling during the minority of Louis XIV) eventually restored order, the crown's intransigence left lasting scars throughout all the layers of French society. War with Spain and economic crises—not to mention famine and plague—exacerbated the government's intolerance for any kind of deviance and unorthodoxy. The perceived heresy of Jansenism and the eccentric behavior of the nuns at Port-Royal made them a natural target for the government's backlash.[13]

The most serious crisis for the Jansenists came in 1653, when Rome decided to get involved in the controversy. At the instigation of the Sorbonne and the French court, Pope Innocent X issued the papal encyclical *Cum occasione*. The Pope had been following the Jansenist affair with some concern, but he hesitated to condemn the movement, in part because he was reluctant to inflame traditional French resentment against Roman interference in Gallican ecclesiastical matters. He did, however, condemn as heretical five propositions that he asserted were in Jansen's *Augustinus*. Among these propositions are the claims that it is impossible for even a just individual to carry out the commandments of God without grace, and that in the state of fallen or corrupt nature an individual cannot resist the operation of grace.

Arnauld and his fellow Jansenists refused to accept the judgment of the encyclical. They granted Innocent's right as Pope to decide infallibly all matters of faith (*questions de droit*), such as whether or not certain propositions were heretical. But, Arnauld insisted, every rational individual is free and capable, with his own God-given abilities, to decide for himself matters of fact (*questions de fait*), such as whether or not certain propositions are contained in a particular book. He granted that the propositions that the Pope had singled out were indeed heretical, but he denied that those propositions were to be found in Jansen's work. He argued that

> it is to the truth that one dedicates his belief, and not to authority unless it is identified with the truth. Otherwise, when that authority is in error, as all the world knows it is possible for popes and bishops to be in matters of fact, one would be obliged to believe in falsehood in deference to authority. And therefore, when for a number of reasons we determine by our judgment that a lesser authority has the truth on its side, and that a much greater authority does not, it is to act against both God's order

> and against the nature of our mind not to place ourselves
> on the side that possesses the clearest indication of the
> truth.[14]

Because of his stubbornness over the five propositions, Arnauld was expelled from the faculty of the Sorbonne in 1656. Soon after, he was on the run again, hiding in various locations in and outside of Paris. At one point he found asylum in the *hôtel* of the Duchesse de Longueville, a cousin to the king but a friend to the Jansenist movement.[15] By 1660, matters had reached a fever pitch as Port-Royal found itself under attack on three flanks: from the French Church, the French court, and the Vatican. In 1661, it was decreed that all clergy in France (including nuns and even lay schoolteachers, such as the *solitaires*) had to sign a formulary pledging to submit to the terms of *Cum occasione* and condemning the *Augustinus*. This caused a serious crisis of conscience within the Jansenist ranks. Mère Angélique's nuns and the *solitaires* debated about whether to sign the formulary, if only to show their humility before the king and the Church and regain the peace they so ardently desired. Many (including Arnauld, Pascal, and others who taught in the "little schools" associated with Port-Royal) did not sign, and they suffered grievously for their resistance. The uncooperative nuns of Port-Royal de Paris were harassed and threatened for their obstinacy, and the new bishop of Paris, less impressed by their piety than his predecessor, refused them access to the sacraments or confessors. Some were even physically removed from the convent and placed elsewhere. Those who did sign the formulary and make the required public renunciation found the spiritual anguish just as hard to bear.[16]

The quarrel over the five propositions was the beginning of an extended period of persecution for French Jansenists. It also created deep fissures in France's religious life and even society at large, and not only between Jansenists and anti-Jansenists: there were many in the kingdom not associated with Port-Royal who nonetheless sympathized with the nuns' predicament and who believed that Rome had no right to interfere in French religious affairs. In 1669, Pope Clement IX and Louis XIV, fearing for the stability and unity of French Catholicism, agreed to what became known as the Peace of the Church. According to the terms of this truce, further discussion of the issues related to the *Augustinus* was forbidden, no further disciplinary actions were to be taken against those who refused to sign the formulary, and the nuns of Port-Royal were once again allowed to return home and partake of the sacraments. Arnauld and other Jansenists were able to come out of hiding, or (as in the case of Nicolas Fontaine and one of Arnauld's nephews, Isaac-Louis Le Maistre de Sacy) were released from the Bastille. The feelings of goodwill and the sense of security, while short-lived, were strong enough to allow Arnauld to gain an audience with the king himself; he was presented to Louis by his nephew, Simon Arnauld de Pomponne.

The same logical acuity and intellectual rigor that made Arnauld such a strong theological polemicist and effective defender of Jansenism also made him a profoundly good philosopher. He was not an original and systematic thinker, as Descartes, Malebranche, or Leibniz was, but he did excel in philosophical disputation, especially when it bore on issues with theological ramifications. When the Jansenists' opponents accused them of undermining human freedom (and thus moral responsibility) with their extreme view of the essential corruption of fallen human nature, the infallibility of sin, and the irresistible efficacy of grace, Arnauld responded with careful analysis. Like a good philosopher, he recognized that his first commitment was to truth, not authority, and he was willing when necessary to depart from Jansen's and Saint-Cyran's views, which—because they claimed that human beings were absolutely *incapable* of not sinning without grace or of sinning with it—he thought could not properly account for freedom.

Arnauld distinguishes between the necessity of something whose opposite is absolutely impossible, the necessity that derives from external constraint, and the necessity that is really just infallible determination from within. The first two kinds of necessity are incompatible with freedom. But the infallible causation of one's choices and actions by one's character and habits, which are deterministic and ensure that one will not do otherwise, leaves a person free and responsible for his actions.[17]

> There is no one who does not see that there are certain sins to which bad habits or a wicked disposition infallibly determine a person, such as a desire for vengeance in a man who has been cruelly wronged or offended. If a prince is presented with a beautiful woman with whom he is hopelessly in love and also has a vehement passion for pleasures of the flesh, he will infallibly satisfy his passion . . . One acts freely even if one is infallibly determined to commit a sin through a bad habit or criminal passion. This kind of determination, which God employs in us through the most efficacious grace, through which he operates in us to will and to act, does not undermine our freedom.[18]

Contrary to what the followers of Molina believe, Arnauld argues, freedom of the will does not require an absolute indifference or a total lack of determination in the will—something that, in Arnauld's view, exists neither before nor after a person receives grace. Rather, all it requires is that the person maintain the power or capacity to do the opposite of what he actually chooses to do (what Arnauld calls *potestas ad opposita*), even if that power is infallibly prevented from being exercised, either by the intense physical desires of concupiscence or by grace. Neither the sinner's fallen nature nor the grace received by the elect extinguishes this power. The sinner sins not because he is *incapable* of not sinning—that is, not because of the absolute impossibility of not sinning or because of "natural necessity"—but because, given his corrupt nature, he does not *want* not to sin. Correspondingly, if he should receive grace, this would (infallibly) invest him with a will not to sin, to choose good works, all the while leaving him with his capacity to act otherwise and thus commit a sin intact—a capacity that will, as long as this person enjoys grace, remain unexercised.[19]

Arnauld's skill with perennial problems of philosophy was manifest early in his career and attracted notice in high intellectual circles. In 1641, Descartes's friend and corresponding secretary Father Marin Mersenne invited the newly minted Sorbonne doctor to be among those commenting on the manuscript of the *Meditations*. Arnauld brought up metaphysical issues about the nature of the human mind, the operation of causality, and Descartes's proofs for the existence of God. He was also the first to comment on a logical—and potentially fatal—problem at the heart of Descartes's epistemological project in the *Meditations*. Descartes seeks in that work to establish solid foundations for the sciences and for general human knowledge. To do so, he must first overcome certain doubts that have been historically raised about the reliability of human reason. Above all, he wants to show that when we use our cognitive powers in the proper way, by giving assent only to what we "clearly and distinctly perceive" with the intellect, and by never making rash judgments based on the misleading testimony of the senses or the imagination, we arrive at true and certain knowledge. He does this by demonstrating that God exists, that God is benevolent and veracious and thus not a deceiver, and that God created us with our rational faculties; this is supposed to guarantee that those faculties are inherently trustworthy and, as long as we exercise them with care, will lead us to real knowledge.

Arnauld points out that because Descartes needs God to have philosophical confidence in his reason, he cannot use the resources of his reason to demonstrate God's existence and benevolence; that amounts to circular reasoning.

> I have one further worry, namely how the author avoids reasoning in a circle when he says that we are sure that what we clearly and distinctly perceive is true only because God exists. But we can be sure that God exists only because we clearly and distinctly perceive this. Hence, before we can be sure that God exists, we ought to be able to be sure that whatever we perceive clearly and evidently is true.[20]

The problem of the "Cartesian circle" has bedeviled commentators for generations.

Arnauld also addresses in his objections "points that may cause difficulty for theologians," including the troublesome question of the compatibility of Descartes's metaphysics of body with Catholic dogma on the Eucharist.[21] Descartes was not one to be generous with praise for his contemporaries or easily to concede an opponent's point, but he willingly pronounces Arnauld's objections to be "the best of all," mainly because they are the "most penetrating."[22] In a letter to Mersenne, he summarizes the changes he wants made in his text based on Arnauld's objections, "to let it be known that I have deferred to his judgment."[23] Arnauld was "acute and learned, [and] I shall not be ashamed to be worsted in argument or to learn from him."[24] In his formal response to Arnauld published with the *Meditations*, Descartes says, "I could not possibly wish for a more perceptive or more courteous critic of my book."[25] This public praise from the famous philosopher did much for the relatively unknown Arnauld's reputation.

As a result of an extended correspondence in the 1640s with Descartes on his "metaphysical meditations," and a close study of his other philosophical, mathematical, and scientific writings, Arnauld soon became a convert to Cartesianism. Although he had some reservations about Descartes's personal piety and certainly did not think that all aspects of the system were in accord with the Catholic faith, Arnauld was one of the new philosophy's strongest champions in the seventeenth century.[26] Arnauld believed that Descartes's mind-body dualism, by making the soul a simple substance ontologically distinct from the perishable body, offered the surest foundation for the soul's immortality, and that his mechanistic account of body guaranteed great progress in the sciences. He was particularly impressed by Descartes's response to the questions he had raised regarding Eucharistic transubstantiation, and he wrote a number of pieces defending Descartes on this score. When Descartes's works were placed on the Index in 1663, Arnauld composed a critical broadside lambasting the censors for condemning a thinker whose ideas so well supported the true principles of the Catholic religion.[27] And when the king issued his 1671 writ forbidding the teaching of Cartesian philosophy, an angry Arnauld wrote his "Several Reasons for Preventing the Censure or Condemnation of Descartes's Philosophy," in which he argues that Descartes dealt with the Eucharist and other issues "in a satisfying manner which should offend no one."[28]

Arnauld's increasing commitment to and public defense of Descartes, however, did not sit well with his Jansenist colleagues. They feared that their leader's open association with the suspect philosophy would only compound their troubles, and that Port-Royal would be seen by its enemies as a redoubt of Cartesianism.

They were right.

In November 1671, Arnauld received a letter from Germany, a long, rambling piece written in florid Latin. He did not personally know the author of the letter, a young man with grand philosophical pretensions who professed a good deal of admiration for the now-famous forty-nine-year-old Jansenist. It was clear, however, that the writer was seeking to impress Arnauld and perhaps begin a correspondence on matters of substance. In the letter, the author, to establish his credentials, drops the name of "the most illustrious Baron von Boineberg," with whom he knew Arnauld to be acquainted. He then outlines, at great length, his own many and various intellectual projects. These include work in physics on the motion and cohesion of bodies; mathematical problems, mainly in geometry; metaphysical questions about the nature and imperishability of the mind; and what he calls "moral problems and . . . the foundations of justice and equity."[29] The author of the letter takes issue with the Cartesian identification of body with extension; suggests that thought is a kind of *conatus* or striving in the mind, not unlike motion in a body; and offers tantalizingly cryptic remarks to the effect that "a body can be understood as a kind of momentaneous mind, albeit one devoid of memory." Above all, he discusses his efforts to shed some philosophical light on the problem of transubstantiation and "to demonstrate the possibility of the mysteries of the Eucharist, or, which is the same thing, to so explain them that we might finally arrive, through a sustained and unobstructed analysis, at a knowledge of the first principles of divine power."[30]

The author of the letter is, of course, Leibniz. It was just one of a number of letters he sent at this time to well-known thinkers throughout Europe. He had written to Thomas Hobbes in England a year earlier; and just a month before the letter to Arnauld, he wrote to the philosopher Spinoza, the author of the scandalous *Theological-Political Treatise*, a work widely attacked for its radical theses about the mundane origins of Scripture and the naturalistic account of its interpretation.[31] Leibniz wrote to Spinoza on the pretext of discussing Spinoza's recent work in optics, and he included a copy of his own "Note on Advanced Optics."[32] But in this and the other cases, what Leibniz was really up to was self-promotion. He was seeking to ingratiate himself with those of renown in the world of science and letters.

It was the Catholic convert Boineberg who had suggested that Leibniz write to Arnauld, and Boineberg took responsibility for sending the letter to his friend Louis Ferrand in Paris, who in turn forwarded it to Arnauld.[33] It arrived at a potentially opportune moment. Arnauld would almost certainly have been interested at least in Leibniz's general remarks on the Eucharist, since Arnauld himself was working on this problem from both a religious and a philosophical perspective in the second volume of his *Great Perpetuity of Faith on the Eucharist* and in a defense of Descartes's philosophy.

It made perfectly good sense for Leibniz to approach Arnauld. He was, as Leibniz notes, "world famous," and despite the persecution that he and his Jansenist colleagues had been experiencing, he was an authoritative figure in the Republic of Letters. Even at the French court—at least as long as the Peace of the Church was in effect—Arnauld was known as "le plus grand homme du Royaume."[34] If Leibniz wanted a chaperone to the world of French intellectuals, and especially to the philosophical scene, there was no better candidate than Arnauld. Moreover, as the uncle of Simone Arnauld de Pomponne, Arnauld could be useful in facilitating talks about the Egyptian project—as he was ultimately, in a small way, by providing Leibniz with the letter of introduction to his nephew.

Most important, Arnauld seemed to Leibniz and to Boineberg to be a potentially valuable confederate for their ecumenical project of reuniting the Catholic and Protestant churches. He was a prominent member of the Catholic Church in France, and it may be that the quasi-Protestant flavor of the Jansenist account of grace encouraged Leibniz to think of Arnauld as a Catholic who would be amenable to giving Protestantism a fair hearing in any kind of reconciliation. Because Leibniz believed that the key to Christian unity was reform in practice, not dogma, he was encouraged by what he took to be Arnauld's similar sentiments. Writing to Johann Friedrich, the duke of Hanover, in March 1673, he says that Arnauld's

> aim is not only to illuminate hearts with the clarity of religion, but, further, to revive the flame of reason, eclipsed

by human passions; not only to convert the heretics, but, further, those who are today in the greatest heresy—the atheists and libertines; not only to vanquish his opponents, but, further, to improve those of his persuasion. His thoughts, then, come to seeking how, so far as it is possible, a reform of abuses, frankly wide-spread among dissidents, would overcome the cause of the division.[35]

Writing a few years later and looking back on his efforts, Leibniz recalls how the late Boineberg "believed that [Arnauld's] opinions could carry great weight" in this matter.[36]

In fact, Leibniz and Boineberg were quite naïve in their thinking about Arnauld's potential to play a sympathetic role in the plan to close the Catholic-Protestant divide. Arnauld's unorthodox views and embattled position within the Church, in spite of the temporary easing of tensions, made him a poor and hardly influential representative of French Catholicism. Moreover, he was deeply devoted to the Counter-Reformation principles of the Council of Trent and was as harsh in his attacks on Protestantism as he was in his critique of the Jesuits. If Leibniz was looking for an ally in ecclesiastic reconciliation, someone of irenic temperament, Arnauld was certainly not his man.

Unfortunately, Arnauld seems not to have responded to Leibniz's initial overture. Ferrand counseled Leibniz not to expect anything from the energetic but overburdened Arnauld. "I delivered your epistle to Arnauld, but he did not give me any response to your letter; nor will he, in my opinion, for that learned man is constantly focused on books, and I hear that he hardly ever responds to any correspondence."[37]

A few months after sending his letter, Leibniz was in Paris. Arnauld was at the top of his list of people to meet, and he wasted no time in trying to see Le Grand Arnauld in person. Leibniz wrote to

Ferrand in April 1672 to ask where both Arnauld and his Jansenist colleague Pierre Nicole lived—Leibniz was no doubt familiar with their jointly written "Port-Royal Logic"—and he must have been disappointed to learn that "the men whose addresses you wanted are not currently in Paris . . . I have learned that Monsieur Nicole was at St. Denis, a city two leagues from Paris and that Monsieur Arnauld has retreated to Chantilly to study more conveniently."[38]

We do not know when Arnauld returned to Paris. But by mid-September, he and Leibniz had already seen each other "three or four times to talk philosophy."[39] At their first meeting, Leibniz carried with him a letter of introduction from Boineberg. They probably met at Arnauld's residence on the rue des Postes in the Faubourg St.-Jacques, near Port-Royal de Paris. Arnauld frequently held intellectual gatherings in his apartments, which functioned as a kind of salon. These activities became a source of concern to the authorities shortly after Leibniz returned to Germany. At one point, Arnauld de Pomponne conveyed a warning to his uncle that there was talk at the court about the "heretics, of whom Arnauld was the leader . . . and that this doctor Arnauld, a man of intrigue and cabal, held gatherings at his home that were prejudicial to the state and to religion." Pomponne was instructed by the king to tell Arnauld that such meetings were now forbidden.[40]

Judging by their reports to others, the two men were very impressed with one another. "I know Monsieur Leibnitz [sic]," Arnauld wrote years later to Count Ernst von Hessen-Rheinfels, Leibniz's new patron, whom Arnauld had met in Paris in 1670. "He came to see me often in Paris. He is of a very fine mind and very knowledgeable in mathematics."[41] For his part, Leibniz told the duke of Hanover, Johann Friedrich, that "Arnauld is a man of the most profound and solid thought that a true philosopher can have."[42] He recognized in Arnauld a man who was motivated, above all, by "the love of truth" and said that "I have infinite respect for his merit."[43]

Arnauld and Leibniz had a lot in common and much to talk about.

Like Leibniz, Arnauld was a man with broad interests in philosophy, theology, mathematics, science, linguistics, politics, and pedagogy, and he regretted how little time his involvement in religious polemics allowed him for these other pursuits. "We often discussed the sciences," Leibniz says, "for he [Arnauld] was no less great a geometer than a theologian."[44] And Arnauld was familiar with his friend Pascal's mathematical writings, which Leibniz had a great desire to discuss. In return, Leibniz shared with the coauthor of the "Port-Royal Logic" his ideas for a "universal characteristic" to resolve all problems of reasoning and kept him informed on his progress on his calculating machine. They also, as Arnauld puts it, "talked philosophy."

As wide-ranging as their conversations were, Leibniz nonetheless told Ernst in 1685 that "we did not touch on matters of religion."[45] This is hard to believe. Leibniz was an expert dissimulator, and he admits that he was circumspect with Arnauld concerning his religious views and projects. He claims that Boineberg's death caused him to place his grand Christian reconciliation plan on hold, and so he temporarily gave up the idea of enlisting Arnauld's help with the Catholic side. Referring to the project, he said, "I did not explain myself to Monsieur Arnauld."[46] But from what Leibniz told Malebranche in a letter of 1679, it is clear that the philosophical question of free will arose in his discussions with Arnauld.[47] In the seventeenth century, when philosophical questions easily led into theological ones, and when an argument with a Jansenist about the nature of *libertas* could not but involve the efficacy of grace, religion must have been a subject that was at least touched on in the conversations on the rue des Postes.

Above all, Leibniz and Arnauld would have broached a philosophical and theological problem that was of great concern to both of them—one whose potential solution constitutes the centerpiece of Leibniz's philosophy and on which he had just begun to formulate his ideas: the problem of evil. The two men must have found treading on this potentially troublesome ground practically irresistible. For Leibniz, there could have been no better audience than the penetrating

Jansenist theologian for his argument that God chose to create this world, despite all of its apparent evils and imperfections, because it is the best of all possible ones. And the pious Arnauld, while certainly engaged in other, more pressing matters, would have wanted to know what his new, brilliant young friend had to say about sin and divine justice; he was no doubt intrigued when Leibniz handed him a short and recently composed piece, the "Confession of a Philosopher," that bore on these themes.

Despite the dearth of concrete evidence for much of what went on between Arnauld and Leibniz in those early meetings in Paris, then, we can be sure that certain metaphysical, theological, and moral matters that later became the focus of their correspondence—when Leibniz was back in Germany and Arnauld in exile in the southern Low Countries—occupied at least some of their time. Leibniz's long, sometimes contentious, but always fruitful relationship with Arnauld was of enormous importance to the development of his mature philosophical views. In the 1680s especially, he sought Arnauld's opinion on his views of the nature of substance and reality, freedom, truth, contingency, and human nature, and on their theological and religious implications. This correspondence, one of the most philosophically fertile exchanges of letters in history, was a continuation of a dialogue that started in the summer of 1672.

Within a couple of years of its commencement—but well after Leibniz had given up on his Egyptian plan and while Arnauld and Port-Royal were enjoying their temporary respite from persecution—that dialogue became a three-way conversation. Somewhere in the middle of Leibniz's Paris sojourn, Malebranche joined the party.

First, Leibniz got to know Arnauld. Then, when he realized that Malebranche was someone worth knowing, Leibniz got to know Malebranche. Before Leibniz appeared on the scene, Arnauld knew Malebranche; the Oratorian, like most of his educated contemporaries, had been familiar with the Jansenist by reputation. He might have caught his first sight of the fellow *sorbonnard* at one of Paris's many Cartesian gatherings. But it was a mutual acquaintance who first introduced the two men formally. Malebranche reminisces, in 1687, that

> the first time that I had the honor of meeting Mr. Arnauld, it was because one of my best and oldest friends lived in the same house as he; and because I often went to see this friend, and because Mr. Arnauld was certainly someone whom I was anxious to meet, it was my duty to give myself the honor of greeting him, even though this was only through the courtesy of our common friend.[48]

It is unclear how close the two men were. In a series of letters in 1685, Arnauld calls Malebranche "an old friend."[49] He speaks of Malebranche's "having shown me much friendship," and of how "over seven or eight years, we saw each other often, with much familiarity and openness of heart."[50] Malebranche, perhaps a little too conveniently given Arnauld's harsh attacks on his system in the intervening years, remembers things differently. "Since that time, I do not think that I have seen him more than two or three times over the years, although I often saw those who lived in the same house as he. Moreover, when I did have the honor of being with him, it was always or almost always in the company of others." It was not, Malebranche suggests in a letter of direct reply to Arnauld in which he rejects Arnauld's characterization of their relationship, a matter of "seeing each other with much familiarity and openness of heart."[51]

In 1685, Leibniz recalled that Arnauld and Malebranche "were such good friends when I was in Paris."[52] And while we know that Leibniz met with Arnauld and Malebranche individually, the three men, all traveling in the same social and intellectual circles and all working on the same philosophical questions, must have come together at least a couple of times as a threesome in the course of Leibniz's four years in Paris.[53] After Leibniz's departure for Hanover and Arnauld's exile from France, with Malebranche alone remaining in

Paris, the philosophical relationships shifted to the more public—and, important for us, more extant—domain of letters, reviews, and treatises. On paper, the exchanges became more heated, the expression of ideas more insistent, and their differences more acute.

Leibniz, Arnauld, and Malebranche constitute the Great Triumvirate of Continental intellectual life in the second half of the seventeenth century, matched perhaps only by Hobbes, Locke, and Newton in England. And what they have to say to and about each other on the problem of God and evil—something on which all three have very much to say, first in person and later in writing—touches on some of the most important and disputed questions of philosophy and religion in the period, and indeed, in all time.

4

Theodicy

The *Journal des sçavans*—"Journal of the Learned"—was the first European periodical created expressly for the public communication of philosophical and scientific matters. Its inaugural issue appeared in January 1665, under the editorship of Denis de Sallo, a counselor to the Parlement of Paris and a member of the circle around Colbert; the king's finance minister was one of the sponsors of the journal. While in some sense a forerunner to the modern academic journal, each weekly issue of the *Journal des sçavans*—available from booksellers for five sous—contained an eclectic mix of book reviews; accounts of experiments, discoveries, and curiosities; scientific, philosophical, theological, and literary articles; and obituaries. Along with its competitors, the journal helped move scholarly exchange in the late seventeenth century beyond the realm of personal correspondence and contributed enormously to establishing an international community of intellectuals through the sharing of news and ideas. This high-profile and prestigious publication, to which Leibniz began contributing during his days in Paris, was the natural venue for him to introduce his mature metaphysical thoughts to a learned public.

Leibniz's "New System of the Nature and Communication of Substances, as well as the Union Between the Soul and the Body" appeared in the journal in the June 27 and July 4, 1695, issues. This was Leibniz's first published presentation of his views on substance and preestablished harmony, and it came after years of developing his ideas in the light of critical exchanges with Foucher and others. Leibniz begins the short piece by announcing that "it is some years since I conceived this system and began communicating with learned men about it, especially with one of the greatest theologians and philosophers of our time"—that is, Antoine Arnauld.[1] This is followed by an outline of the various scientific and philosophical motivations that led Leibniz to reject the Cartesian picture of matter and to reintroduce Aristotelian substantial forms into corporeal substances, a discussion of the differences between rational souls and the "forms or souls" constituting lesser substances, and, above all, an explanation of the "perfect spontaneity" that necessarily characterizes substances. He says, "I found no way to explain how the body causes anything to take place in the soul, or vice versa, or how one substance can communicate with another created substance." That the lawlike coordination in the states of things *appears* to be due to real causal interaction is undeniable; but independent, created substances and their properties, in all metaphysical rigor, cannot causally depend in any way on other created substances. The "system of occasional causes" of Malebranche and other Cartesians might seem to offer a way out of this dilemma, with God working ceaselessly to keep up a regulated order of things, but Leibniz criticizes that theory on the ground that such constant causal activity by God is nothing but a retreat to a deus ex machina, one that introduces perpetual miracles into nature.

He concludes that the only reasonable explanation of the phenomena of nature is his own theory of the causal independence and spontaneity of substances and the preestablished harmony that accounts for their correlations in appearances.[2] Leibniz insists that this "hypothesis [whereby] God . . . gives to each substance in the beginning a nature or internal force that enables it to produce in regular order . . . everything that is to happen to it" also has the advantage of providing a sound account of human freedom, understood not as a complete lack of determination (something that Leibniz regards as a fiction) but rather as spontaneity and autonomy, the self-regulation of a being through its own nature.

Not everyone was as impressed with Leibniz's innovations as Leibniz himself. Critical reaction came quickly, and from just the kind of source from whom Leibniz was hoping to receive feedback.

Pierre Bayle, the founding editor of one of Europe's first popular literary reviews, the *Nouvelles de la république des lettres*, and author of the celebrated (and vilified) *Historical and Critical Dictionary*, was the Continent's premier intellectual impresario. Born to a Huguenot family in France in 1647, Bayle converted to Catholicism while still a young man. He soon returned to the Calvinist fold, however, which (according to French law) made him a "relapse" and subject to prosecution. He left France for Geneva, but surreptitiously returned by 1674, eventually to teach philosophy at the Protestant academy of Sedan run by Pierre Jurieu. When the school was closed in 1681, he and Jurieu, a highly orthodox Protestant figure who became Bayle's nemesis, moved to the safer and more tolerant environment of the Netherlands. Bayle settled in Rotterdam and, the consummate man of letters, devoted himself to writing and editorial work. He labored with particular passion on the defense of toleration and of a reasonable approach to religion and morality. Although he was a committed Calvinist, Bayle was not a dogmatic thinker. He soon became known as *le philosophe de Rotterdam* and had a reputation throughout Europe for his skeptical cast of mind and his critique of philosophical and religious rationalism. In his monumental *Dictionary*, ostensibly a series of entries on a variety of historical and fictional figures from antiquity through the early modern period, but in fact an opportunity for Bayle to offer his own, usually unsystematic and always critical thoughts on a wide range of philosophical, literary, and religious questions; in his *Diverse Thoughts on the Comet*; and in his many letters and reviews, Bayle makes a case for the general incapacity of human reason to resolve any crucial problems of philosophy and theology. He insists that while philosophy is perfectly adequate within a circumscribed domain, faith alone can provide the certainty of belief that we need for both deeper intellectual satisfaction and spiritual comfort, as well as for salvation.[3]

In intellectual terms, there was no one more unlike Leibniz or Malebranche than Bayle. Where they were builders of grand philosophical systems, Bayle was, above all, a severe critic of philosophy's pretensions in constructing such rationalistic edifices.[4] Nonetheless, Bayle was, in many respects, an admirer of Malebranche's philosophy. In a review of Malebranche's *Treatise on Nature and Grace* in May 1684, in one of the first issues of his *Nouvelles*, Bayle says that "there has never been, developed in so short a time, so tight a system . . . there has never been a more vast, extensive, penetrating and sound a mind as his."[5] Bayle was especially impressed by the theory of occasional causes, which he saw as properly respectful of God's omnipotence and of the dependence of creatures on divine power, although he had doubts about how God's direct causal role in every state of affairs, including events in the human mind, could be reconciled with an adequate account of human freedom.

Bayle thus took issue in the first edition of his *Dictionary* (1697) with Leibniz's critique of occasionalism.[6] Contrary to Leibniz's charge, Malebranche's system does not, Bayle insists, fill every corner of nature with miracles, since God's ubiquitous causal activity is always in accordance with the laws of nature. But Bayle makes his most extensive comments not in defense of Malebranche's theory, but to criticize in particular the doctrine of spontaneity and preestablished harmony. Leibniz's views are "full of impossibilities," he says. In Leibniz's complex world of independent substances but coordinated appearances—

with its "perfect harmony between two substances that do not act upon one another"—"the power and intelligence of divine art [are raised] above what we can conceive."[7] Not even God, Bayle is saying, can do what Leibniz proposes. How could God possibly arrange it so that the states of one substance (for example, the soul of Julius Caesar) conveniently modify themselves to reflect the states of other substances (such as the body of Julius Caesar) without having those substances interact or without directly bringing about the desired changes Himself? Even Leibniz admits, as a fundamental principle of nature, that "a thing always remains in the state it is in, if nothing happens that makes it change"; and yet now he insists that a thing will spontaneously change its state without being caused to do so by anything else.

Leibniz, pleased to be sparring with someone of Bayle's caliber—he notes that "it is a pleasure to have to do with an opponent who is at once as just and as profound as M. Bayle"[8]—responded with a "clarification" published the following year in the journal *L'Histoire des ouvrages des sçavans* by extending his critique of Malebranche's occasionalism and further defending preestablished harmony.

> Let us see whether the system of occasional causes does not in fact imply a perpetual miracle. Here [in Bayle's article] it is said that it does not, because God would act only through general laws according to this system. I agree, but in my opinion that does not suffice to remove the miracles. Even if God should do this continuously, they would not cease being miracles, if we take this term, not in the popular sense of a rare and wonderful thing, but in the philosophical sense of that which exceeds the powers of created beings.[9]

Bayle replied to Leibniz with additions to the second edition of the *Dictionary* in 1702,[10] to which Leibniz—no more willing than Bayle to allow someone else to have the last word—responded that same year with what was initially a personal letter to Bayle but was then published in the periodical *L'Histoire critique de la république des lettres.*[11]

The intense but ever cordial exchanges between the German archrationalist and the exiled French skeptic continued until Bayle's death in 1706. At a certain point in their dialogue, however, the metaphysics of substance and causality gave way to more imperative issues about God, nature, and the relative values of faith and reason. Above all, Leibniz and Bayle opened up a debate on a particularly troublesome series of moral and theological questions regarding the relationship between God and His creation. Some of these problems had been of great concern in medieval religious philosophy and even in pagan antiquity. But they took on new urgency in the sixteenth and seventeenth centuries, as the Reformation movements and their Catholic opponents fought bitterly over the proper doctrines and practices of Christianity.

The Bible says that Job is a blameless and upright man (in Hebrew, *tam ve-yashar*), that he fears God and turns away from wrongdoing. When his tribulations begin, he accepts them unshaken in his faith and is unwilling to speak ill of God. "If we accept good from God, shall we not accept evil?" (Job 2:10). He suffers the loss of his family and property with patience and humility. Ultimately, however, it is too much even for him. When Job is finally overcome by his suffering, when he has been robbed of everything that was dear to him and his body is covered with sores, when all seems lost, he raises his voice to complain to God about the way he, a righteous individual, has been treated. While Job recognizes God's wisdom and power, he nonetheless questions God's justice. God, he insists, "rains blows on me without cause . . . He destroys blameless and wicked alike" (Job 9:17–22).

The Book of Job, while not a work of systematic philosophical thinking, is perhaps the most personal and immediate presentation in all of literature of the problem of evil. The conundrum is familiar to anyone who has ever wondered why bad things happen to good people or good things happen to bad people. Stating the question in this simple way, though—why do bad things happen to good people?—does not pose a real problem. Why should it be puzzling that good and bad things happen to the virtuous and the vicious alike? Why think that nature should exhibit any providential care for the righteous? To generate the problem of evil, a number of conceptual and empirical ingredients are required. First, there is the claim that there is a God and that God is the creator of the world. Second, there is the claim, supported by everyday experience, that there is evil in God's creation. Whether what is at issue are small-scale miseries, monumental disorders, or ethical lapses, there is undeniably imperfection in the world, especially relative to human beings and their well-being. Sometimes the defect is the body of sins committed by moral agents. At other times, it consists of the suffering of the innocent and the flourishing of the wicked. Birth defects, natural disasters, criminal behavior, and undeserved affliction are all evident features of the world.

In and of themselves, these facts about the world are disturbing, but they are not yet philosophically or theologically troubling, even with the premise that the world was created by God. They generate the questions that constitute the problem of evil only when taken in conjunction with a number of claims about God's nature. First, there is the idea that God is omnipotent: God can do whatever He wills to do, and God's will is of infinite scope, limited perhaps only by the logical law of noncontradiction. Second, God is omniscient: God knows everything, including the alleged defects in His work.[12] Third, God is wise, benevolent, and just, and He wills only what is good.

Now there is a problem. How can the existence of imperfection, disaster, evil, and undeserved suffering in the world be reconciled with the belief that the world was created by a just, wise, good, omniscient, omnipotent, and free God? It cannot be said that God knows about the evils and would like to do something about them but is unable to, because this is inconsistent with His omnipotence. Nor can it be said that God can and would do something about those evils if only He knew about them (but does not), because this implies that God is not omniscient. Finally, God's goodness seems to rule out the possibility that God knows about the evils and could do something about them but simply does not care to do so.

One need not subscribe to the Judeo-Christian conception of God to recognize the conundrum. The ancient Greek philosopher Epicurus (341–271 BCE) put the problem in a particularly succinct way:

> God either wishes to take away evils and he cannot, or he can and does not wish to, or he neither wishes to nor is able, or he both wishes to and is able. If he wishes to and is not able, then he is weak, which does not fall in with the notion of god. If he neither wishes to nor is able, then he is both envious and weak and therefore not god. If he both wishes to and is able to, which alone is fitting to god, whence, then, are there evils and why does he not remove them?[13]

When later philosophers in the Western Latin tradition, such as Augustine and Thomas Aquinas, as well as Jewish and Arabic philosophers, such as Maimonides and Averroës, approach the problem of evil, they tend to distinguish between different species of "evil" in the world. First, there are the calamities of the physical world (floods, droughts, earthquakes, tsunamis) and the incapacities and inconveniences (pain, disability, suffering) that ordinarily affect human beings through their bodies. The world is not physically perfect, particularly from the perspective of human needs, desires, and ambitions. Second, there is sin and moral shortcomings among rational agents. As they lie, cheat, steal, murder, and wage war, human beings are involved in ceaseless violations of God's commandments. Why does God allow such things to happen when He can so easily prevent them? (Related to the issue of sin is a problem concerning human freedom. God's omnipotence implies, for many thinkers, that God is constantly and intimately causally involved in the world, actively concurring in all events, including the sinful actions undertaken by human beings. Not only does this seem to implicate God directly in these sins, but God's inviolably powerful involvement in the actions of sinners seems to undermine the freedom of human agents and, consequently, to absolve them of any responsibility for their behavior.) Finally, there is the problem that the world God created does not seem to be a very just place. Virtuous people often lead lives of poverty and pain, while vicious people, precisely because of their vices (such as greed and dishonesty), frequently prosper. Why would a just God permit such injustice?

In addition to these general aspects of the problem that are recognized by thinkers of various religious persuasions, Christianity, with its powerful doctrine of grace, introduces a wholly new dimension. God, according to Christian Gospels, wants all human beings to be saved (1 Timothy 2:3–4). And yet not everyone receives salvation, either because they have not made proper use of the grace given to them by God (according to the standard Roman Catholic version) or because they are not among the elect who are predestined to receive the grace that is necessary and sufficient for faith and, consequently, beatitude (according to some Reformed doctrines). How can it be, then, that the salvific grace whose source is an omnipotent, omniscient, and beneficent God is not given to all and does not always have its intended effect? And why is grace sometimes given by a just God to people who do not deserve it, and at other times to people who, as God knows, will fail to make proper use of it?

Proposed solutions to the problem of evil take many forms. One early approach, initially attractive to Augustine but later condemned by him as heresy, is to insist that there are, in fact, two funda-

mental, active principles in nature. According to Manicheanism—
a doctrine derived from the thought of the ancient Persian prophet
Mani—the good principle, God, must contend with an independent,
equally real and powerful force of evil, Satan. The dynamic generated
by these opposed powers, with created things involving a mixture of
good and bad, is supposed to account for the presence of particular
evils in the world in a way that absolves God of responsibility for
them.

Aquinas, who, like all orthodox Christian thinkers, rejects Mani-
chean dualism, is concerned mainly with the problem of God's physical and moral involvement in human events because of His universal
causal concurrence in all things. To the question of whether God is in
fact the cause of sin, Aquinas replies—like Augustine before him—
that evil is not something real and positive, but only an absence of
good; since God is supremely good, He can be the source only of the
positive features of a thing, not of an absence. "God is not the author
of evil because He is not the cause of not-being."[14] In the case of sin,
God is responsible for what is real in the act—its being as an act—but
not for what is lacking (or the "deformity") in it. "God is a cause of
the act in such a manner that He is in no way the cause of the defect
accompanying the act; and, hence, He is not the cause of sin."[15]

The most popular philosophical approach to evil begins with the
idea that the entire problem stems from too narrow a view of things.
If one only broadened one's perspective on events, and on the world
at large, one would see either that what appeared to be evil was not
in fact evil, or that the evil was real but that it formed an essential
and therefore necessary element in something larger that was, on the
whole, good.[16]

Sometimes this "consider the whole" approach has a quantitative
form. The more expansive perspective provides a realization that the
universe is not in fact on the whole evil. The number of bad things
is far outweighed by the number of good things. This is how Maimonides, the great twelfth-century rabbi and philosopher, occasionally

addresses the problem. Sometimes he means that while evils may numerically outweigh the good in the human arena, this domain forms such a small and insignificant part of the whole universe that it is of no real consequence in judging the overall character of God's creation. "If man considered and represented to himself that which exists and knew the smallness of his part in it," Maimonides says in his *Guide of the Perplexed*, "the truth would become clear and manifest to him. For this extensive raving entertained by men with regard to the multitude of evils in the world is not said by them to hold good with regard to the angels or with regard to the [heavenly] spheres and the stars or with regard to the elements and the minerals and the plants composed of them or with regard to the various species of animals . . . Now the true way of considering this is that all the existent individuals of the human species . . . are of no value in comparison with the whole that exists and endures."[17] Maimonides also insists that when one takes a long view of history and a wider view of the state of the world, one will see that the number of evils even within the human domain is not as great as many believe, and that, in fact, it is far outweighed by the number of good things. "You will find that evils of this kind that befall men are very few and occur only seldom. For you will find cities, existing for thousands of years, that have never been flooded or burned. Also thousands of people are born in perfect health whereas the birth of an infirm human being is an anomaly, or at least . . . such an individual is very rare; for they do not form a hundredth or even a thousandth part of those born in good health."[18]

This quantitative solution to the problem of evil is not very satisfying, however, and Maimonides and other philosophers partial to it recognize this. Trying to decide whether the number of good things is greater than the number of evils must ultimately lead to an endless numbers game, with empirical disputes over the counting and normative disputes about how to evaluate states of affairs. More important, it leaves the fundamental question at the heart of the problem of evil unresolved: Why is there any evil *at all* in God's creation? And why is there exactly this much evil and not an iota less? If considering the whole or taking a larger perspective on things is supposed to help us understand why there are defects and sins in the work of an omnipotent, omniscient, and perfectly benevolent deity, it must draw our attention to something beyond the evident facts of nature itself, to something that only metaphysical inquiry can reveal.

Throughout his philosophical career, Leibniz was occupied, even obsessed, with the problem of evil. Elements of his famous solution to the puzzle appear in his writings from before the Paris period and in pieces he was working on the year he died, and the fundamental structure of that solution remained basically the same for almost fifty years. Indeed, Leibniz's entire philosophy revolves around his concern with providing a theodicy (from the ancient Greek words *theos*, God, and *diké*, justice[19]), a term that Leibniz coined for the rational justification or vindication of God's ways.[20] His ongoing dialogue with Bayle, however, is what gave him the occasion to compose his most sustained treatment of the problem in the only philosophical book that he would publish in his lifetime.

Bayle's skeptical tendencies, mocking manner, and generally opaque approach to theological matters earned him a name in some quarters as a freethinker and a heretic, even an atheist. At one point, practically goading his critics, he suggests that a society of atheists can be more moral than a society of professed Christians. The fact that he was perceived to be sympathetic to Manicheanism did not help his reputation. It was a mistaken impression, but not without some basis. In the first edition of the *Dictionary*, there is an entry on "Manicheans" in which Bayle notes that the sect "taught what should have struck everyone with the greatest horror . . . a false doctrine . . . incapable of being maintained as soon as one accepts Scripture."[21] He goes on to explain how difficult it is to refute this system, a comment that his opponents immediately attacked. But Bayle's point is not to defend the Manicheans; rather, it is to show that reason alone is not capable of undermining such a heresy. "Human reason is too feeble for this. It is a principle of destruction and not of edification. It is only proper for raising doubts, and for turning things on all sides in order to make endless disputes."[22] The only way to defeat the theory—the only way to come to a proper defense of God's attributes and a belief in the justice of God's ways—is through faith, "the light of revelation." The quest for a rational theodicy, Bayle believes, is hopeless.

Even if he were unprompted, Leibniz would never have left Bayle's challenge unanswered, especially regarding a set of issues he had long considered to be of the greatest import. But Leibniz says that he was urged to respond to Bayle by the queen of Prussia. Sophie Charlotte, the daughter of Leibniz's employer, Ernst-Auguste—Johann Friedrich's brother and successor as duke of Hanover—and the wife of Frederick of Brandenburg, was, Leibniz says, "delighted with meditations."[23] She also very much enjoyed reading Bayle, whom she had met personally during a visit to the Netherlands. As she and Leibniz sat together in her country estate outside Berlin in the summer of 1702, no doubt in the company of others with a taste for philosophical conversation, she wondered how her father's counselor would reply to the various "difficulties" raised by Rotterdam's charismatic skeptic.

That same summer, Leibniz wrote his "Reply to the Thoughts on the System of Preestablished Harmony Contained in the Second Edition of M. Bayle's Critical Dictionary, Article 'Rorarius,' " which he published in *L'Histoire critique de la république des lettres*. He insists that Bayle's mocking talk of "a ship that guides itself to port without a pilot, or of a machine that carries out the functions of man without having intelligence" does not offer serious counterexamples to the claim that God can provide every substance with a faculty and internal force for spontaneously bringing about its own states of being; for such a contrivance is achievable even for finite spirits—as is clear from the kinds of things that human-made machines can do. "There is no doubt whatever that a man could make a machine capable of walking about for some time through a city and of turning exactly at the corners of certain streets."[24] Satisfied that he has sufficiently answered Bayle's objections to the spontaneity of substances and the preestablished harmony, Leibniz turns at the end of the essay to matters from other entries in the *Dictionary* that must have been nagging at him since first reading it. Here Leibniz broaches their differences on the problem of evil. It is a tantalizingly brief sketch of his views, but Leibniz explicitly announces his endorsement of reason in the struggle to reconcile God with evil, and in particular his adoption of the "consider the whole" approach to theodicy:

> To say something about the articles of M. Bayle that I have just mentioned and whose subject matter has many connections with this question [of preestablished harmony], it seems that the reason for permitting evil rests in the eternal possibilities, in accordance with which the kind of universe that allows evil and has admitted it to actual existence is found to be more perfect, considering the whole [*en somme*], than all other possible kinds.[25]

It is, Leibniz says, all a matter of "taking a step back, so to speak, in order to leap forward better." From that more distant perspective, one sees that in creating the best of all possible worlds, God must admit evil.

The following year, Bayle took up the challenge with his *Response to a Provincial's Questions*, an extremely long work that took him over two years to complete. It is directed at writings on the origin of evil by a number of his contemporaries, including the Englishman William King and the Frenchman Jacques Bernard, but it is clearly intended for Leibniz as well. Bayle's general rejection of rational theology was motivated by his fideism, an epistemological submission to faith and a belief that when truths discovered by reason alone clash with revealed truths, it is reason that must give way. His particular criticisms of the kind of theodicean strategy favored by Leibniz persuaded Leibniz that it was time to mount a full-scale defense of his views.

Unfortunately, Bayle died in 1706, before Leibniz got started on the project.[26] This was not the first time Leibniz found himself in such a predicament. Two years earlier, as he finished composing a point-by-point response to John Locke's *Essay Concerning Human Understanding*, Locke died. Leibniz, out of consideration, refrained from publishing his *New Essays on Human Understanding*. Bayle's criticisms, however, were too important not to answer publicly because they were directed not only at central elements of Leibniz's philosophy but also at the whole notion of a rational defense of God's attributes. Moreover, unlike the relationship with Locke, who had not written anything against Leibniz specifically, this was a matter of responding to published criticism of his ideas. Leibniz was also eager to put out something on what he knew to be a subject of great public interest: "[M. Bayle] has left us," Leibniz says. "But the matter is on the rug, and clever men continue to work on it, and the public is expectant."[27] Leibniz therefore composed an extended reply to Bayle—in French, so it would reach a broad readership—and at the same time presented an overview of his metaphysical system to the public.

The *Essays of Theodicy, on the Goodness of God, the Freedom of Man and the Origin of Evil* (its usual title in English is simply *Theodicy*) were published anonymously in Amsterdam in 1710.[28] The "Preliminary Dissertation" of the work, on "the conformity of faith with reason," is devoted to refuting Bayle's view that faith could require one to believe something that is logically incoherent or inconsistent with reason itself. "After all," Leibniz insists, "one truth cannot contradict another, and the light of reason is no less a gift of God than that of revelation."[29] Leibniz defends a classic rationalist credo: that there is only one body of truth, that it includes the claims of both metaphysics and theology, and that all the propositions contained therein are accessible to, or at least consistent with, reason. Above all, he insists that the principles that govern divine justice and explain God's modus operandi must be sufficiently like our own conception of justice to allow them to be transparent to human reason. "His goodness and His justice as well as His wisdom differ from ours only because they are infinitely more perfect."[30] The way is now clear for a rational defense of that justice and goodness.

Leibniz concedes that the problem of evil is one of enormous difficulty. Along with the problem of the continuum, it is one of the "two famous labyrinths on which our reason founders," a conundrum that "perplexes almost all the human race."[31] It is, he says, a question of natural theology "how a sole principle, all-good, all-wise and all-powerful, has been able to admit evil, and especially to permit sin, and how it could resolve to make the wicked often happy and the good unhappy."[32] It is not so much that God is the direct cause of sin—although God appears to cooperate positively in the production of evil—but that He allows it to occur. "Even though there were no co-operation by God in evil actions, one could not help finding difficulty in the fact that He foresees them and that, being able to prevent them through his omnipotence, He yet permits them."[33] Most troublesome is the problem that arises "in relation to God's dispositions for the salvation of men," that is, in the realm of grace. According to the doctrine of original sin, all human beings are innately corrupt and capable only of evil; grace alone (at least for a Lutheran such as Leibniz) allows one to perform good works. Why, then, are some saved and others left to damnation?

> There are few saved or chosen; therefore the choice of many is not God's decreed will. And since it is admitted that those whom he has chosen deserve it no more than the rest, and are not even fundamentally less evil, the goodness that they have coming only from the gift of God, the difficulty is increased. Where, then, is his justice (people will say), or at least, where is his goodness? Partiality, or respect of persons, goes against justice, and he

who without cause sets bounds to his goodness cannot
have it in sufficient measure.[34]

The resolution of this set of problems is, for Leibniz, to be found in
the consideration of God's rationality, wisdom, and goodness. He has
chosen to create this actual world rather than any of infinitely many
other possible ones, even though it includes evil and sin, simply because it is the best of all possible worlds. Indeed, part of what makes
this the best of all possible worlds is the fact that it contains just the
quantity and character of things (including evils) that are present
within it. "God cooperates morally in moral evil, that is, in sin, without being the originator of the sin, and even without being accessory
thereto. He does this by permitting it justly, and by directing it wisely
toward the good."[35]

God, in His infinite, eternal intellect, knows an infinity of possible
worlds. Each possible world is a concatenation of possible substances
and their relationships, a conceptual representation of an unfolding of
things and events in time. Some of these worlds vary only minimally
from one another, perhaps by one single feature—such as a particular
person having blue rather than brown eyes;[36] others are radically unlike
one another, having entirely different laws of nature. (Imagine, for example, a world in which bodies, rather than being attracted to each
other according to Newton's inverse square law of gravitation, repelled
each other according to the same formula.) The eternal essence of
each world is present in God's understanding only as an idea, as a possibility, one that strives for existence with all the other equally possible
worlds but that, without a positive creative act by God, will forever
remain only an unactualized notion.

Surveying all of these possible worlds in His understanding and
contemplating each one, God compares them with one another. In
doing so, He takes note not only of their descriptive variations but
also of their normative differences. Some worlds are, from God's perspective, better than, hence preferable to, others. Leibniz argues that

there is, in fact, one world that is qualitatively superior to all the others, one world that is the best of all. Because God is infinitely wise, he infallibly knows which world is the best; and because He is infinitely good, He creates that one.

> The wisdom of God, not content with embracing all the possibles, penetrates them, compares them, weighs them one against the other, to estimate their degree of perfection or imperfection, the strong and the weak, the good and the evil. It goes even beyond the finite combinations, it makes of them an infinity of infinites, that is to say, an infinity of possible sequences of the universe, each of which contains an infinity of creatures. By this means, the divine Wisdom distributes all the possibles it had already contemplated separately, into so many universal systems that it further compares the one with the other. The result of all these comparisons and deliberations is the choice of the best from among all these possible systems, which wisdom makes in order to satisfy goodness completely; and such is precisely the plan of the universe as it is.[37]

The idea that there *is* a best of all possible worlds is not philosophically uncontentious. Aquinas, for example, argues that there is not and cannot be such a thing. No matter how good any given world may be, it is always possible for God to make a world that is better. If there really are infinitely many possible worlds, Aquinas says, then there cannot be one that is the best of all.[38]

To anyone who would question whether there *is* a best of all possible worlds, and moreover whether the actual world is the best, Leibniz has a response based on a priori reasoning. It is inconceivable, he insists, that an infinitely good and perfect God could choose anything less than the best. "This supreme wisdom, united to a goodness that is no less infinite, cannot but have chosen the best. For as a lesser evil is a kind of good, even so a lesser good is a kind of evil if it stands in the way of a greater good; and there would be something to correct in the actions of God if it were possible to do better."[39] This means not only that if God creates a world, he will choose to create the one that is the best, but also that if there were no world that was the best, then God will not create a world at all. For if there were no world that was uniquely the best, then there would be no compelling reason for God to create a world and no basis for choosing which world to create, and without such reasons, God would simply not create. "If there were not the best (*optimum*) among all possible worlds, God would not have produced any . . . [T]here is an infinitude of possible worlds among which God must needs have chosen the best, since He does nothing without acting in accordance with supreme reason."[40] As a matter of fact, God did create a world: the present world, the one that actually exists. Therefore, there must be a world that is the best of all possible worlds, and it must be the actual world.

In his satire *Candide*, published in 1759, Voltaire has a good time at Leibniz's expense. The story's hero, Candide, experiences all manner of evil, every sin, vice, and perversion imaginable. Throughout his wanderings, he confronts dishonesty, treachery, greed, starvation, war, pestilence, earthquake, rape, murder, theft, dismemberment, bestiality, and even cannibalism. Rather than shake the young man's sanguine outlook, however, these encounters only serve to confirm the lessons he learned from his tutor, Dr. Pangloss. Consider the whole, he has been told. And he does so, literally, as he travels extensively in many lands. His manservant points out that evil seems to be evenly spread throughout. "You see, this half of the world is not better than the other. Take my advice, let's head back to Europe by the shortest route possible." Candide, however, sees that, despite his tribulations, it really is the best of all worlds, because everything seems to work out for some good, if not right away then at least in the long run. Initially remorseful over having killed the brother of his beloved in a fit of anger, he later reflects on the subsequent course of events, and especially on his success at having escaped alive from a wild tribe in the New World when they realized he was not a Jesuit: "If I hadn't had the good fortune to run Miss Cunégonde's brother through with a hefty thrust of my sword, I would have been eaten, and without remission of sentence." In fact, as Pangloss points out to him at the end of the story, everything ultimately does turn out well for Candide: he is happily married to his love and living a life of comfort. "All events form a chain in the best of all possible worlds. For in the end, if you had not been given a good kick up the backside and chased out of a beautiful castle for loving Miss Cunégonde, and if you hadn't been subjected to the Inquisition, and if you hadn't wandered about America on foot, and if you hadn't dealt the Baron a good blow with the sword, and if you hadn't lost all your sheep from that fine country of Eldorado, you wouldn't be here now eating candied citron and pistachio nuts."

Candide is supposed to constitute one long reductio ad absurdum of Leibnizian optimism. To Leibniz's claim that this world is the best, Voltaire answers with a sharply written, highly sardonic "Really?" Voltaire's point is that Leibniz's a priori answer to the problem of evil—that this is the best of all possible worlds, and therefore it does not impugn God's justice and wisdom—runs headlong into obvious empirical difficulties. Anyone familiar with the world would, like Pangloss, have to be wearing very thick rose-colored glasses to continue to think that things could not possibly be better. If Leibniz is going to succeed in his theodicean project, he has to explain just *how* this is the best of all possible worlds and in what way the persistence of sin and suffering is consistent with this world's optimality. Otherwise, all he has done in the face of the problem of evil is beg the question.

Leibniz is acutely aware of the pervasiveness—but not necessarily of the predominance—of evil in the world. "It must be confessed, however, that there are disorders in this life that appear especially in the prosperity of sundry evil men and in the misfortune of many good people."[41] He agrees with Aquinas that evil is nothing real and positive in ontological terms; it is only a negation or a lack of good. Everything that exists is good, although each individual may fall short of its optimal condition. In this sense, for Leibniz, nothing is in itself truly evil. But he still needs to explain why this lack exists and why God, even if he does not directly cause it, nonetheless allows it to be and to have the consequences it does.

Leibniz divides evil into three categories. Metaphysical evil consists in the limitation and imperfection that necessarily characterize any finite, created being; this species of evil is an unavoidable part of the nature of things because anything God creates will, simply by virtue of being created, be less perfect than the absolutely perfect, uncreated being. Physical evil, by contrast, is suffering, and moral evil is sin. Physical and moral evil are not, by themselves, necessary elements of creation, although they are essential parts of many possible worlds. They exist in the actual world because God, by choosing to create this world while being fully aware of everything it involves, permits them. The question is, why?

Leibniz does *not* have in mind what Voltaire accuses him of claiming. Candide believes that to say that this is the best of all possible worlds means that everything in this world turns out for the best *for him*, and, presumably, for any other creature. One may suffer through pain and misfortune, but only because they eventually lead to felicity. This is not Leibniz's view, however. On his account, it is not that everything will turn out for the best for me or for anyone else in particular. Nor is it necessarily the case that any other possible world would have been worse for me or for anyone else. Rather, Leibniz claims that any other possible world is worse *overall* than this one, regardless of any single person's fortunes in it.[42]

Leibniz does not think that in the best of all possible worlds every creature will ultimately experience happiness and well-being, although the path thereto may be rocky. On the contrary, Leibniz concedes that in the best world many will know nothing but suffering. He denies that "what is the best in the whole is also the best possible in each part."[43] Not every particular evil or series of evils will, in the end, lead to a particular good result. Sometimes a miserable life will end miserably. But without the specific evils that the world does contain, without the physical suffering and moral sins that we experience and inflict on one another, this world would not be the world that it is. And if this world were not the world that it is, it would, for just that reason, not be the best of all possible worlds, and God would not have chosen to create it.

> God has ordered all things beforehand once for all, having foreseen prayers, good and bad actions, and all the rest; and each thing *as an idea* has contributed, before its existence, to the resolution that has been made upon the existence of all things; so that nothing can be changed in the universe (any more than in number) save its essence or, if you will, save its numerical individuality. Thus, if the smallest evil that comes to pass in the world were missing in it, it would no longer be this world; which, with nothing omitted and all allowance made, was found the best by the Creator who chose it.[44]

The desirability of the world from God's perspective is determined by its contents. Among those contents are many actions and events that are evils, either because they involve the suffering of some creature or the violation of God's commandments. There are infinitely many possible worlds that have fewer such things; but it is, among other reasons, just *because* these worlds have less pain or sin than the actual world that they fall short of being the best, and therefore are unworthy of God's choice.[45] "It is true that one may imagine possible worlds without sin and without unhappiness, and one could make some like Utopian or Sevarambian romances: but these same worlds again would be very inferior to ours in goodness."[46] For God to have chosen a world with even one less instance of evil would mean creating a world with less overall goodness, because all things are connected and every single aspect of the world makes a contribution to its being the best world. Similarly, for God to step in even on one small occasion miraculously to forestall a natural disaster from happening to one person (or to prevent human evil from destroying six million people) would represent an abrogation of this world's laws of nature or an interference with human freedom; it would be to change the world, a world whose principles and their results God is committed to sustaining. "Shall God not give the rain, because there are low-lying places that will be thereby incommoded? Shall the sun not shine as much as it should for the world in general, because there are places that will be too much dried up in consequence?"[47] God, foreseeing everything that will unfold over time as a result of His choice, opted to create this world precisely because it includes these items that, from our perspective, are imperfections, but which from His eternal and penetrating point of view go toward making it the very best.

Sometimes, Leibniz seems to mean that the bad elements (those things that have a lesser degree of perfection) accentuate the good, and that particular evils are required to bring into relief particular goods. Like chiaroscuro in painting or dissonances in music, the contrast makes those goods shine even brighter, thereby also rendering our appraisal of the whole more positive. "Is it not most often necessary that a little evil render the good more discernible, that is to say, greater?"[48] In an essay of 1697, Leibniz gives an elegant statement of this version of the "consider the whole" approach.

> If we look at a very beautiful picture but cover up all of it but a tiny spot, what more will appear in it, no matter how closely we study it, indeed, all the more, the more closely we examine it, than a confused mixture of colors without beauty and without art. Yet when the covering

is removed and the whole painting is viewed from a position that suits it, we come to understand that what seemed to be a thoughtless smear on the canvas has really been done with the highest artistry by the creator of the work. And what the eyes experience in painting is experienced by the ears in music. Great composers very often mix dissonances with harmonious chords to stimulate the hearer and to sting him, as it were, so that he becomes concerned about the outcome and is all the more pleased when everything is restored to order. Similarly, we may enjoy trivial dangers or the experience of evils from the very sense they give us of our own power or our happiness or our fondness for display.[49]

This kind of aesthetic contribution that evil makes to our evaluation of the whole by heightening our perception of the good and enhancing the overall beauty of the world does have an important role in Leibniz's thinking. But it is not the main point of his theodicy. And while Leibniz sometimes plays with the quantitative version of the "consider the whole" approach, what makes this world the best is not the fact that good outnumbers evil.[50] The best-ness of the world is not a straightforward empirical matter, accessible to anyone with a superior appreciation of the light and the shadows or a direct grasp of the number of good things. Nor, finally, are evils justified by good consequences that may follow them in the course of events, as when the end is claimed to justify the means; for sometimes there are no such good consequences, and a good person will end his days in grief and sorrow.[51] Rather, the evil, like the good, makes a positive contribution to the overall optimality of the world by constituting a part of its contents.[52] It belongs to the conception of the best of all possible worlds that it involves a large number of wonderful, good things. But it also belongs to the conception of that world that it involves a determinate number of evils, including certain human beings committing certain sins; these, too, contribute to the fact that this world is "found to be the best by the Creator who chose it."[53] Because God is compelled by His goodness and wisdom to create the best world, He must also allow—with what Leibniz calls a "permissive will"—those sins to come into existence. "For God, having found already among things possible, before his actual decrees, man misusing his freedom and bringing upon himself his misfortune, yet could not avoid admitting him into existence, because the general plan required this."[54] "God, having found among the possible beings some rational creatures who misuse their reason, gave existence to those who are included in the best possible plan of the universe."[55] In short, there is sin and suffering in a world created by an all-wise, all-powerful, all-good God because that God can achieve His will to create the best of all possible worlds only by allowing the sin and suffering it contains to come into existence with it. As Leibniz puts it, God may in a sense be the ultimate physical cause of evil, but He is not the moral cause; the sinner is the author of his own sins.[56]

In the end, Leibniz realizes that philosophical understanding of these matters can go only so far. If one persists in seeking an explanation for the existence of evil by asking just *how* evil is connected with the best, in demanding an account of exactly what contribution evil makes to the overall goodness of the world, then one is engaged in a futile enterprise. This insight transcends human understanding. Responding to Bayle's demand for "a detailed explanation of how evil is connected with the best possible scheme for the universe," Leibniz replies that "M. Bayle asks a little too much . . . there is no obligation to do that which is impossible for us in our existing state. It is sufficient for me to point out that there is nothing to prevent the connection of a certain individual evil with what is best on the whole. This incomplete explanation, leaving something to be discovered in the life to come, is sufficient for answering the objections, though not for a comprehension of the matter."[57]

Still, even in this life, something can be said about what the best of all possible worlds is like and what makes it the best. When Leibniz says that this world is the best, he does not primarily mean this in an aesthetic sense, such that it is the most pleasing or satisfying to behold, although this may be true. Nor does he intend the claim to be understood in ethical terms, whereby this world is morally preferable to any other world, although this, too, is true of the world in his thinking.[58] What makes this world the best of all is that it is *metaphysically* superior to all other possible worlds.[59] The actual world contains the highest degree of perfection, insofar as it realizes the maximum level of created being or reality. (In the seventeenth century, *perfection* is often understood not as a normative term but as a descriptive and ontological one, equivalent to *positive reality*; thus, one thing has more perfection than another if it has more reality. So a mere property of a thing is less real, and therefore has less perfection, than the thing to which it belongs and upon which it depends; the color of a horse is less real than the horse itself. And an infinite being is more perfect or contains more reality than a finite being.) No other world contains as much positive reality, measured in terms of both quantity and variety of essence, as this world. The best possible world is, in its own essential nature, populated by the greatest number of beings that can possibly co-occupy a world over time without contradiction, and exhibits the greatest possible variety of kinds of beings.

What makes possible such fullness and richness of being is what Leibniz calls the "order" employed by God to govern the phenomena of the world. God, he says, faces in creation a problem of engineering. Given the means available, He must find a way to produce the maximum amount of perfection, or reality, possible. He is "like a good architect who utilizes his location and the funds destined for the building in the most advantageous manner, leaving nothing that shocks or that does not display the beauty of which it is capable."[60] Leibniz compares God's creative challenge to a tile puzzle; it consists in discovering an order and principle for arranging things that allows for the greatest amount and variety of being to be included. And he believes that the order that is most productive of the greatest amount of reality and the greatest richness of phenomena consists in the simplest and most universal laws of nature. "God has chosen the most perfect [world], that is to say, the one that is at the same time the simplest in hypotheses and the richest in phenomena."[61] "God makes the maximum of things he can, and what obliges him to seek simple laws is precisely the necessity to find room for as many things as can be put together; if he made use of other laws, it would be like trying to make a building with round stones, which make us lose more space than they occupy."[62] The best world is characterized by the maximal simplicity of laws and maximal quantity and richness of effects, just because the most superior laws are also the most fecund.[63]

This perfect match among simplicity of law and maximization of being and richness of phenomena is what Leibniz calls "harmony." An exceedingly important element of Leibniz's philosophy from the beginning of his career, harmony is defined as "similarity in variety,"[64] or a great quantitative and qualitative multiplicity of beings brought together and systematized by some law or principle. "Harmony is when many things are collected into a certain unity. For where there is no variety, there is no harmony . . . On the other hand, where variety is without order, without proportion, there is no harmony."[65] If God's choice of a world results in the maximization of any single value, this is it. "Harmony is just this: a certain simplicity in multiplicity. Beauty and pleasure also consist in this. So for things to exist is the same as for them to be understood by God to be the best, i.e., the most harmonious."[66] One of Leibniz's favorite illustrations of harmony is a highly complex, continuous curved line that, to all appearances, seems random and without reason but whose construction, in fact, can be captured and brought to order by a mathematical equation.[67]

Harmony is not a visible aspect of the world; Leibniz's claim about what makes this world the best goes beyond any empirical evidence. Appearances sometimes seem even to contradict the metaphysical truth of things as Leibniz sees it. Leibniz does not hesitate to assert that sometimes the world presents "a confused chaos."[68] The harmony characteristic of the best of all possible worlds is accessible only to those who, given to metaphysical speculation, can "look more deeply" and see beyond the hodgepodge of appearances in order to grasp the invisible order that unifies them. The best world is a plenum of being, with each substance an active, organic unity that spontaneously generates its own states, albeit in perfect conformity with what is happening in all of the other substances—in other words, a thoroughly Leibnizian world populated by causally independent substances and characterized by preestablished harmony.

As for human happiness, it is unclear whether or not Leibniz believes that this, too, is maximized in the best of all possible worlds. At times he admits that it is certainly possible to conceive of other possible worlds in which more human beings enjoy happiness, even in which there is no unhappiness whatsoever.[69] Elsewhere, however, he suggests that the most harmonious universe maximizes the objective conditions for the virtue and happiness of rational minds—who enjoy their supreme felicity in contemplating such harmony—and therefore contains the greatest amount of happiness possible.[70] Either way, what is certain, as experience shows, is that in the best world not everyone is virtuous and happy; more troublesome from a theodicean perspective is the fact that not even every virtuous person is happy (at least in this lifetime; Leibniz suggests, though, that any undeserved suffering among the virtuous in this life is compensated for by an eternal reward in the hereafter: "It is true that one often suffers through the evil actions of others; but when one has no part in the offence one must look upon it as a certainty that these sufferings prepare for us a greater happiness"[71]).

It is not that God does not want every person to be happy. On the contrary, God, being perfectly beneficent, desires that every rational being enjoy happiness, just as He wants everyone to be saved. But He desires this only with what Leibniz calls an "antecedent will," that is, a highly abstract volition for something, a volition that is so "detached"

from all other considerations that it does not take into account anything except the thing desired—like wanting a triple-scoop ice-cream
cone without considering its cost or its effects on one's health. All
things being equal, God wants a world without evil; He wants everyone to enjoy happiness and all people to be saved. But all things are
not equal, and there are other antecedent wills in God that are contending for realization. God wants the world to be governed by simple, universal laws that do not allow for exceptions, even when the
ordinary course of nature leads to the suffering of virtuous individuals.
God also wants the world to be populated by free agents who are
morally responsible for their actions, and thus who may act in such a
way that they sin and therefore deserve punishment. All of these antecedent wills exist absolutely in God, but because some of them are
inconsistent with others, not all of them will have their proper effects.
Even God cannot bring it about that the world is governed by the
most simple laws *and* that everyone is happy. Compromises have to be
made so God can accomplish as much as possible of what He wants
to accomplish. The final outcome of this struggle among God's antecedent wills is a kind of maximization solution that optimally reconciles the various antecedent wills. This is God's "consequent will," and
it consists in the volition to create this world rather than any other.

> This will is called *antecedent* when it is detached, and con-
> siders each good separately in the capacity of a good. In
> this sense it may be said that God tends to all good, as
> good . . . and that by an antecedent will. He is earnestly
> disposed to sanctify and to save all men, to exclude sin,
> and to prevent damnation. It may even be said that this
> will is efficacious *of itself*, that is, in such sort that the ef-
> fect would ensue if there were not some stronger reason
> to prevent it: for this will does not pass into final exercise,
> else it would never fail to produce its full effect, God be-
> ing the master of all things. Success entire and infallible

belongs only to the *consequent will*, as it is called. This it is which is complete; and in regard to it this rule obtains, that one never fails to do what one wills, when one has the power. Now this consequent will, final and decisive, results from the conflict of all the antecedent wills, of those that tend toward good, even as of those that repel evil; and from the concurrence of all these particular wills comes the total will.

To Leibniz's opponents, many of them concerned to safeguard divine omnipotence, it seemed, shockingly, that he was saying that God does not get to accomplish everything He wants to accomplish or that God must tailor His work to the limited means available. This makes God remarkably like *finite* agents, like human beings, and not like the infinite being He is supposed to be. Leibniz, however, maintaining even in old age an optimistic and ecumenical outlook, found a characteristically positive way of summarizing his position: "God wills *antecedently* the good and *consequently* the best."[72]

5

The Kingdoms of Nature and Grace

In the fall of 1676, Leibniz was not a happy man. His employer, Duke Johann Friedrich of Brunswick, was growing impatient. He wanted his new counselor at court. Leibniz could delay his departure from Paris no longer, and in October he finally left for Hanover, a German backwater of ten thousand souls. He hoped he would not have to abandon his philosophical projects and the world of letters, and he had in hand a letter to the Catholic duke from Le Grand Arnauld, who recommended that Leibniz be given freedom to pursue his studies.[1]

Leibniz was determined to stay in touch with his French friends. Over the next four decades, he exchanged correspondence and writings with Malebranche, Arnauld, Foucher, Huet, and others, and kept abreast of developments on the Parisian intellectual and scientific fronts. Leibniz followed closely Malebranche's growing reputation as a leading, if highly unorthodox, Cartesian philosopher,[2] and was concerned about Arnauld's personal troubles and forced exile in the Netherlands. Malebranche himself told Leibniz that "Arnauld [is] in hiding . . . some say [he] went to Rome, but I do not believe that that is true."[3]

Leibniz was a man of enormous energy and persistence. Though he never again saw Malebranche or Arnauld in person, and despite the many time-consuming projects in which he was involved—some of them far-flung assignments on behalf of the House of Hanover, including designing windmills—he made great efforts to keep his erstwhile Parisian colleagues within his philosophical circle. Doing so was essential if his ideas were to receive critical examination from the period's leading thinkers.

Malebranche and Leibniz especially remained in sporadic but reasonably close contact. There are more than twenty letters extant between the two from 1675 to 1712—not a large number, particularly for an indefatigable correspondent like Leibniz, but enough to maintain a regular dialogue.[4] Leibniz studied Malebranche's books closely; he usually obtained copies soon after they appeared and made extensive remarks as he read them. Leibniz wrote to Malebranche in January 1679, for the purpose of "maintaining the advantage of your acquaintance," as well as to acknowledge having just received a copy of Malebranche's recently published *Christian Conversations*.[5] In his reading notes to this, Malebranche's second work (published just two years after the *Search After Truth*), Leibniz says that "this book, without a doubt, merits being read with care, not only because of its author, whom I know to be a clever man, but because it deals with an important matter in a very ingenious and very profound manner."[6] That same year, Leibniz, replying to Malebranche's request that he explain more fully "the things you say about Monsieur Descartes," sent to Malebranche two long letters in which he offers "without dissimulation" his critical assessment of Descartes's philosophy, to which he knew Malebranche was still wedded. Leibniz is especially harsh in his treatment of what he sees as Descartes's morally impoverished conception of God. "Descartes's God or perfect Being is not a God as one imagines Him and as one wishes, that is, just and wise."[7] The Cartesian God, Leibniz complains, does not act for the sake of any good ends, and thus "provides us with no consolation" in a universe governed by necessity rather than providential care.

Over the ensuing years, the two men exchanged letters on questions of mathematics, philosophy, and physics, with Leibniz doing most of the work in trying to draw the more reserved Malebranche out on metaphysical matters. In their communications to each other and to third parties (including Bayle), as well as in treatises and notes, they discuss the nature of substance, disagree about the proper conception of the laws of nature, and debate the respective advantages of occasionalism and the preestablished harmony. As to Leibniz's charge, for example, that Malebranche's doctrine introduces perpetual miracles into nature, it emerges from these writings that they in fact disagree as to what exactly constitutes a miracle: for Malebranche, while all events are directly caused by God, a miracle is an extraordinary state of affairs that He brings about in violation of the laws of nature; for Leibniz, an event is miraculous if its occurrence is something that exceeds the power of created substances.

Then, in 1711, Leibniz sent Malebranche a copy of the *Theodicy*. Leibniz says that he was generally pleased with the public's response to the book. In a letter of May 1715, to Christoph Joachim Nicolai von Greiffencranz, he notes that it was well received among "excellent theologians from the three religions" (that is, Lutherans, Calvinists, and Catholics).[8] It even won approval from the Jesuits in Paris, who had it reprinted. Evidently, he was now also looking for the Oratorian's approval of the book, or—even better—to begin a philosophical exchange concerning its contents.

The *Theodicy* includes strong objections to central elements of Malebranche's system. It was written around the same time that Leibniz composed his "Conversation of Philarète and Ariste," a self-styled sequel to Malebranche's own *Dialogues on Metaphysics and on Religion* (1688). Leibniz called the book "a little dialogue on some opinions of the Reverend Father Malebranche," and in it he continued his assault on the Cartesian conception of matter and on Malebranche's doctrine of the Vision in God.

Malebranche, thin-skinned as he was, was also possibly the most forgiving and charitable thinker of his time. When a fellow ecclesiastic, a man from Lyons named Vaugelade, offered to publish a second edition of Malebranche's *Christian Conversations* with the addition of his own preface, Malebranche, not particularly impressed by the man's work, nonetheless allowed it to go through. The book appeared with Vaugelade's name as author, however, and no mention of Malebranche anywhere. Vaugelade subsequently took no steps to correct the "error" and reportedly even accepted compliments on the book. Malebranche decided not to make a fuss about the incident. One contemporary wrote that "seeing that truth did not suffer, and that his book, while under a foreign banner, brought him each day new conquests, he kept silent. He believed that charity required him not to reveal to the public his brother's shame."[9] It is a striking instance of benevolence, particularly in the seventeenth century, and reveals Malebranche's kindhearted and pious nature. It is hard to imagine Leibniz, concerned as he was with his worldly reputation and with making an impression among his peers and potential patrons, responding in the same way.

With the *Theodicy*, Leibniz presented Malebranche with a book in which he repeatedly criticized occasionalism and other Malebranchian doctrines. To share criticism of another's work in this way was a classic gesture of respect in the seventeenth-century intellectual world, and Malebranche, ever the polite and accommodating correspondent and perhaps mellowed even further by old age, did not completely disappoint his German friend. To Leibniz's regret, Malebranche failed to offer much in the way of a philosophical reply or the opening of an extended conversation on theodicean strategy. And Malebranche told Leibniz, in the last extant letter he wrote him, that he hoped that God would reward Leibniz for such a fine work by bringing about his conversion to Catholicism—a remark to which Leibniz did not take very kindly. But Malebranche also said to him that "you very well prove a priori, Monsieur, that of all the possible plans of works that God discovers in his wisdom, He must choose the best."[10]

Leibniz probably expected this. He no doubt believed that Malebranche would overlook their minor differences, consider the whole, and see the common ground between them. In the *Theodicy*, Leibniz notes that "Father Malebranche's system . . . amounts to the same as mine."[11] There is a bit of disingenuousness in this statement, and ultimately Malebranche himself took issue with the claim. But Leibniz knew that he and Malebranche agreed on certain fundamental philosophical and theological truths. They adopt similar approaches to the problem of evil; they offer compatible accounts of the distribution and efficacy of divine grace (no small feat for a Catholic and a Lutheran to accomplish in the seventeenth century); and above all, they share the most basic assumptions about the nature of God and His modus operandi. Perhaps the reason why Malebranche did not feel the need to say more in reply to Leibniz at this late point was because he had already, and at great length, made clear his views on the matter.

In May 1684, the readers of Bayle's *Nouvelles de la république des lettres* were treated to a glowing review of "a wonderful book" that was then already four years old.[12] "This book," Bayle writes, "made such a commotion that everyone who was capable of this kind of reading has already read it." Nonetheless, he continues, it is worthwhile to "send readers back to it" and say some things about this new edition, with its appended elucidations. Bayle summarizes the work and praises the way in which it successfully depicts God as intimately causally involved in the world and also allows us to understand why He permits "so many monstrous and irregular things" in nature. "Never before . . . has there been so well constructed a system on so profound a theological matter as the mystery of grace, and one would fail to render it any justice if one did not acknowledge that there could not be a more vast, extensive, penetrating, and sharp genius than what is possessed by this system."[13]

The object of Bayle's admiration was Malebranche's *Treatise on Nature and Grace*. Malebranche had only hinted at theodicean issues in the *Search After Truth* proper, but did offer some extensive reflections in the elucidations appended to that work's third edition, in 1678, as well as in the *Christian Conversations* the previous year. But it is in the 1680 *Treatise*, devoted to justifying "the wisdom and goodness of God despite the disorders of nature," that Malebranche first gives the problem of evil his full and undivided attention. He wrote the book, he says, as a response to certain current Jansenist beliefs. The fifth of the contentious Five Propositions attributed to the Port-Royalists is the following claim: "It is a semi-Pelagian opinion to say that Jesus Christ died or that he shed his blood for all men without exception." According to the Jansenists (at least as their enemies in the Church understood them), God does not will to save all men, and anyone who says otherwise is a heretic. Arnauld, in fact, had argued on behalf of Jansenism that the Scriptural statement "God wants to save all men" must not be taken literally, *au pied de la lettre*, and that to be properly understood it must be interpreted figuratively. It certainly does not mean, he insisted, that God positively wills that each and every human being be saved. Rather, the phrase "all men" refers to all *kinds* of human beings, and thus the general claim means that while God has elected to save only certain individuals, they are drawn "from all sorts of conditions, ages, sexes, and nationalities"; the rest of humanity is to be left "in the common mass of perdition."[14]

Malebranche was astonished by the audacity of such an opinion, so contrary to Scripture's apparent intent (as well as to God's infinite mercy). With the *Treatise* he intended to defend the true universality of God's salvific will. Despite the entreaties of his friends, not to mention the urgings of his conscience, he was initially reluctant to publish anything on such a potentially incendiary matter, being, as his biographer Father André notes, "extremely adverse to confrontations" and taken by a "mortal fear when obliged to mount the stage and speak to the public."[15] But he was sufficiently troubled by the Jansenist onslaught—in his eyes, a Protestant fifth column in Catholic France, with its claim that only a preelected few are given God's grace—that he felt a religious duty to demonstrate that God does indeed desire the salvation of all individuals and, at the same time, to show just why, as tradition testifies, not everyone is actually saved.[16] Like Leibniz, however, he realized that addressing this issue requires a more general investigation into God's ways in the realms of both nature and grace, with the damnation of so many (including virtuous individuals presumably deserving of salvation) counting as only one (albeit a particularly important one) of a variety of evils or imperfections in creation.

In the *Dialogues on Metaphysics and on Religion*, published in 1688 to provide the public with an accessible and entertaining overview of the multifarious parts of his philosophy, Malebranche offers an elegant and succinct statement of the problem of evil. As Theodore, his spokesman, exclaims, "The universe is the most perfect God can create? What! So many monsters, so many disorders, the great number of impious people; does all this contribute to the perfection of the universe?" Aristes, his interlocutor, is thereby led to question either the efficacy of God's will or the benevolence of God's intentions:

> You confuse me, Theodore. God wills to make the most perfect possible work. For the more perfect it is, the more it will honor Him. That appears evident to me. But I clearly conceive that it would be more accomplished if it were free of the thousands and thousands of defects

which disfigure it. That is a contradiction that stops me
short. It seems that God has not executed His plan or has
not adopted the plan most worthy of His attributes.[17]

In essence, as Theodore explains, Aristes gets it wrong. God does not
will to make the most perfect work. Or, to put it in Leibnizian terms,
this is not the best of all possible worlds.

The key to Malebranche's theodicy lies in what he sees as the generality of God's will and in the recognition that making a world that is
perfect in all of its details—without sin and evil—is, for God, secondary to acting in a way that is most worthy of His attributes. This is
true for his solution to the problem of evil both in the realm of nature
(when it comes to physical and moral evils) and in the realm of grace
(where not everyone who is deserving of ultimate felicity will enjoy it).

Before creating the world, Malebranche's God, like Leibniz's, surveys in His eternal understanding an infinite number of possible
worlds. In addition to the worlds that He may create, however, Malebranche's God must also consider the variety of possible means of creating and sustaining a world, since presumably one and the same
world might be brought about in very different ways. "The wisdom of
God reveals to Him an infinity of ideas of different works, and all the
possible ways of executing his plans."[18] What Malebranche has in mind
are the laws that govern a universe. As guides to God's ubiquitous
causal activity, these are partly responsible for bringing about all the
phenomena of that world and for keeping things running in a regular
manner.

At this point, an important theodicean question, distinct from the
problem of evil per se but no less pressing, arises: Why should a perfect, eternal, and self-sufficient God create anything in the first place?
Nothing God creates could possibly equal Him in perfection and be
truly worthy of His will; the finite goodness of the world is incom-

mensurable with the infinite goodness of God, and thus can offer God no compelling reason to choose to create it. As Malebranche puts it, "God has no need of His creatures."[19] For Malebranche, the problem becomes particularly acute because he believes that God never pursues any end outside Himself. God acts only for His own glory, and He finds that glory in the first instance only in His attributes. Malebranche, however, has a solution to this difficulty: the Incarnation. This is what dignifies the world, elevating it to a level sufficient for God's choice. God's glory finds its highest expression in creation in the establishment of His Church; and what makes the establishment of that Church possible is the presence in the world of Jesus Christ. "If you join Jesus Christ to his Church, and the Church to the rest of the world, from which it is drawn, you will then raise to the glory of God a temple so august and so holy that you will be surprised that the foundations of it were laid so late."[20]

But the Incarnation and the establishment of the Church might have taken place in any number of possible worlds. What made the actual world most worthy of God's choice is the fact that it is the one world that is most consistent with God's character, and thus most expressive of His attributes. This is not because the actual world is without any imperfections. Malebranche concedes that the world is full of real defects—an opinion that inflamed many of his critics (who, like Leibniz, preferred to believe that the world's imperfections were only apparent). "When I open my eyes to consider the visible world, it seems that I discover there so many defects, that I am once again led to believe something that I have nevertheless denied so many times, that the world is the work of blind Nature, which acts without design."[21] In fact, Malebranche insists, the actual world does not even contain fewer evils than any other possible world. Thus, what primarily makes the actual world the most worthy of choice in God's eyes has nothing to do with the phenomena of the world per se. Rather, it is the fact that the laws that govern the universe and its phenomena are of maximum simplicity.

An excellent workman should proportion his action to his work; he does not accomplish by quite complex means that which he can execute by simpler ones, he does not act without an end, and never makes useless efforts. From this, one must conclude that God, discovering in the infinite treasures of his wisdom an infinity of possible worlds (as the necessary consequences of the laws of motion that he can establish), determines Himself to create that world that could have been produced and preserved by the simplest laws, and that ought to be the most perfect, with respect to the simplicity of the ways necessary to its production or to its conservation.[22]

According to Malebranche's doctrine of occasionalism, God is the sole efficient cause in nature. Even after the world is first created, God, through an ongoing creative activity, will continue to be responsible for generating all natural phenomena. Thus, God's primary consideration in selecting and creating a world is that His means of acting in that world, His ordinary operation in bringing things into being and sustaining them and effecting all changes does not dishonor his attributes. And this can be ensured only if things are governed by the simplest laws imaginable. These alone would be "the design most worthy of Him." As examples of such maximally simple laws, Malebranche offers the inertial law of rectilinear motion and an impact principle inspired by Descartes's rules for the distribution of motion during the collision of bodies.

I am persuaded that the laws of motion that are necessary to the production and the preservation of the earth, and of all the stars that are in the heavens, are reducible to these two: the first, that moved bodies tend to continue their motion in a straight line; the second, that when two bodies collide, their motion is distributed in both in proportion to their size, such that they must afterwards move at an equal speed. These two laws are the cause of all the motions that cause that variety of forms that we admire in nature.[23]

The picture is not yet complete, however, because the simplest laws, just because of their simplicity and generality, can give rise to a wide variety of worlds (even if these are restricted to worlds containing the Incarnation). From different initial states of creation, with the same set of basic laws, different subsequent courses of events—different worlds—follow. Malebranche says that God, "from an infinity of possible combinations of causes with their effects," looks to create that one world "that most felicitously reconciles the physical and the moral."[24] This is a world in which justice predominates as much as it can, given the simplest laws, and as many people as possible receive their proper deserts—where rewards and punishments ("the physical") are closely related to deeds ("the moral").[25] Thus God, after setting upon the simplest laws, looks for the most perfect world that can arise from such laws. He then creates an initial state of the universe, knowing that from that state, in accordance with those laws, He will get the world He wants.

This opens the way for the first step in Malebranche's theodicy. For it is now clear why the world created by God is not the best of all possible worlds. The divine need to establish and follow the simplest laws possible represents a constraint on God's choice and a limitation on how good the world can be. The actual world is not the most perfect world absolutely speaking; rather, it is only the most perfect world possible relative to those maximally simple laws.[26]

A work perfect to the degree of eight, or that bears the character of the divine attributes to the degree of eight, produced by means that only express those attributes to the degree of two, provides a total expression of those attributes only of ten. But a work perfect only to the degree of six, or that expresses only to the degree of six the divine attributes, but produced by means that express those attributes also to the degree of six, provides a total expression of those attributes to the degree of twelve. Thus, if God made a choice of one of these two works, He would choose the less perfect: since the less perfect [work] joined to those means would better express the character of His attributes . . . In a word, God is honored as much by the wisdom of His ways as by the excellence of His works.[27]

In the actual world, not every virtuous person is rewarded nor every wicked person punished. There are many other possible worlds with closer connections between "the physical and the moral," where more of the virtuous enjoy happiness and more of the wicked suffer misery. But all of those other worlds involve more complex laws—for example, laws that make exceptions for virtuous individuals to escape some harm that, by the ordinary course of nature, they would suffer. And achieving those more perfect worlds may even require God to act often in improvised ways, outside the prescriptions of any law whatsoever—for example, to save a prophet from being eaten by lions into whose den he has been thrown, which (by the laws of nature) is what would ordinarily happen. In short, God wills to accomplish as much justice and goodness as He possibly can, not absolutely but consistent with the simplest laws. "God can act only according to what He is, only in a way that bears the character of His attributes; thus He does not form His plans independently of the ways of executing them, but chooses the work and the ways that all together express the perfections, which He glories in possessing, better than any other work in any other way."[28]

With the laws in place and the absolute simplicity of God's ways guaranteed, Malebranche can explain not just the imperfection of the world at large but also the particular evils contained therein. The conceptual centerpiece of Malebranche's theodicy is the claim, so frequently found in his writings, that a wise, simple, eternal, and constant God acts only by "general volitions" and (almost) never by "particular volitions."[29] A general volition is a will to do something that is in accordance with some law or general principle. A law of physics, for example, specifies that if a body of a certain size at rest is struck by a body of a certain size in motion, then it will be moved in a certain way. When Malebranche's God then moves a body in the appropriate way on the occasion of its being struck by another body, He is acting by a general volition. Similarly, if God causes a feeling of pain in some person on the occasion of his being pricked by a needle, this is done through a general volition, since it is in accordance with the laws of mind-body union that He has established. A particular volition, on the other hand, does not obey any law, but is ad hoc. If God were to move a body without its having been struck by another body, or if He were to cause pain in someone without anything having happened to that person's body, He would be acting by a particular volition.[30] Malebranche insists that such arbitrary acts by God, just because they are not regulated by general laws of nature, are miracles.[31] Thus, Malebranche's God not only institutes the simplest laws but also is bound by his own nature—as a wise, good, immutable, and absolutely simple being who acts with perfect constancy—to follow those laws in the causal operations through which He makes nature function.

In addition to the logical, a priori reasoning that Malebranche provides for this claim about the generality of God's will, based on the consideration of God's attributes, Malebranche adds a secondary argument based on more practical considerations. If God acted by particular volitions—that is, if He regularly brought about events not because they were, given the antecedent conditions, demanded by the laws of nature but because He simply and directly wanted those particular events to happen—then it would always be a sin not to accept passively everything that happens. A person caught in a burning building would sin against God were he to try to escape from that building, since the building's collapse on him would be something willed very specifically by God Himself, and not just something that happens to be brought about in the law-governed, ordinary course of nature.[32]

Why, then, is there evil in the world? Why are individuals born without limbs, why are there floods and droughts, why is there sin and suffering, and why do virtuous people sometimes suffer while vicious people prosper? And why, especially, are not all human beings saved by the grace of God?

Malebranche believes that it is important, above all, to bear in mind that God does not will any of these evils with a particular volition. God does not choose them for their own sake and regardless of what else happens to be the case.

> If rain falls on certain lands, and if the sun roasts others; if weather favorable for crops is followed by hail that destroys them; if a child comes into the world with a malformed and useless head growing from his breast, and makes him wretched; it is not that God has willed these things by particular wills.[33]

These unfortunate events occur because God allows them to occur— or, rather, brings them about—as a part of the ordinary course of nature as this is regulated by its most simple laws. General laws have a wide variety of effects. As anyone whose plans have ever been disturbed by the weather knows, these laws, which on the whole make for an orderly and predictable world, cannot take into account the convenience and wishes of particular individuals. Birth defects, earthquakes, and other natural disorders are but the "necessary consequences [of] laws so simple that they serve to produce everything beautiful that we see in the world."[34] God, obliged as He is to following the laws of nature, "makes it rain on fallow lands as well as on those that are cultivated," because that is the meteorological result to which the laws lead. Likewise, if a person should be "dropping rocks on the heads of passers-by, the rocks will always fall at an equal speed, without discerning the piety, or the condition, or the good or bad dispositions of those who pass by."[35] Just as the rain falls where it must, regardless of what lies underneath, so the rocks, falling as rocks do, will land on the heads of the virtuous and the vicious alike. In these and other cases, God is simply carrying out the natural consequences of the laws of nature—laws that are so simple that they admit of no exceptions and that specify that when certain things occur, other things must happen.

God, then, is more committed to acting in a general way and to a nature governed by the simplest laws than He is to the well-being of individuals. As the universal cause, He follows those laws, come what may to those affected by them. For this reason, Malebranche says that God "permits disorder but He does not create it, He does not will it."[36] But the word *disorder* is ambiguous. An event is a disorder in one very relative sense if it frustrates the ends or ambitions of an agent. A rock falling on one's head is certainly a disorder for the injured party. But from a more global perspective, such an event is perfectly ordered, since it follows from the sequence of previous events in a lawlike way. "It is no disorder for lions to eat wolves, wolves sheep, and sheep the grass that God tends so carefully that He has given it all the things necessary for its own preservation."[37] For Malebranche, nature is perfectly well ordered—and that is exactly why disorders happen.

God, of course, could step in at any time and forestall these unfortunate things from occurring. He could prevent droughts, keep fruit from rotting on trees, and stop rocks from falling on the heads of virtuous people. But this would involve His constantly interfering with the operations of the laws of nature through particular volitions, and thus violating the generality of His ways. It would be asking God perpetually to perform miracles to "correct" nature. But, Malebranche cautions, "it is a weakness to change one's mind, it shows a lack of enlightenment or of firmness . . . Thus one must be careful not to

demand miracles from God, or to attribute them to Him at every moment."[38] In the *Dialogues*, even the sometimes slow-witted Aristes,
having well learned his lessons from Theodore, can wax eloquent on
the inappropriateness of demanding that God "multiply his volitions"
for the sake of reducing the number of evils in the world.

> God could convert all people and prevent all disorders.
> But He must not thereby upset the simplicity and unifor-
> mity of His action. For He must be honored through the
> wisdom of His ways as well as through the perfection of
> His creatures. He does not allow monsters; it is He who
> makes them. But He makes them only in order to alter
> nothing in His action, only out of respect for the gener-
> ality of His ways, only to follow exactly the laws of na-
> ture He has established and has nonetheless established
> not for the monstrous effects they must produce, but for
> those effects more worthy of His wisdom and goodness.
> For He wills them only indirectly, only because they are
> the natural consequence of His laws.[39]

One might reply that, instead of operating outside the laws of nature
through miracles, God could also have simply instituted different laws,
ones that do not lead to so many "disorders." But such laws would,
Malebranche insists, have to be more complex than the ones actually
established, and thus inconsistent with the simplicity of God's ways.

> God could, no doubt, make a world more perfect than
> the one in which we live. He could, for example, make it
> such that rain, which serves to make the earth fruitful,
> fall more regularly on cultivated ground than in the sea,
> where it is unnecessary. But in order to make this more
> perfect world, it would have been necessary that He have
> changed the simplicity of His ways . . . Our world, how-

ever imperfect one wishes to imagine it, is based on laws
of motion which are so simple and so natural that it is
perfectly worthy of the infinite wisdom of its author.[40]

This is not the best of all possible worlds. It is a defective world, one
full of imperfections, sins, and inequities. But given the constraints set
by the simplest laws, it is the best God can do. And that is enough to
vindicate God in the face of the world's evils. The reason why bad
things happen to good people and good things to bad people is not
because God, through particular volitions, wants it to work out that
way. That would seriously put in question God's goodness and justice.
Rather, all people, the virtuous and vicious alike, are subject to the
vicissitudes of nature's lawlike ways; no one, no matter what his character, can be fully immune to the slings and arrows of outrageous
fortune.

Divine grace is a pleasure, at least as Malebranche conceives it. It is
a delectation that has God as its object and that sets the human
will in motion toward its true good. The product of grace is a love of
God.[41] Adam and Eve naturally knew through reason alone that God
was their true good; they had no need of pleasure to be led toward
Him. With the Fall, this original cognitive condition was lost, with
the result that individuals are now led by sensory delights and their
wills are turned toward the material goods that occasion those delights. Through grace, God uses pleasure to counteract base desires
and turn postlapsarian human beings back toward Himself.

As a supernatural phenomenon, the distribution of grace is something that transcends the laws of nature. And as a pure gift, one would
naturally expect it to be given by God on an individual basis to those
whom He wants to save, regardless of desert. Unlike the phenomena
of nature, then, it might seem that the phenomena of grace are governed by God through particular volitions, independently of any laws.

And yet, as Malebranche notes, "Holy Scripture teaches us on the one hand that God wills that all men be saved, and that they come to a knowledge of the truth; and on the other, that He does everything that He wills: and none the less faith is not given to everyone; and the number of those that perish is much greater than that of the predestined." Here, once again, is the conundrum. "How," he wonders, "can one reconcile this with His power?"[42] Moreover, there are many individuals who, though perfectly just, do not receive grace, while many of those who do receive grace fail to make the proper use of it and remain among the mass of the damned.

This "disorder" in the realm of grace is, in Malebranche's eyes, sufficient evidence that even here God does not act by particular volitions. An omnipotent God acting by particular volitions would not find His will failing to have its intended effects. And a wise and just God acting by particular volitions would not give to an individual less grace than is needed to overcome his devotion to the pleasures of the senses. "If God gave grace by particular wills, no doubt he would not take it into His head, in order to convert a sinner who has four degrees of concupiscence, to give him three degrees of spiritual delectation, supposing that those degrees were not sufficient to convert him . . . For to what purpose is it to give three degrees of spiritual delectation to one for whom four degrees are necessary, and to refuse them to him to whom they would be sufficient to convert him?"[43]

In grace, as in nature, God acts only by general volitions and according to maximally simple laws that He is devoted to following. Grace is diffused among human beings in the same ordered manner as the rain is diffused upon the earth. And just as rain will occasionally fall futilely on fallow ground or destructively on swollen rivers, so, too, the divine gift will often fall on souls undeserving of its rewards or unprepared to make the proper use of it.

> Thus, as one has no right to be annoyed that the rain falls
> in the sea where it is useless, and that it does not fall on

seeded grounds where it is necessary . . . so too one ought not to complain of the apparent irregularity according to which grace is given to men. It is the regularity with which God acts, it is the simplicity of the laws which He observes, it is the wisdom and the uniformity of His conduct, which is the cause of that apparent irregularity. It is necessary, according to the laws of grace, that God has ordained, on behalf of His elect and for the building of His Church, that this heavenly rain sometimes falls on hardened hearts, as well as on prepared grounds. If, then, grace falls uselessly, it is not the case that God acts without design . . . Rather, the simplicity of general laws does not permit that this grace, which is inefficacious in this corrupted heart, fall in another heart where it would be efficacious.[44]

To ask God to ensure that grace falls only on "prepared ground" and therefore has the ultimate effect for which it is intended—the conversion of the sinner—is, once again, to ask God to act by more complex means than His nature allows, to violate the simplicity of His ways, to interrupt the laws of grace and operate through particular volitions: in short, to perform miracles.[45] A God acting in a general way according to simple laws will sometimes, even often, bring about unhappy consequences, whether it is a matter of natural disasters or a matter of a sinner not receiving enough grace to overcome his attachment to sensory pleasures. But that is the price to be paid for an orderly world governed by a deity who acts as a perfectly wise, just, and simple being must.

God does want everyone to be saved, but only with what Malebranche calls a "simple volition." Much like Leibniz's "antecedent will," this is a desire that something occur regardless of all other considerations.[46] If God acted on these simple desires—thereby making them "practical volitions"—then everyone would be saved. But such abstract volitions or wishes in God do not necessarily get fulfilled; Malebranche's God does not get to do everything He wants to do. He has to take into account all those other considerations, as well as the laws that govern them. Just as God moves a body only when it is struck by another body, as dictated by the laws of physics, so God gives grace to a soul only when the requisite conditions—those speci-fied by the laws of grace—obtain. Grace, like motion, is distributed according to the system of occasional causes. And those laws of grace stipulate that this supreme gift is to be given to an individual not on the occasion of that individual's desiring or earning it—this would be tantamount to Pelagianism—but only when Jesus Christ, the Re-deemer, who is responsible for building the Church, wills (with a par-ticular volition) that the specific person should receive it. It is Christ who prays for the salvation of individuals. Unfortunately, Christ, with his human nature, while endowed with his Father's infinite knowledge of all things, is still a finite being whose actual, conscious thoughts at any given moment are limited. He is therefore not always aware of the use to which a person will put the grace he is given. "[Jesus Christ] does not see . . . if a just person will or will not follow the movement of grace." While potentially knowledgeable about every facet of an in-dividual's character and condition, he does not in fact always "pene-trate their hearts."[47] Thus, he will sometimes desire that grace be given to a person—and thereby "occasion" God, the true cause, to provide grace to that person—whose heart is so hardened that the grace does not have its ultimate effect, the overcoming of concupiscence. God could remedy this with but a single particular volition, but—as Male-branche never tires of reminding his readers—that would be to expect Him to act in a manner unworthy of His nature.

Malebranche believed that his system did full justice both to God's beneficence and to Christ's redemptive role. Bishop Jacques-Bénigne Bossuet, one of Malebranche's more important critics, was less

satisfied with the arrangement. Bossuet was confessor to Louis XIV
and tutor to the Dauphin, and thus a man of some consequence. He
found the *Treatise on Nature and Grace* to be "total gibberish," and
objected to the way in which Malebranche's God fails to show a particular providence for each and every individual. "God leads each
thing to the end that He proposes for it by the means which He follows."[48] Bossuet was especially troubled by the way Malebranche dis-
tanced God from the distribution of the necessary aids for salvation. A
man always ready with the appropriate bon mot, he suggested that,
in Malebranche's view, "we would all be saved, if we did not have a
Savior."[49]

In his *Theodicy*, Leibniz notes that "the excellent author of *The Search
After Truth*, having passed from philosophy to theology, published finally an admirable treatise on Nature and Grace."[50] Leibniz was impressed by Malebranche's demonstration that events—in particular,
evils—that follow from God's enforcement of general laws are not
necessarily things that He wills especially. "I agree with Father Malebranche that God does things in the way most worthy of him."[51] Leibniz reads Malebranche as saying, in effect, that the result of God's
creative act is the best of all possible worlds.

> The ways of God are those most simple and uniform: for
> he chooses rules that least restrict one another. They are
> also the most productive in proportion to the simplicity
> of ways and means. It is as if one said that a certain house
> was the best that could have been constructed at a certain
> cost. One may, indeed, reduce these two conditions, sim-
> plicity and productivity, to a single advantage, which is to
> produce as much perfection as is possible: thus Father
> Malebranche's system in this point amounts to the same
> as mine.[52]

Upon reading this in 1711, Malebranche demurred. When he wrote to Leibniz that December, he suggested that there was an important difference in their respective views.

> I am persuaded, as you are, that God has produced for his creatures all the good that He can produce for them, acting nonetheless as He must act, that is to say, acting according to His law that can only be the immutable order of His divine perfections, which He invincibly loves and that He can neither violate nor neglect. And thus His work [*Son ouvrage*] is the most perfect it can be, not absolutely, however, but in relation to the means in accordance with which it is executed. For God is honored not only by the excellence of His work, but also by the simplicity and the fecundity, by the wisdom of His ways.[53]

Writing back a month later, Leibniz acknowledges that he may have oversimplified things and explains to Malebranche why he, Malebranche, may have been misled into thinking there was a substantive difference in their views: "In effect, when I consider the work [*l'ouvrage*] of God, I consider his ways as a part of the work, and the simplicity joined to the fecundity of the ways form a part of the excellence of the work, for in the whole the means form a part of the end [and the simplicity of the means forms a part of the excellence of the work]."[54] Toward the end of the letter, Leibniz recaps some important points of agreement and suggests once again that the difference between them is really just nominal. Leibniz says that God creates the best of all possible worlds; there may be many other possible worlds with fewer sins and sufferings, but these worlds are inferior to the actual world God has created, and this is in part because they involve more complex laws. Malebranche says that God does not create the best of all possible worlds; there are many other possible worlds that are more perfect than the actual world because they contain fewer evils, but God does not create them because to do so He would have to violate the simplicity and generality of His ways.

In short, according to Leibniz, he and Malebranche disagree on whether or not this is the best of all possible worlds only because Malebranche uses the term *world* or *work* more narrowly than Leibniz does. For Malebranche, *world* refers only to the created product itself, the phenomena of nature (and grace), exclusive of the laws governing it. This allows Malebranche to declare that the goodness of the world is not absolute but only relative to God's means in making and preserving it. For Leibniz, on the other hand, *world* includes both the created product and the laws that generate and sustain it. Leibniz's point is that, terminological differences aside, he and Malebranche agree that the composite of product design and laws is, taken as a whole, the best overall and the most worthy of God's wisdom and benevolence, even if the product design itself, exclusive of the laws, seems fraught with imperfections. Malebranche should be able to accept this conciliatory assessment, at least to a degree, because he says that "God chooses the work and the ways that all together express the perfections that He glories in possessing better than any other work and way."[55] Just as for Leibniz this world combines maximally simple and fruitful laws with as much goodness and happiness for creatures as those laws will allow, so for Malebranche this world is governed by the simplest laws and reconciles to the highest degree possible, relative to those laws, "the physical and the moral."[56]

In spite of this agreement, there is no getting around the fact that Leibniz, unlike Malebranche, does believe that the world, considered even independently of the laws, is absolutely the best of all. It contains sin, suffering, and other inconveniences for creatures. But it also contains the maximum amount of perfection and happiness a world can contain, just because of the simplicity and fecundity of the laws governing it. Malebranche, by contrast, believes that there in fact are many other possible worlds that, in terms of intrinsic perfection, surpass the actual world. For Leibniz, the absolute bestness of the world is not just consistent with "the most fitting" laws but is made possible by them. For Malebranche, there is a tension between the simplicity of the laws and the quality of the product they generate; the beauty of the effect can be improved, but only at the cost of the simplicity of the means.[57]

The ecumenical Leibniz has strong motivation for glossing over any differences with Malebranche.[58] After all, if he can achieve some kind of theological common ground with a French Catholic, and especially on so important a topic as the justification of God's ways, then perhaps some life yet remains in his grand reunification project. Thus, it is hard not to believe that he is being devious when he claims that their views are so similar. There are important points of disagreement between the two philosophers on the problem of evil, as Leibniz well knew. Malebranche objected to Leibniz's view that the apparent evils of the world actually make a positive contribution to its overall goodness, in part by accentuating the good things to make them shine even brighter. An evil is an evil, he insists in a piece published in 1686 that Leibniz must have read, and its presence cannot serve to make anything better by contrast.

> One can certainly say, against the Manicheans, that monsters constitute a kind of beauty in the universe, and that God makes use even of impious people and demons for the execution of His designs. For everything enters into the order of Providence, even disorder. But disorder always remains what it is. God permits it, because He can put it to various uses. But He does not will it, because He has not established His laws in order that it happens . . . Shadows are necessary in a painting, and dissonances in music. Thus, women must abort and create an infinite number of monsters. What an absurd consequence, I strongly reply to the philosophers![59]

In the *Dialogues*, when Theotimus suggests that "the irregularities of nature, monsters, and even the impious are like the shadows of a painting, which lend force to the work and relief to the figures," Aristes, taking his lead from Theodore, replies that "such a thought has an 'I know not what' that pleases the imagination, but the mind is not satisfied by it. For I understand quite well that the universe would be more perfect if there were nothing irregular in any of the parts comprising it, and on the contrary there is almost no place where there is not some defect."[60] For Malebranche, the world truly is defective; for Leibniz, despite its many evils and imperfections, it is not. For Malebranche, the evils in the world really detract from the character of God's product. "I do not agree that there is evil only in appearance; I think that there is evil, that God permits it."[61] As he says in the *Treatise*, "it would be better if these [monstrous deformities] did not exist."[62] For Leibniz, so-called evils are really just lesser degrees of perfection that appear to be defects only when we take too narrow a perspective on things and fail to see the contribution they make (aesthetic or metaphysical) to the overall goodness of creation.

Leibniz, in turn, was explicitly critical of Malebranche on just this point in his *Discourse on Metaphysics*, composed in 1686 but still unpublished by the time of their exchange of letters in 1711. "I am unable to approve of the opinion of certain modern writers who boldly maintain that what God has made is not perfect in the highest degree, and that he might have done better." Mere "comparative perfection," he insists, "is wholly inconsistent with the glory of God."[63]

And then there is the basic difference in the aims and intentions they attribute to God. Unlike Leibniz's God, Malebranche's God is not concerned with producing as much good as possible; He is not trying to balance or even maximize two values to produce the best outcome overall. Rather, for Malebranche, the simplicity of God's ways takes precedence over everything else. "His wisdom in a sense renders Him impotent; for because it obliges Him to act by the most simple ways, it is not possible for all humans to be saved, because of the simplicity of His ways . . . God loves His wisdom more than His work . . . because His wisdom prescribes means that most bear the character of His attributes."[64] Borrowing terms from moral philosophy, one can almost reduce the difference between the Gods of Malebranche and Leibniz to that between an agent following a deontological ethics, for whom a particular value or way of acting must be pursued no matter what the consequences (Malebranche's God, with simplicity being supreme), and an agent devoted to consequentialism, who chooses his actions to bring about as much total good as possible (Leibniz's God).[65]

Nonetheless, Leibniz was on to something. These differences, significant as they are, should not obscure the more fundamental agreement between the two philosophers. They do provide the same basic explanation for *why* there is evil and imperfection in the world: God permits evil for the sake of a higher value. He allows suffering, sin, and damnation because to forestall them would require Him to violate superlative principles that He has wisely set in place to govern the world. Intervening to prevent an evil or rectify a situation brought about by the laws of nature and grace would entail some loss for God, either in terms of the overall goodness of creation or in terms of what He owes Himself. As Leibniz says in a letter to Malebranche in 1679, which he wrote just after reading the *Metaphysical Meditations* and well before ever conceiving his book on God's justice, "I find very true what you say about the simplicity of God's decrees being the cause of the existence of particular evils, since God would otherwise be obliged to change the laws of nature at each moment."[66]

Even more important than this point of theodicy is a shared assumption about the nature of God and His ways of operating. Both Malebranche and Leibniz are committed to the view that God is a rational being who does things for an intelligible and objective purpose. As natural and unremarkable as this assumption may seem, it constitutes a crucial point of contention in the seventeenth century, one that ultimately divides two different conceptions of the universe, of the human being's place therein, and of the nature of and the path to true happiness and well-being.

A rational being is one for whom reasons matter. Such an agent is motivated teleologically by aims; he acts for the sake of achieving something. And he strives to achieve what he does because he recognizes it as good, as desirable in its own right. Moreover, his rationality is instrumental: he selects means toward his desired goal because he believes, with justification, that those means are the most efficient way to it. To pursue ends that one does not believe to be good, or to follow a path toward one's end that one knows not to lead there, or to lead there inefficiently, is to act irrationally.

Now consider Leibniz's God. He contemplates an infinite number of possible worlds and recognizes that one of them (the one that contains the simplest laws and the greatest amount of perfection) is, in absolute terms, the best of all. His desire is to produce as much perfection as possible, and so He brings that best of all possible worlds into existence. The optimality of that world provides Him with a compelling reason to create it; and had there been no such compelling reason, Leibniz's God would not have created a world at all. The principle of sufficient reason is binding even upon God. As Leibniz says, "[God] does nothing without acting in accordance with supreme reason."[67] This is true for all of God's choices, large and small. It is beautifully reflected in Leibniz's argument for his famous law of the identity of indiscernibles, which says that "there is no such thing as two individuals indiscernible from each other." The reason why there are not and cannot be two distinct things in nature that are absolutely identical—two leaves, or two snowflakes, "without any difference within themselves"—is because, in the complete absence of any differences between the two, God would have no compelling reason to put one of them in one place and the other in another place, rather than vice versa. Consequently, God, "who never does anything without wisdom," will not create such things.[68] "I infer from [the principle of sufficient reason] . . . that there are not in nature two real, absolute beings, indiscernible from each other, because if there were, God and nature would act without reason in treating the one otherwise than the other; and that therefore God does not produce two pieces of matter perfectly equal and alike."[69]

God, then, is never indeterminate; He never acts without knowledge of what He is doing and without being determined by reasons to do it. "His will is always decided, and it can be decided only by the best." God can never have what Leibniz calls a "primitive particular will," that is, an ad hoc volition that is independent of any rational law or principle. "Such a thing would be unreasonable. [God] cannot determine upon Adam, Peter, Judas, or any individual without the existence of a reason for this determination; and this reason leads of necessity to some general enunciation. The wise mind always acts according to principles; always according to rules, and never according to exceptions."[70]

Leibniz recognizes that this amounts to a kind of constraint on God, but insists that it is no more than the ordinary kind of determination that reasons bring to rational choices. His critics, less sanguine about the consequences of putting the restrictions of reason on God than Leibniz was, were concerned that if these reasons lead God "of necessity," then God loses His freedom of choice. Bayle argues that Leibniz subjects God to a kind of fate: "There is therefore no freedom in God; He is compelled by His wisdom to create, and then to create precisely such a work, and finally to create it precisely in such ways. These are three servitudes that form a more than Stoic *fatum*, and that render impossible all that is not within their sphere."[71]

But the necessity that binds God, Leibniz says, is "a happy necessity," because it has its source in God's own nature. "This so-called *fatum*, which binds even the Divinity, is nothing but God's own nature, his own understanding, which furnishes the rules for his wisdom and his goodness."[72] Contrary to Bayle's accusation, other possible worlds still remain possible, logically speaking. Each, considered in and of itself, involves no logical contradiction (as would be the case, for example, with a world in which both Napoleon is the French emperor and Napoleon is not the French emperor). However, these possibilities will, with certainty, *not* be chosen by God, and thus do not remain live options for His creative will. On the issue of God's freedom, Leibniz is what philosophers call a "soft determinist," or "compatibilist": God is determined to choose the best, but this does not mean the choice is not free. The determination is characterized only by what Leibniz describes as a *moral* (as opposed to a logical, metaphysical, or absolute) necessity, the necessity of reasons that compel choice in a rational being—a being who, because of His goodness and wisdom, is moved infallibly to choose the best. "There is always a prevailing reason that prompts the will to its choice . . . The choice is free and independent of [absolute] necessity because it is made between several possibles, and the will is determined only by the prepondering goodness of the object."[73]

In his early works, Malebranche often seems more interested in defending the sheer power of God's will than its wisdom and rationality. "God is a being whose will is power and infinite power," he wrote in the *Christian Conversations*.[74] But even in the *Search After Truth*, and especially in the *Treatise on Nature and Grace*, it is clear that Malebranche's God—like Leibniz's God—does not act arbitrarily. This is true in the ordinary course of nature (and grace), where God's causal activity is guided by laws. But the fact that God must choose the simplest laws for the world He creates, and then strive to produce as just and perfect a world as possible relative to those laws, shows that there is a higher authority than His will alone. God, Malebranche says, "cannot act against Himself, against His own wisdom and light." He may be indifferent as to whether or not anything other than He exists, indifferent as to "what He does external to Himself"—in other words, indifferent about whether or not to create at all. But having decided to create, "He is not indifferent, although perfectly free, in the way in which He does it; He always acts in the wisest and most perfect way possible. He always follows the immutable and necessary order."[75]

God's power is in itself infinite and incomprehensible. However, once God does decide to act "external to Himself," that power is subordinated to His wisdom, and especially to what Malebranche calls Order. Order consists in the eternal, immutable verities that stand above all things. These are pure logical and mathematical truths, absolutely true with the highest degree of necessity, but also moral and metaphysical principles about what Malebranche calls "relations of perfection." They determine the relative value of various kinds of being, and even of God's own attributes. Order shows that a soul is more noble than a body, and a human being more worthy than a dog; and it proclaims that, as important as God's mercy is, the simplicity and generality of His ways are even more important, and therefore cannot be violated, even to save a good person from drowning or damnation.[76] Order is "the exemplar of all God's works," and his volitions must conform to its principles. The dictates of Order serve God as universal reasons for everything He does. Even if, on some rare occasion, God must act by a particular volition and violate the laws of nature or grace to perform a miracle, this will be only because Order demands it.[77]

Thus, when God, considering the infinite possibilities in His understanding, chooses to create a world, Order sets one of His attributes (simplicity) above the others. Simplicity will in turn determine which laws God will establish for the world, and then how, given those laws, He can establish as much perfection as possible in the relationship of the physical to the moral. Malebranche says:

> Assuming that God wants to act, I contend that he will always do it in the most wise manner possible, or in the manner which most bears the character of his attributes. I insist that this is never an arbitrary or indifferent matter

for Him . . . Immutable Order, which consists in the
necessary relationship that exists between the divine
perfections, is the inviolable law and the rule of all His
volitions.[78]

God's wisdom, the dwelling place of Order, stands above his will and
guides it. "In Himself God has good reasons for everything He
does."[79]

Like Leibniz, Malebranche is concerned that his account of divine
rationality might be seen as compromising God's freedom. He even
concedes that, in a manner of speaking, it does. "The wisdom of God
renders Him impotent in the following sense, that it does not allow
Him to will certain things, nor to act in certain ways . . . God is impotent in the sense that He cannot choose ways of acting unworthy of
His wisdom, or that do not bear the character of His goodness, of His
immutability, or of His other attributes."[80] But, once again, this is only
the *moral* impotence of a perfectly rational being to act contrary to
unassailable reasons. God's choices are compelled; there are standards
that God is bound to observe. But these standards lie in God's wisdom, and the obligation to obey them comes from His nature alone.

In his critical remarks on Malebranche's system, published in 1686,
Bernard Le Bouvier de Fontenelle complains that the Oratorian's
principles make God out to be a very poor workman, one unable or
unwilling to achieve all his ends—above all, the goal of saving all human beings.[81] But this is wrong. It is not that Malebranche's God cannot achieve all His ends. Rather, there are certain ends He might wish
for, all things being equal, but that He ultimately does not want to
achieve, at least not at any cost. God does want to save all human beings. But God also knows that the salvation of many must be sacrificed
for the sake of higher, more important principles. God, like any rational agent, recognizes priorities and acts accordingly, even if this
means compromising on some of His "simple" or antecedent prefer-

ences. The best workman, as Malebranche sees it, is the one who knows which compromises to make.

Questions of influence in the history of philosophy are always difficult, and never more so than in the case of contemporaries. Leibniz was impressed by what he read in Malebranche's writings. It may be that, as some scholars have argued, Leibniz appropriated for his own theodicean purposes the picture of God he found there: a rational agent whose choices are guided, even determined, by a prior and infallible conception of the good; a wise, divine strategist seeking to maximize certain values (for Malebranche, the ratio of the physical to the moral; for Leibniz, perfection) within constraints set by His nature.[82]

On the other hand, Leibniz seems already to have had the important elements of his conception of God's modus operandi in place before Malebranche published a single word. In the unpublished dialogue "The Confession of a Philosopher," composed soon after his arrival in Paris, most likely in the fall or winter of 1672, Leibniz states his commitment to the rationality of God's choices: "The will of God is not the reason why God wills something (for what leads someone to will is never his willing to will but rather his believing that the thing merits it); the reason why God wills something is rather the nature of the things themselves."[83] Even before his Paris sojourn, Leibniz was convinced that what moves God to make the choices He makes, what counts as the sufficient reason for his will, is the principle of the best. Writing to Magnus Wedderkopf in 1671, he notes that "the ultimate basis of the divine will [is] . . . the divine intellect. For God wills those things that He perceives to be the best and, likewise, the most harmonious; and he selects them, so to speak, from the infinite number of all the possibles . . . Because God is the most perfect mind, it is impossible that He is not affected by the most perfect harmony and thus must bring about the best by the very ideality of things. But this does not detract from freedom. For it is the highest form of freedom to be forced to the best by right reason."[84]

When Leibniz arrived in Paris, then, he was already convinced that God is not an arbitrary being. He knew at the time, as well, that the key to unraveling the problem of evil lay in that divine rationality, especially in God's choice of the best of all possible worlds. This could not have failed to come up in his conversations with Malebranche on the rue St.-Honoré, as it must have been clear to both men that they were kindred spirits on some of the most basic of theological questions.

Their mutual friend Arnauld, however, was of another mind altogether. If the Jansenist firebrand was present in the Maison de l'Oratoire during these discussions, then he would have made his views known—and most likely not in a very politic way.

6

"Touch the Mountains and They Smoke"

During the early years of his exile from France, Arnauld, trying to stay a step ahead of his enemies, never remained in one place for very long. From the summer of 1679 through mid-1680, he sought refuge in a number of cities in the southern Low Countries. While these were still a Catholic domain, they belonged to France's bitter Hapsburg foe, Spain, and thus were not a particularly hospitable place for French spies. Over the course of several months, Arnauld lived in Mons, Brussels, then back in Mons, then in Ghent, and, in February 1680, back in Brussels. Still, he knew that the French authorities, aided perhaps by local Catholic ecclesiastics hostile to Jansenism, were on his trail, so he kept a low profile wherever he went. Writing to a friend at the end of May 1680, Madame de Sévigné notes that "poor M. Nicole [Arnauld's fellow Port-Royalist, also in exile] is in the Ardennes, and M. Arnauld has gone underground, like a mole."[1]

By July 1680, Arnauld had ventured north into the relatively safe environment of the Calvinist provinces of the Dutch Republic, where

religious toleration—and a resentment of outside meddling, especially
by Catholic authority—was the rule. While in Amsterdam, Arnauld
(still trying to keep his whereabouts a secret, even to sympathizers)
sent his personal secretary, Léonard Guelphe, to the publisher Daniel
Elzevier to supervise the printing of one of his writings. Guelphe
brought back to his employer a piece of shocking news: Elzevier was
in the process of printing a work by Malebranche with the title *Treatise
on Nature and Grace*. What was particularly galling to Arnauld was
that Malebranche was supposed to wait for comments from Arnauld
on this work, and had promised he would not publish it until he saw
what his Jansenist friend had to say.

Arnauld had been an early fan of Malebranche's *Search After Truth*
and sang its praises to others soon after its publication in 1675. "Monsieur
Arnauld is charmed with [your work]," the Marquis de Roucy
wrote to Malebranche that year. "He cites it all the time, he praises it
everywhere, he reads it to everyone."[2] What most pleased Arnauld
about the treatise was that Malebranche did not tread on matters of revealed
theology and respected the all-important divide between things
amenable to rational inquiry and things embraced on faith alone. Arnauld
also believed that the philosophical doctrines of the *Search* were
consistent with Jansenist sentiments, and even that its author was a
friend to the Port-Royal cause.

Arnauld was accordingly quite taken aback when Malebranche
managed to convert Michel Le Vassor, a young Oratorian highly sympathetic
to Jansenism who lived with Malebranche at St. Honoré, to
his novel views on grace—only lightly hinted at in the *Search*—and to
a general anti-Jansenist position.[3] This might have remained a minor
matter had Le Vassor not taken to proclaiming publicly the falsity of
Jansen's views and the truth of Malebranche's. There was much grumbling
over the affair among Port-Royalists and even within the Oratory
itself, where some of the priests had Jansenist leanings.

Le Vassor, discomfited by the turmoil he was causing, especially the falling out of old friends, decided that the best thing to do would be to bring Arnauld and Malebranche together for a tête-à-tête, preferably in a quiet and friendly setting. The Marquis de Roucy volunteered his home for the event, and in May 1679 the three men, along with Le Vassor and several others, met for dinner and an attempt at a reconciliation. The discussion lasted no more than two hours. Apparently, things did not go as well as Le Vassor had hoped.[4] As soon as Malebranche began to present his views, Arnauld attacked him, "interrupting continuously and at every moment."[5] According to Father André, the Oratorian "had hardly opened his mouth to speak when M. Arnauld's vivacity did not permit him to proceed further." Regarding Malebranche's opinion that God acts in the realms of nature and grace only by general volitions and never by particular volitions, Arnauld "did not want to hear either proof or explanation . . . He was constantly interjecting a question here, a conclusion there, even throwing in passages from St. Augustine." Malebranche was overcome by the force of Arnauld's considerable personality. "M. Malebranche did not have either the forcefulness or the linguistic volubility of his adversary, and was obliged simply to listen." It was, Father André concludes, "a heated dispute," although he says that in the end everyone parted as good friends.[6]

Arnauld, not surprisingly, remembers things differently. He recalls hearing Malebranche out and then offering his criticisms—objections that he believed everyone else in the room (except Le Vassor) shared—in a constructive and cooperative manner. He professes to have had no other intent than to see his friend set rightly on the path to Christian truth. Writing to De Roucy, he notes that "everything went off without much heat, and we all departed from your home as good friends as when we arrived."[7]

Whether or not the evening ended on a cordial note, it seems that Malebranche never really got the opportunity to give his views the exposition and defense he felt they deserved. Everyone agreed before parting that he should put it all down on paper and provide Arnauld with a copy, so that he might be able to study it at his leisure and in greater depth; Arnauld was then to offer his objections in writing as well.

Within a month of the dinner, however, Arnauld was in flight. When Malebranche had a complete draft of his new treatise on grace in August 1679, Arnauld was on the move in the Spanish Netherlands and not easily reached. Malebranche, apparently unaware of Arnauld's departure, gave a copy of the work to De Roucy to send to Arnauld, but it took a long time to reach its destination. Arnauld later said that he did not receive the manuscript until April of 1680, when he was settled in Brussels, and even then he did not acknowledge receipt. Malebranche thus heard nothing from Arnauld for many months after fulfilling his part of the agreement. He was initially annoyed by the silence and the inconvenience and delay it had caused him in bringing his book to publication. But after learning of Arnauld's exile, he was more understanding. Father André wrote that "as soon as he learned that M. Arnauld had left France and that his treatise followed him soon thereafter, he found it easier to accept the silence of his censor."[8]

Malebranche's patience, however, lasted only so long. He wrote to Arnauld in March of 1680 to nudge him, but did not receive a response.[9] Eventually, pressed by his opponents on one side and urged by his friends on the other, he decided to go ahead with the printing and sent the manuscript to Elzevier in Amsterdam.

Arnauld, for his part, admits that reading the draft of Malebranche's treatise was not his top priority at this time. He was in the middle of seeing some of his own work through the press. Moreover, the stress and difficulties of exile did not leave him much time or energy to devote to a serious reading of a philosophical discussion of nature and grace. Writing to his friend the Jansenist Pasquier Quesnel in April 1680, Arnauld says that "it has been impossible for me to read [Malebranche's] system. Since he wants me to read it without prejudice, I must also do it without distraction; and in order to fully understand such sublime thoughts, my mind must not be occupied with other things. I am afraid that I am not yet in that right condition, since I find myself about to undertake a short voyage that will last more than a month."[10] With all that he had to worry about, Arnauld says to De Roucy, "I did not feel myself obliged to drop everything in order to examine with greater leisure the *Treatise on Nature and Grace*."[11] He assumed that Malebranche, respecting their agreement, would simply wait to hear from Le Grand Arnauld before publishing the work.

It was therefore a great and unpleasant surprise when Guelphe returned from Elzevier's that day in July to report to Arnauld that his manuscript would have to wait its turn, as the presses were currently occupied with the printing of Malebranche's *Treatise on Nature and Grace*. Arnauld immediately sent his secretary back to the publisher to persuade him to halt the presses temporarily and give him copies of the few pages that had already been run off, along with the rest of the manuscript. Elzevier agreed, reluctantly, but allowed Arnauld only two days, after which he wanted everything back.

Arnauld had to work quickly—"with much precipitation," he said. He was alarmed by what he read. The treatise was, he insists, "full of audacious things." He found "so many things that I could not approve, and that I judged would be very poorly received."[12] He tried to persuade Elzevier to suspend publication, "having in view only the interest of the truth." He immediately wrote to Malebranche through a mutual friend who had also been at the De Roucy dinner to persuade him to abandon the project altogether, or at least until Arnauld could give it a more careful reading and provide the necessary corrections— something that he now promised to do "with all due care" and as soon as possible.

Malebranche, not surprisingly, declined the offer. He was anxious to see the work, an important follow-up to the *Search*, in print, and within a couple of months it was available to readers. Arnauld was greatly put off by this. He accused Malebranche of acting "with great haughtiness." "It seems to me that, after having asked for my judgment, it was not within the rules of decency to then go ahead and publish it without first receiving either [that judgment] or my refusal to provide it."[13]

Arnauld wanted his friends to be in no doubt about his intentions. He bore Malebranche no personal ill will, despite Malebranche's having composed a work so "prejudicial to religion." Writing to De Roucy on May 26, 1681, and knowing that the letter would be shown to Malebranche, Arnauld says that he will give the work the attention it deserves, thoroughly refuting its scandalous principles but doing so "with so much courtesy and moderation that [Malebranche] will have no cause to take offense."[14] That's the way it should be among "honest men, who must be able to be of different minds without this causing any harm to their friendship, especially when it comes to Christian truths, which everyone is obliged to defend according to the lights that God has given him." The sharp-witted Arnauld, however, cannot keep up this gentlemanly restraint, and the rest of the letter drips with sarcasm. Anticipating the backlash against his own contentious views on grace that Malebranche's book will occasion, Arnauld says that

> [Malebranche] himself has provided a fine example of [this proper way of conducting oneself], namely, through the consideration he has shown for those whom he has professed to love and who consider it an honor to be his friends by not having refrained from publishing his book, despite the fact that he well knew that it was highly contrary to their doctrines and that he could also easily see that this would provide an occasion for their enemies to attack them, abandoned as they are by those who

used to pass themselves off before all the world as their comrades.[15]

Writing again later that day, in a letter not for Malebranche's eyes, he assures De Roucy that, while "the things in his work that I cannot approve of do not at all diminish the affection that I have, and will always have, for him," he will not hold back in his retaliation.[16]

In the end, Arnauld let loose with a merciless fury.

The Arnauld–Malebranche debate was one of the great intellectual events of the seventeenth century. These two giants of philosophical theology, so unlike each other but each brilliant in his own way, opposed each other on a wide range of central issues in metaphysics, theology, natural philosophy, epistemology, and logic.[17] Their long battle, lasting almost fifteen years and comprising an extraordinary number of pages in treatises, reviews, and letters—written both by themselves and by others—is a rich and fascinating source for early modern views on knowledge, causation, the nature of the human mind, the morality of pleasure, and human freedom, as well as on God, grace, and miracles. The dispute is also full of misunderstanding and misrepresentation and is poisoned by vitriol and harsh invective. Things turned personal very quickly, and any pretense of maintaining a friendship despite their philosophical differences immediately dissipated as soon as Arnauld composed his first polemical treatise. Many leading thinkers of the century—including Newton, Locke, Bayle, and, above all, Leibniz—took great interest in the exchanges, choosing sides and following the debate as sport.

What is striking about the falling-out between Arnauld and Malebranche is not just the vehemence with which these onetime friends argued their respective positions. After all, this was the seventeenth century, when intellectual disputations were often fueled by religious differences and pursued with particular fervor. Rather, it is the fact that the protagonists had so much in common, socially, religiously, and intellectually.

Temperamentally, the two men could not have been more different. Unlike Arnauld, who was never really suited to the quiet life of a Jansenist *solitaire* and seemed to have a particular relish for battle, the reticent and retiring Malebranche only reluctantly engaged in disputes; he much preferred the reflective confines of the Oratory and always seemed to regret being dragged out into public debate. But personalities aside, Arnauld and Malebranche came from the same world. They were baptized in the same church in Paris, Sainte-Marie; they came from the same social class, the scions of families who belonged to the *noblesse de robe*; and quite significantly, both were Catholic priests, albeit of different orders. Even more important, they shared a basic set of philosophical and theological commitments. Both Arnauld and Malebranche were deeply devoted to the thought of Augustine, their mentor in religious questions, and to the philosophical principles of Descartes, their guide in matters metaphysical and epistemological. In fact, theirs was in many ways a fight over the Augustinian and Cartesian legacies: Whose interpretation would prevail? Whose account of grace was more faithful to Augustine's views, particularly their anti-Pelagianism? And whose understanding of human nature and knowledge better represented the spirit (if not the letter) of Descartes's philosophy?[18]

Despite his many engagements, not to mention the constant menace of his enemies, which was a matter of concern even in exile, Arnauld was too committed to a defense of *la vérité*—philosophically and theologically—not to take on the burden of publicly putting Malebranche and his ideas in their place. In turn, Malebranche, who so disliked confrontation, recognized that he had to defend himself against the onslaught of so formidable and respected an opponent. "Arnauld is too illustrious a critic to treat like others," he wrote soon after Arnauld's opening salvo.

That first shot came in the form of a relatively short but severe treatise called *On True and False Ideas*. Published three years after the appearance of Malebranche's *Treatise on Nature and Grace*, the "little book on ideas" is a work that shows Arnauld at his analytical best.[19] Arnauld intended ultimately to carry out a thorough refutation of Malebranche's system, and especially of his views on grace and on God's way of acting. However, before he could begin addressing the more important elements, the opinions he believed most likely to offend theologians, he needed to strike at the philosophical foundations of Malebranche's thought, and especially at the doctrine of the Vision in God.

Arnauld found highly objectionable Malebranche's theory that the ideas that serve human beings in their apprehension of eternal truths, and even in their ordinary knowledge of things in the world, are none other than God's own. He believed the doctrine was based on the flimsiest of arguments, and he also thought it was a gross misreading of both Augustine and Descartes. Arnauld does not dispute the claim that human beings know things by way of ideas, mental items that represent external objects. This is a seventeenth-century philosophical commonplace. If one knows the sun, it is only because one has an idea of the sun present to the mind. But this idea or concept, Arnauld insists, belongs to the human mind—it is nothing but one's own thought or perception of the sun. It is certainly not, as Malebranche claims, some eternal "third being," distinct from both the mind and the sun, that exists in the divine understanding and that stands as an ideal intermediary between the human knower and a perceived object.[20] As Arnauld says at one point, Malebranche's doctrine leads to the conclusion that the human mind is in fact completely cut off from the physical world and resides instead in an entirely other realm, surrounded by a "palace of ideas." "According to [Malebranche], we do not ever see the bodies that God has created, but only intelligible bodies, which he says are God Himself, and thus we see only God."[21]

As becomes clear in his subsequent writings against Malebranche, however, what bothers Arnauld most about the Vision in God is not just that Malebranche gets the elements and structure of human cognition wrong; this was something a theologian like Arnauld could live with. Rather, it is that Malebranche eliminates any differences between the way God knows things and the way human beings know them.[22] If Malebranche is right, then God's ideas are our ideas, and thus we know truths exactly the same way God knows them. And if Malebranche is right, then we have access to divine wisdom. This means that we, no less than God, are free to make pronouncements concerning the demands of Order and to judge on that basis God's works and ways.[23] This, Arnauld believes, represents the height of human presumption. It also terribly misrepresents both the nature of God and the character of our relationship to Him. Arnauld's initial, small-scale attack on Malebranche's "way of ideas" is, then, more than a critique of his epistemology. It sets the stage for the theological onslaught to come.

Having demolished Malebranche's theory of knowledge to his own satisfaction, Arnauld turns to the heart of the matter. This he does in the monumental *Philosophical and Theological Reflections on the New System of Nature and Grace*, published one year after *On True and False Ideas*.

One of the first things that must have struck Arnauld on his initial quick reading of the manuscript of the *Treatise on Nature and Grace* in Amsterdam is Malebranche's claim that sometimes, like the rain falling on fallow ground, divine grace lands uselessly on a soul unprepared to make proper use of it. To Arnauld's Jansenist mind, the idea that God's grace is not always and necessarily efficacious, and that to bring about its intended effect it requires the cooperation of the individual to which it has been granted, is Pelagianism.[24] God, he insists in the *Reflections*, does not always give a person enough supernatural aid to overcome his concupiscence, and thus the gift of grace does not always lead to the ultimate goal, a conversion of the heart. But this does not mean that grace does not always have its intended effect, namely, countering concupiscence to a specific (if not always sufficient) degree.[25] On the other hand, if God wants a person to have faith and do good works, then He *will* give that person enough grace to overcome the pleasures of the body. But it is inconceivable to Arnauld that God would give a person enough grace to resist those base urges and turn to God and yet that this might not result in his full conversion.

Equally troubling to someone who prizes God's omnipotence and the essential and absolute efficacy of His providential will is Malebranche's failure to deal adequately with the conundrum arising from the fact that although, as Scripture proclaims, God wills to save all people, not everyone is actually saved. If Malebranche had understood the true meaning of the Bible's words here, Arnauld argues, then there would be no need for introducing into God the torturous and degrading distinction between simple volitions—which Arnauld dismisses as mere inconsequential "wishings"—and practical volitions. God wills to save "all men," Arnauld claims, only in the sense of willing to save all *kinds* of human beings, people from all walks of life; and He does so with a volition that, like all of God's volitions, is completely efficacious and terminates in its intended effect.[26]

And then there is Malebranche's notion that the realm of grace is just as law-governed as the realm of nature. How, Arnauld wonders, can grace be the true gift that it is, distributed gratuitously, without any regard to merit, if God is determined to give it according to a set of laws based on the desires that Christ has to save this or that person? Malebranche appears to Arnauld to be naturalizing the supernatural by reducing God's provision of grace to a process of occasional causation no different from that which explains how one billiard ball moves another.

Much of Arnauld's attack on Malebranche's *Treatise* is clearly inspired by what he sees as an offensive and unorthodox account of grace, a misconstrual of the nature of grace that is completely unworthy of God. As Arnauld says, "the reason why I have undertaken to attack what he has written . . . is that the *Treatise on Nature and Grace*, which he published against my advice, does not at all agree with what I believe on the matter of grace. This is assuredly the cause of my anger against the author of the *Search After Truth*; except for this, I would never have conceived the project of criticizing him as I have."[27]

But the issue of grace, as important as it is, and while it provided the necessary stimulus for Arnauld to initiate his campaign against Malebranche, is only part of the story. Arnauld was troubled by a lot more than Malebranche's way of explaining the distribution of *auxilium Dei*. To his mind, the errors on grace were symptomatic of much deeper, more systemic problems.

On the matter of theodicy, ostensibly the main topic of Malebranche's book, Arnauld had many of the same intuitions as Leibniz. He was willing to accept that the evil in the world makes a real contribution to its overall optimality. This is the best of all possible worlds—not because there are no evils in it but because it is the world each of whose details is an expression of God's providential care. Thus, the alleged imperfections only *appear* to be defects because of a narrowness of vision, a failure to look at the big picture to see how all things fit together to make a beautiful whole. Quoting Aquinas, he condemns those who judge things only because of their inconvenience for this or that creature. "The corruptions and defects that occur in the world are such only relative to particular natures (that is, they are not real defects); they are a part of the plan and the intention . . . of God."[28]

Arnauld, then, adopts the "consider the whole" approach to theodicy. A broad perspective on things reveals that any evil is, in fact, a kind of good.

> The primary thing that God wants, above all with respect
> to corporeal nature, is the goodness of the order of the

universe, in which its beauty consists . . . He thus wills, positively and directly, everything that contributes to that beauty. Thus, monsters contribute to it, through the consent of the Creator.

Using the same analogy as Leibniz, Arnauld continues,

> Nothing is more contrary to music than dissonances, which are otherwise called "false agreements." And yet, a dissonance, mixed in among many consonances, is what makes for the most excellent harmony. And thus, will one dare say that there is no evidence that this musician positively and directly wanted to put this dissonance, although a bad agreement, into his composition? The relevance of this is clear: A monstrous animal is, if you will, a dissonance in the harmony of the universe; but it does not fail to make a contribution to this harmony.[29]

Arnauld is thus astonished by Malebranche's claim that the world is full of real and consequential imperfections. He refuses to see in the universe the defects that Malebranche finds therein and that lead Malebranche to infer that God acts only in general ways, and never with particular volitions. Neither the rain falling on fallow ground nor a deformity of birth is, for Arnauld, an imperfection in nature. These are, like everything else, things that God wills in particular and that serve a purpose in His design, whether we know that purpose or not. The claim that there are real evils, disorders, and irregularities in nature "must hurt Christian ears," he says.[30] "There are no defects in God's work," he repeats many times in his writings; only ignorance can lead one to believe otherwise.[31]

This assault on Malebranche's conception of the status of evil reflects a real difference between the two thinkers on the nature of God's activity. The most problematic aspect of Malebranche's theodicy, for Arnauld, is also its most central one: the idea that God acts only by general volitions and never by particular ones. Such a claim, which relieves God of having to take responsibility for everything that happens in the universe, is what allows Malebranche to concede that some elements of God's handiwork really are imperfect or defective. But as Arnauld explains at great length in the *Reflections*, it also undermines God's providence by removing Him from a direct and immediate care for every part of His creation. And this, Arnauld believes, no good Christian can tolerate.

Whatever God wills, Arnauld insists, He wills in particular, by a "positive, direct and particular volition." This applies to everything in the world, no matter how small or insignificant, regardless of its apparent beauty or deformity. Every natural disaster, monster, and failed ambition, every life and every death—and, above all, every soul's salvation or damnation—is, as Leibniz agrees, an intended part of God's plan. "God makes every drop of rain fall with a particular volition." To suggest otherwise, as Malebranche does, is to compromise the universality of divine governance. "Nothing happens in the world— be it a leaf or a fruit falling from a tree, or, more importantly, the birth or death of an animal, except by the will of God applied to each event . . . by the particular commands of His providence."[32]

We do not always know why God wills this or that event. Often the purposes of God's volitions escape our finite understanding. We may not be able to see a reason why the rain falls on unseeded soil or an already swollen river. But this does not justify the conclusion that such events are defects of nature or not something willed positively by God, by whom everything in particular is ordained. Arnauld insists that this is what "everyone who has read Scripture for thousands of years" knows. Only Malebranche feels the need to provide a figurative or metaphorical interpretation of the Bible's words when it speaks of God acting in particular ways; Malebranche alone, he says with typical sarcasm, believes that Scripture employs "a language so extraordinary that it has misled everyone who has read these divine books for more than a thousand, two thousand, three thousand years, and that it has not been intelligible except to only one man, who, after so much time of error and illusion, has found the secret to interpreting these puzzles."[33]

The unfortunate but necessary conclusion of Malebranche's view that "God acts only by general volitions," Arnauld claims, is that God's true providence manifests itself only in miraculous events. In these cases alone, where the ordinary course of nature as determined by its general laws is violated, does God will something directly and by a particular volition.[34] But Arnauld believes that God's providence is revealed in every single and particular aspect of the world. All of nature, from the smallest detail to the largest cataclysm, is a direct expression of God's power and other attributes.

This does not mean that God is constantly acting in ad hoc and unpredictable ways. Divine providence, at least in the realm of nature, plays itself out in a perfectly lawlike manner. God, Arnauld says, accomplishes his eternal designs "under the appearance of inferior [i.e., natural] causes and through the ordinary course of things in the world."[35] The difference is that whereas Malebranche's God acts *by* general laws, through volitions whose content is general and does not regard anything in particular[36]—such as a distant king issuing broad commands about how his subjects should behave in general, come what may and without paying any attention to individual subjects— Arnauld's God acts (in nature) *according to* or following general laws through particular volitions directed at specific things and events. Like a king who directly orders an individual subject to perform a certain action because that is how the king wants people to behave in general, Arnauld's God sees to it that a leaf falls under certain circumstances (a strong wind, decreasing hours of daylight) because that is the regular way in which He desires nature to proceed.

In the realm of grace, wherein Arnauld's God dispenses with laws and generalities altogether and acts to save individual souls only through infinite mercy, the unreasonableness of Malebranche's position and its inappropriateness for God are even more evident. Malebranche grants that there are rare times when God's wisdom, as expressed by Order, requires Him to act by a particular volition and to perform a miracle—for example, to aid the children of Israel or to cause or forestall some disaster of nature. Moreover, he maintains that the creation of the world itself, including all the individual beings it initially contained, as this is described in the opening chapters of the Bible, must have taken place through particular volitions. This is because until God first creates something, there are no natural events to get the system of general laws working. God can act by general volitions only if there are particular occasional causes to determine Him to bring about consequent events; God must create the earth, Adam and Eve, and the beasts surrounding them through particular volitions because until He does so, there is no world nor any creatures whose activities occasion the working of the laws governing nature and living beings. But, Arnauld asks, if God can act by a particular volition to keep Daniel from being eaten by the lions or to create a lowly fly, then surely He would act by a particular volition to save a soul, a much more momentous and important achievement, especially if, as Malebranche insists, His ultimate aim is to build His "Eternal Temple." If anything could justify God's departure from "the most simple and general ways," it would be the salvation of a soul that God wants to save but that is destined for damnation by the laws of grace.

> We are not talking here about preventing an overabundant rain from flooding a field of wheat, or an animal from having six feet instead of four. It is a matter of the salvation of those whom God presumably wants to save, and of the sanctification of those whom He presumably wants to sanctify. And will one dare say that, if God acted in these cases by particular volitions, then the effect of

each volition—that is, the eternal salvation of a soul that God wants to save, and that was worth the sacrifice of [the son of] God—would not be worth the action by which God would save that soul, if He had to accomplish that salvation by a particular volition?[37]

Only a God acting by particular volitions—in nature and in grace—is a true providential God. "God orders all things," Arnauld reminds Malebranche, "this is what His providence consists in."[38] Only this conception of God's action—which makes Him directly responsible for everything that happens—is conducive to the proper worship of God, to the love and fear of Him alone.[39]

Malebranche's fundamental problem, as Arnauld sees it, is that he construes God as showing more concern for His own manner of acting than for the quality of the work He is producing. To deny that "God prefers the greatest perfection of the work over the greatest simplicity of means," to insist that God gives a higher priority to the process of creating and sustaining the world than to the intrinsic perfection of the world itself, strikes Arnauld as simply absurd. "It is a total reversal of order to insist that [God] primarily and directly wants to act by the most simple means, but only indirectly wants each of the works thereby formed."[40] In all cases of workmanship, the end is always more important than the means. Any craft is primarily oriented toward the product and only secondarily to the tools and their use. "The means are for the product, not the product for the means," Arnauld reminds Malebranche.[41] This is obviously true in the case of human workmanship; how much more so is it in the case of God? Of course, human artisans often have to tailor their ambitions and proportion their work to the means available. If only a certain amount of funds are available for the building of a house, then one cannot build any house one desires; one will have to economize on size and materials. But such means-imposed restrictions on the product cannot possibly apply to the work of an omnipotent creator, for whom *all* means are equally easy. "It suffices that God will in order for His volition to be executed."[42]

Much about Arnauld's critique of the *Treatise on Nature and Grace* suggests that he, no less than Malebranche, is committed to the rational defense of God's ways. In his refusal to concede the reality of defects in God's creation, and his recommendation that one broaden one's perspective and "consider the whole" to see the contribution that evils make to the overall beauty of things, Arnauld sometimes appears wedded to a particular kind of theodicean strategy—one not very different from Leibniz's, although, in keeping with Arnauld's Jansenism, it emphasizes the infinite distance between God and human beings and the ultimate inscrutability of His wisdom.

Part of what bothers Arnauld about Malebranche's philosophy is the central assumption of the Vision in God, that the eternal ideas in the divine understanding are revealed to human beings. This gives Malebranche the temerity to make bold judgments about the quality of God's creation and especially about its conformity to the principles of Order, as well as to speculate about the reasons that guide God in the realms of nature and grace. This picture of a God whose wisdom is accessible to human knowledge and whose reasons are transparent to finite minds is, to Arnauld, intolerable. "We believe that God's providence extends to all things; this is one of the primary truths of the Christian religion. But to know how this happens and in what way everything that happens in the world is directed, regulated, and governed by the secret orders of this infinite providence is something that infinitely surpasses our intelligence."[43]

Throughout the *Reflections*, Arnauld insists on the "inscrutability" and "incomprehensibility" of God's judgments.

> What could be more bold and more presumptuous of
> blind human beings, full of shadows, and so little capable

of discovering on their own what is hidden in God, than to try to judge for certain, solely by the idea of the perfect being, without the aid of any divine revelation, what is more or less worthy of His wisdom.[44]

It exceeds the natural cognitive capacities of human beings to assess God's ways of acting on the basis of His attributes. This applies to God's behavior both in the realm of nature and in the realm of grace. Why, contrary to what Malebranche claims, does not God will—even with a simple volition—to save all individual human beings? And why does God not always give to a person who receives grace an amount sufficient to overcome his concupiscence? In these and all other cases, Arnauld seems to be saying that God has His reasons, but that they must remain hidden, *cachées*, in his "incomprehensible designs."[45]

And yet, as troubling as it is to Arnauld to see Malebranche try to "provide reasons for the impenetrable judgments of God" and so casually plumb the depths of His infinite wisdom, his objections to the "new system of nature and grace" run deeper than a common enough worry about divine transparency. Arnauld is fond of quoting St. Augustine on "the profound abyss of God's judgments."[46] But what he has in mind is something more radical even than what his fellow Port-Royalist Pascal, writing in the *Pensées*, called "man's nothingness" and "unworthiness" to know God. For Arnauld, the incomprehensibility of God's action is not merely due to the infinite chasm between human wretchedness and divine eternity. It is explained by the very nature of God.

Despite appearances, Arnauld does not really offer a theodicy at all. In fact, he regards the whole project of theodicy as misguided and grounded in human presumption, and not just because he believes the wisdom that guides God's activity to be inaccessible to us. Rather, for Arnauld, a rationalist theodicy is based on an altogether improper conception of God's nature and a thorough misunderstanding of the structure of divine agency. God's actions cannot be justified by God's wisdom—even a wisdom beyond human apprehension—because that is simply the wrong way to think about how God acts.

Malebranche's God is a rational being. Led by practical reason, He deliberates and chooses in a manner akin to human agency, doing things for an intelligible purpose and selecting that which He recognizes to be the objectively preferable option. Reasons matter for Malebranche's God; His actions are guided by His wisdom.

When Arnauld's attention is focused more narrowly on the issue of particular versus general volitions—and especially what must be Malebranche's God's lack of providential care for all aspects of creation—he sometimes speaks as though his God were no less rational an agent than the Oratorian's deity. "God does not act capriciously," he insists. "It is not at all true that God acts without an end or design."[47] In a letter to Malebranche from 1685, Arnauld asks rhetorically: "How will you prove that God did not have any reason to distribute among men their prosperity or adversity by particular volitions?"[48]—while in the *Reflections* he relies on the words of Augustine: "Who will dare to say that God has created all things without reason [*irrationabiliter*]?"[49]

But it is clear that Arnauld ultimately wants to defeat Malebranche's whole way of conceiving the relationship between will and wisdom in God. For Arnauld, God does not "consult His wisdom," as Malebranche would say. This is a false and thoroughly improper way to think of the relationship among God's attributes and the nature of God's activity.

> Did he [Malebranche] really think that this was an expression perfectly conforming to the idea of the perfect being, to say of God that He consults His wisdom? One consults only when one is in doubt; and one consults about how to accomplish one's desires only when there may be some difficulty in achieving what one desires.

Neither the one nor the other can be said about the perfect being, whose knowledge is infinite and whose will is all-powerful.[50]

Part of Malebranche's problem, according to Arnauld, is that to distinguish wisdom from will in God and have His wisdom guide His will by providing compelling reasons for its choices is to undermine divine freedom. Malebranche repeatedly says that "God's wisdom renders Him, in a sense, impotent" by determining Him to choose one world rather than another.[51] Malebranche takes comfort in the "in a sense" qualification, as well as in God's original indifference as to whether or not to create a world in the first place, and so is not particularly troubled by the implications of this for His freedom. Arnauld, however, is. He conceives of God's freedom as consisting in an absolute "liberty of indifference," thoroughly undetermined in the creation and governance of things. God's will is not guided by anything whatsoever external to it, not even by the dictates of His own wisdom.

By following Malebranche in the manner in which he conceives God, I do not see how He can be indifferent to creating or not creating something outside Himself, if He was not indifferent to choosing among several works and among several ways of producing them. For God . . . , according to [Malebranche], having consulted His wisdom, is necessarily determined to produce the work that it [wisdom] has shown him to be the most perfect, and to choose the means that it has shown Him also to be the most worthy of Him.[52]

Malebranche's God, Arnauld claims, cannot possibly satisfy what he sees as Aquinas's authoritative demand that the will of God remain perfectly self-determining, never willing anything external to itself *ex necessitate*.[53]

To be fair, despite his deterministic language, Malebranche strives to preserve the ultimate contingency of God's creative act. But—and this is Arnauld's point—Malebranche's account fails miserably; he ends up subjecting God to "a more than stoical necessity."[54] In fact, Arnauld appears to be saying, how could it be otherwise? In a perfectly rational being in whom there are no passions exercising a contrary influence, reasons must determine and necessitate the will and render it "impotent" to choose otherwise. When His wisdom dictates the creation of one world over all the others, Malebranche's God must obey; He *must* create that world, Arnauld insists, and Malebranche apparently agrees. Because they are demanded by Order, not even miracles are freely ordained by Malebranche's God.[55] In the name of divine freedom, Arnauld therefore rejects the thesis, popular among medieval philosophers and now adapted by Malebranche to suit his own theodicean purposes, of the *priority* of divine understanding over divine will. In Arnauld's God, *sagesse* does not rule over *volonté*.

Even more fundamental than the idea that wisdom must not exercise a determining influence on God's will is Arnauld's radical refusal to distinguish between will and wisdom in God in the first place. One should not, he warns, speak of God "consulting His wisdom" before He wills, "as if His will is not His wisdom, as if everything that He wills is not essentially wise as soon as He wills it."[56] Arnauld once again cites approvingly the words of Aquinas: "God's will is God Himself," adding the following gloss: "Note that he does not say that it is the wisdom of God that determines His will . . . but that it is the divine will that determines itself, freely and indifferently, toward all things to which it does not bear a necessary relation, that is, to all things that are not God."[57]

Malebranche's distinction between wisdom and will in God and his rationalistic depiction of God's behavior, Arnauld warns, constitute an anthropomorphization of God's nature and of His ways. It portrays God as if He, like human beings, has a mind constituted by different faculties, with a will that is able to select volitionally only from among the options the understanding presents to it (one can will only what one knows) and that is guided in its choice by the dictates of reason: "[Malebranche] speaks about [God] as if he were speaking about a human, in making Him consult His wisdom on everything He would like to do . . . as if His will, in order to will nothing other than what is good, had need of being regulated by something other than itself."[58] Arnauld sees God as a being in whom will and wisdom are one and the same, and thus for whom the will is a law unto itself. This God indifferently creates reasons through its volitions. He does not, like Malebranche's God, have a will that takes its lead from wisdom's antecedent reasons:

> If we are asked why God has created the world, we should reply only that it is because He wanted to; and . . . if we are asked again why He wanted to, we should not say, as [Malebranche] does, that "He wanted to obtain an honor worthy of Himself." The idea of God does not allow us to accept Malebranche's proposition. We ought rather to say that He wanted to because He wanted to, that is, that we ought not to seek a cause of that which cannot have one.[59]

Arnauld's God is a deity who does not act for reasons at all; who, in the structure of His being, transcends practical rationality altogether. This is a very radical conception of God, one that few other philosophers in history have been willing to adopt.[60]

Arnauld's conception of God and His arbitrary will is motivated primarily not by philosophical considerations but by religious and theological ones. It is intimately connected to the Jansenist view of the nature of grace and its distribution. If God's grace is not to be given to an individual because of anything that individual may have done to deserve it, if it must be an entirely gratuitous gift, unrelated to merit, then it would seem that there cannot be any reasons for God to provide a person with grace at all. Why, then, does God give grace to a person? There is no response to this question by Arnauld's logic other than that God acts with infinite and unmotivated mercy.

To Arnauld's many Catholic opponents, it seemed as if he had broken completely with the Church and crossed the line into Calvinism.

Before the publication of Arnauld's two treatises, Malebranche, having heard only reports from friends about the impending attack, was not very concerned. Writing to Pierre Berrand in May 1683, he notes that "there are always threats coming from M. Arnauld, but this is exactly what I want, for I do not see that he can say anything of great import." As the works appeared in print, however, Malebranche realized that he had underestimated Arnauld and knew that he had to respond—because of not just what was said but also who was saying it. Referring to Arnauld's *On True and False Ideas*, Malebranche admits that "if the book . . . did not bear the name of M. Arnauld, then I would have kept my silence."[61]

Ever sensitive to criticism, Malebranche was stunned by the fury and tone of Arnauld's two-pronged assault. He was hurt by the harsh, overly personal way in which Arnauld expressed his philosophical and theological objections and felt that Arnauld's critique went well beyond the bounds of propriety. He also insisted that Arnauld "either does not understand my views, or is not as moved by the love of truth as he says."[62] Arnauld's *Reflections* had not yet been sent to the publishers when Malebranche set to composing a reply to the book on ideas. His *Response by the Author of the Search After Truth to the Book of Monsieur Arnauld* was published in 1684. Arnauld immediately began to write his *Defense of Monsieur Arnauld, Doctor of the Sorbonne, Against the Response to the Book on True and False Ideas*. Arnauld was not impressed by Malebranche's rejoinder, a copy of which Malebranche himself had sent to him through a bookseller in Rotterdam, along with a "very civil letter." In a note to Pierre Nicole, Arnauld complains that Malebranche "accuses me of writing against him merely out of chagrin . . . The haughtiness and the pride of this good Father is unbelievable . . . and the book has the same air: always proud, boastful, hurtful, and always impertinent."[63]

Malebranche responded to Arnauld's *Defense* with three published letters in 1685, to which Arnauld, taking up some theological themes raised by Malebranche, replied that same year with his *Dissertation of Monsieur Arnauld, Doctor of the Sorbonne, on the Manner in Which God Performed Frequent Miracles of the Ancient Law Through the Ministry of Angels*. Malebranche quickly followed with his *Response to a Dissertation by Monsieur Arnauld*.

At this point, Arnauld's *Reflections* were out, along with his "Nine Letters" in reply to Malebranche's three letters from just a few months earlier. This broadened the debate into the realm of grace and led Malebranche to write a further series of letters in which he replies directly to the charges of the *Reflections*. Two years had not yet passed since Arnauld's first strike, and already the public was inundated with an extraordinary number of pages devoted to an increasingly rancorous (and often repetitive) debate. This continued—in published treatises, in letters in the *Journal des sçavans*, and even in the pages of Bayle's *Nouvelles de la république des lettres*—for another nine years, testing the fortitude and patience of European intellectuals, until Arnauld's death in 1694.

By the end, Malebranche was exhausted and seems to have regretted the whole affair. "It is for a younger man," he complained. Arnauld, in turn, was fed up with Malebranche's intransigence and refusal to see the truth. Malebranche was so blind, Arnauld insisted, that "only a miracle" would make him change his mind.[64]

Readers of the exchanges—and there were many—quickly became partisans, and some of the most illustrious and influential thinkers of the period fell out among themselves according to whose side they favored. John Locke, for one, took up his own pen to argue against Malebranche and the Vision in God doctrine, seeing it as nothing but an expression of religious "enthusiasm,"[65] while Isaac Newton was impressed by Arnauld's rapier-sharp analytic abilities. Malebranche, in turn, after reading Newton's *Opticks* in 1707, said that "though Mr. Newton is no physicist, his book is very interesting."

As for Bayle, his appreciation of Malebranche's occasionalism was, at first, only deepened when he read Malebranche's depiction of God's way of acting in the *Treatise on Nature and Grace*. "The author is right to say that God acts by particular volitions only when He performs miracles," he wrote in a review in the April 1686 issue of the *Nouvelles de la république des lettres*.[66] Even with his skeptic's distaste for rational theodicy, he concedes that

> there is nothing more unworthy of a general cause, who puts all other causes into action by way of a simple and uniform law, than to violate this law at every moment, to prevent the murmurings and superstitions that arise among weak and ignorant people. Nothing provides a more elevated idea of a monarch than to see that having wisely established a law, he maintains its vigor in all cases and against all, not allowing the prejudice of a particular or the interested recommendations of a favorite to bring about some qualification to it.[67]

Bayle in the mid–1680s was an enthusiastic fan of Malebranche's system, one that he found "preferable to all others."

And then he read Arnauld's *Reflections*. The about-face is remarkable. Writing some years later, Bayle maintains that

> this thought [that it is of infinitely greater consequence to change the order of the universe represented by very sim-

ple and very uniform laws than the health and prosperity of a man during the brief duration of this life] has something astonishing about it. Father Malebranche presented it in the clearest light possible, and he persuaded some of his readers that a simple and very fecund system is more worthy of the wisdom of God than a system that, because it is more complex and less fecund, is more capable of preventing irregularities.

He notes that he himself was among these readers "who believed that [Malebranche] put a marvelous end to the debate." But, he continues,

> it is almost impossible to appreciate this position after having read the books of Monsieur Arnauld against this system and after having considered the vast and immense idea of a supremely perfect Being. This idea tells us that there is nothing easier for God than to follow a simple plan, one that is fecund, regular and commodious at the same time for all creatures.[68]

Like Arnauld, Bayle is concerned about the ramifications for divine freedom of Malebranche's conception of God's modus operandi; he, too, is troubled by Malebranche's talk of God's wisdom rendering Him "impotent." And he shares Arnauld's incredulity that a wise and just God would use particular volitions to create rocks, plants, and insects but not to save a human soul.[69] By the time Bayle composed his *Dictionary*, he had concluded that Malebranche's philosophy was nothing but "a pious fraud."

Bayle was not the only one convinced by Arnauld's criticisms. In 1690, at the instigation of Arnauld, the Vatican decided that the *Treatise on Nature and Grace* should join Descartes's works on the Index Liborum Prohibitorum. Despite his own troubled standing among

French Catholic authorities, Arnauld's *Philosophical and Theological Reflections* received no ecclesiastic censure.

In the years immediately after his departure from Paris, Leibniz had no direct contact with Arnauld. What he knew about Arnauld's ongoing troubles, and even about his health, he learned through letters from their mutual acquaintances, including Malebranche. And then, in the summer of 1683, after reading Arnauld's *Second Apology for Jansenius*—in which he found "many very considerable things"— Leibniz tried to reconnect with the exiled Jansenist. Writing to him on the pretext of continuing some mathematical discussions that they had begun in Paris, and using their mutual acquaintance the Landgrave (or Count) Ernst von Hessen-Rheinfels as an intermediary, he sent along some of his recent papers in geometry, hoping for a reply and an opening to engage him on other matters.[70]

The attempt failed. Arnauld, already quite occupied with other affairs, simply could not devote the time necessary for a close study of what Leibniz had sent. Writing back to Count Ernst, he confesses that "I glimpsed some fine things [in Leibniz's pieces], but it would be too much for me to drop everything and devote the time required for completely understanding them."[71] No doubt disappointed, Leibniz tried again in late 1684, this time approaching Arnauld (again through Ernst) with a writing more to Arnauld's current tastes, a short piece called "Meditations on Knowledge, Truth and Ideas" that he had just published in the *Acta Eruditorum*. Leibniz was thinking of Arnauld's polemic with Malebranche, and now told the count that he wanted "to know M. Arnauld's opinion" on this, his first philosophical article to appear in print.

At this time, Leibniz had not yet read either Arnauld's *On True and False Ideas* or any of the ensuing exchanges, although he had heard a great deal about the debate in letters from Foucher—"The disputes between Monsieur Arnauld and Father Malebranche are still going on," Foucher informed him[72]—and followed its course in the book reviews that Bayle wrote for his *Nouvelles de la république des lettres*. The falling-out of these onetime friends took him by surprise. "I am astonished that M. Arnauld and M. Malebranche, who were such good friends when I was in Paris, are now attacking each other in their writings," he wrote in November of 1684 to Walther von Tschirnhaus.[73] He was struck particularly by the vitriolic tone of their dispute. As he said to Ernst several months later, in March of 1685—when, strangely, he *still* had not read what he calls their "reciprocal books"— "it seems to me that they could proceed a little more gently."[74]

Not having studied the principal writings of the debate did not keep Leibniz from having an opinion about them. He favored Arnauld's position, or so he tells his correspondents. "Father Malebranche . . . is very ingenious and has some very good and solid thoughts, but he also has many that are a bit hyperbolic or lightly conceived."[75] "I find [in Malebranche's *Christian Conversations*] many fine thoughts, and yet there are many that have more show than solidity."[76] "Father Malebranche has much spirit, but Monsieur Arnauld writes with more judgement."[77]

Leibniz did not give up his hope of engaging Arnauld in discussion on philosophical and theological issues. Finally, on his third attempt, he achieved success. Once again he had enlisted the help of Ernst, a convert to Catholicism who, in 1680, had stepped in as Leibniz's patron after the deaths of Boineberg and, later, Johann Friedrich and who Leibniz hoped would support him in his Church reunification project. The count was the perfect go-between for Leibniz if he wanted to reach out to Arnauld. Ernst met Arnauld in Paris in 1670 and had exchanged friendly letters with him over the years.[78] He even offered asylum to Arnauld in his German lands near Frankfurt, but Arnauld, in Brussels at the time, preferred to stay where he was. Although no fan of the Jansenists—his conversion had been facilitated by the Jesuits—Ernst was, like Leibniz, of an ecumenical spirit and was interested in ecclesiastic reconciliation. In 1684, he arranged a series of meetings between Arnauld and a leading Jesuit to help foster mutual understanding. Although Arnauld eventually broke off the dialogue because it was going nowhere, he and Ernst never lost their respect for each other.[79] Arnauld's friend, the Jansenist sympathizer Louis-Paul du Vaucel, probably reflecting Arnauld's own views, said of Ernst that "he philosophizes on all things, in a just and Christian manner."[80]

Ernst, unlike Leibniz, knew how to get in touch with Arnauld in exile. Thus, in February of 1686, Arnauld received a short manuscript of Leibniz's, a summary of what is now known as the *Discourse on Metaphysics*. Just as Malebranche had hoped to take advantage of Arnauld's highly critical eye before publishing his *Treatise on Nature and Grace*, so Leibniz wanted Arnauld to have a look at least at the main theses of his new work. "Being at a place lately for several days with nothing to do," Leibniz says to Ernst, "I wrote out a short discourse on metaphysics, on which I would be very glad to have the opinion of Monsieur Arnaud [*sic*] . . . I enclose herewith a summary of the articles which it contains, as I have not had time to make a clean copy of the whole. I therefore beg Your Serene Highness to send him this summary, requesting him to look it over and give his judgment upon it. For as he excels equally in theology and in philosophy, in erudition and in power of thought, I know of no one who is better fitted to give an opinion upon it."[81]

The *Discourse* provides a good overview of Leibniz's philosophical system in this period, especially his metaphysics and his philosophical theology. In the course of the work, he spells out his views on the nature of substance, including its essential spontaneity, and the doctrine of preestablished harmony; his idiosyncratic theory of truth, whereby in every true proposition the concept of the predicate is "contained" in the concept of the subject—much as the concept "unmarried male" is contained in the concept "bachelor"—thus making any truth tantamount to an analytic truth ("A bachelor is an unmarried male");

and his quasi–Aristotelian explanation of the nature of the soul and its union with the human body. He also broaches questions of physics, examining the nature of corporeal things and offering on that basis a correction of the Cartesian account of the laws of nature.

Leibniz may have imagined that what would interest Arnauld the most were the items in the work that treat of God's nature and His manner of choosing among possible worlds. The *Discourse* contains a fine, if abbreviated, presentation of Leibniz's theodicy. In it he shows how "God who possesses supreme and infinite wisdom acts in the most perfect manner not only metaphysically, but also from the moral standpoint" and argues "against those who think that God might have made things better than He has." Leibniz elaborates on the character of this best, "most perfect" of all possible worlds, "the one that is at the same time the simplest in hypotheses and the richest in phenomena," and shows how, despite its apparent imperfections, it is eminently worthy of God's choice.[82]

Much of the content of the *Discourse* dealing with theodicean matters would probably have been familiar to Arnauld from his discussions with Leibniz in Paris. Leibniz says in the *Theodicy* that during his time there, probably in 1673, he gave Arnauld a short item that he had written on the subject. "To the celebrated M. Arnauld I even presented a Latin dialogue of my own composition . . . wherein I laid it down that God, having chosen the most perfect of all possible worlds, had been prompted by his wisdom to permit the evil that was bound up with it, but that still did not prevent this world from being, all things considered, the best that could be chosen."[83] Leibniz is referring here to the "Confession of a Philosopher." If Arnauld read the dialogue, some conversations about God's rational choices and the nature and origin of evil must have ensued.[84]

Arnauld did not see the entire *Discourse*, as Leibniz sent him only a list of the titles of each of the work's thirty-seven articles. It was not much to go on, and Arnauld would have had to fill in a lot of the gaps for himself, although Leibniz offered "to explain myself sincerely and frankly." What Arnauld read, however, was enough for him to make up his mind quickly and firmly.

Perhaps Leibniz had good reason to expect that Arnauld would find much to approve of in the sketch. Among the article titles are several unmistakable swipes at Malebranche, including article twenty-nine ("We think directly by means of our own ideas and not through God's") and article three ("Against those who think that God might have made things better than He has"). And only a month and a half before he sent the *Discourse* summary to Arnauld, Leibniz had been reassured by Ernst that, contrary to Ernst's expectations, Arnauld's re-action to one of Leibniz's previous letters to Ernst, which the count had forwarded to him for his perusal, was positive: "I remember also that formerly Your Serene Highness sent one of my letters to M. Ar-nauld, with your reflections appended, from which it seemed that you believed that my views went against even the first councils of the Catholic Church, to which M. Arnauld replied to you that my words at least witnessed exactly the opposite."[85]

Arnauld did not read the *Discourse* summary under the best of cir-cumstances. As he says to Ernst in his first, very brief letter of March 1686, he was so busy that he was not able to study even such a short piece until a month after receiving it. Moreover, he was not feeling well. "At the present time I have such a bad cold that all I can do now is to tell Your Highness [my opinion] in a couple of words." He did read it, however, and the words he used were chosen for maximum ef-fect: "I find in his [Leibniz's] thoughts so many things that frightened me and that, if I am not mistaken, almost all men would find so star-tling that I cannot see any utility in a treatise that would be evidently rejected by everybody." It was now Leibniz's turn to be the target of Arnauld's famous temper.

Arnauld in particular objected to a central element of Leibniz's metaphysics, one that suggests a very intimate, even necessary relationship between a thing and its properties. The title of article thirteen of the *Discourse* states that "the individual concept of each person includes once and for all everything that can ever happen to him." Leibniz believed that for every individual substance there is a corresponding concept that captures that substance's essential nature and the properties that necessarily derive from it. The concept of "Adam" specifies Adam's nature and what exactly it is that makes him Adam. But given Leibniz's theory of the spontaneity of substance, an individual's nature is the causal source of *all* of its properties, including even those relational properties that refer the individual to other things; thus, Adam's nature is the reason why he has the property of being the father of Cain, and Leibniz's nature is the reason why he has the properties of being thirty-four years younger than Arnauld and of having resided in Paris from 1672 to 1676 within four hundred meters of the Luxembourg Gardens. It follows that the concept of an individual substance will include in its content a predicate for every single property possessed by that individual. The propositions "Adam is the father of Cain" and "Adam sins by eating the fruit of the tree of knowledge" are true because the predicates "is the father of Cain" and "eats the fruit of the tree of knowledge" are contained in the concept of Adam.

The concept of an individual will, therefore, be distinguished from the concepts of all other individuals by the totality of the properties, states, and actions it contains. To conceive of any single feature of that substance, any moment of its existence, no matter how apparently insignificant, being other than what it is, is in fact to conceive of an entirely different substance, albeit one that is very similar in many other respects to the original substance. As Leibniz says, if the first man had not eaten the fruit of the tree of knowledge, then he would not have been Adam but rather some other individual very much like Adam but lacking one of Adam's properties. Eating the fruit is an essential part of the concept of Adam. Thus, if God creates Adam, Adam will sin; for if he does not sin, then it is not Adam whom God has created.

Arnauld, once again the defender of God's absolute liberty—and this letter was written less than a year after he composed his attack on Malebranche's failure to safeguard divine freedom—insists that if Leibniz is right, then God's first free choices in creation are also His last free choices. For God may have been free to create or not to create Adam—that is, the first human being, whose individual concept presumably includes and thus necessarily implies not just the original sin but everything that succeeds him, including all his progeny (the entire human race and everything that happens to it). But then supposing that God does decide to create Adam, Arnauld insists,

> all that has since happened to the human race or that will ever happen to it has occurred and will occur with a necessity more than fatal. For the individual concept of Adam involved that he would have so many children and the individual concepts of these children involved all that they would do and all the children that they would have, and so on. God has therefore no more liberty in regard to all that, provided He wished to create Adam, than He was free to create a nature incapable of thought, supposing that He wished to create me.[86]

As Arnauld reads Leibniz—or, rather, the titles of the articles of the *Discourse*—if God creates Adam, then not only will Adam sin but also there is nothing that God can do about it.

Whatever Arnauld's response was to Ernst about his earlier exposure to Leibniz's views, the opinion the count received this time was decidedly negative. In Arnauld's eyes, Leibniz's metaphysics of substance and concept-containment account of truth have theological ramifications that no good Catholic could accept. "I cannot refrain from expressing to Your Highness my sorrow at his [Leibniz's] attachment to those opinions, which he has indeed felt could hardly be permitted in the Catholic Church. The Catholic Church would prohibit his entertaining them."[87] The problem is that—much to the regret of both Arnauld and Ernst—Leibniz was not a good Catholic. But all was not lost. Arnauld closes his letter by recommending that Leibniz give up his metaphysical speculations, "which can be of utility neither to himself nor to others," and take care for the salvation of his soul by converting to Catholicism.

Leibniz may have been expecting an insightful, even uncompromising critique. After all, why else would he have sent this summary to Arnauld, whom he (and everyone else) knew to be a rigorous and brutally honest critic? And he was certainly aware of Arnauld's irascibility. But what he did not expect was an intemperate, personally insulting response from someone whom he considered a friend, a response based on what appears to have been a rash and superficial review.

Leibniz was speechless. In a letter to Ernst intended to be shown to Arnauld, he says that "I do not know what to say to M.A.'s letter, and I never would have thought that a person whose reputation is so great and so real and from whom we have such excellent reflections on morals and logic would be so precipitate in his judgments. After this instance, I am not surprised that some are angry at him."[88] In a separate, private letter to Ernst written on the same day, Leibniz suggests that it is no wonder Arnauld does not have any friends left. "I am not surprised now that he has so easily fallen out with Father Malebranche and others who used to be his fast friends." He adds a more unguarded assessment of Arnauld's "severity":

> I have had much difficulty in suppressing a desire as much to laugh as to express pity, inasmuch as the good man seems really to have lost a part of his mind and seems not to have been able to keep from crying out against everything, as do those seized with melancholy to whom everything that they see or think of appears black . . . [One] must take care not to excite his bilious temper."[89]

In closing, he notes that "one of the very reasons why I communicated the summary to M. Arnauld [was] to probe a little to see what his behavior would be. But 'touch the mountains and they will smoke.'[90] As soon as one deviates the least amount from the positions of certain professors they burst forth into explosions and thunder."[91]

Arnauld, after receiving Leibniz's reply, realized that he had crossed the line of civility. In a direct letter to Leibniz, he apologizes, in his own way. "I thought that I ought to address myself to you personally to ask pardon for having given you cause to become angry against me, in that I employed too severe terms when I indicated what I thought of one of your positions." But lest Leibniz think that Arnauld is taking back anything from his objections, he adds that he wants Leibniz to know that "what caused my indiscretion was simply that, having been accustomed to write off-hand to His Highness [Ernst] because he is so good as to readily excuse all my faults, I imagined that I could tell him frankly what I was unable to approve of in one of your opinions because I was very sure it would not pass muster."[92] In other words, Arnauld was just being honest.

Despite this rough beginning, Leibniz and Arnauld settled into a comfortable and frank series of philosophical exchanges. Their correspondence, which lasted until 1690 (with Leibniz doing most of the writing), was of enormous value to Leibniz's philosophical maturation and to the development of his metaphysical views. Arnauld pressed Leibniz on his hylomorphic account of corporeal substances (such as living bodies), and especially on how an immaterial form is supposed to bring organic unity to a parcel of matter, thereby conferring substantiality upon it and making it more than just an accidental collection of parts (which is all that a pile of rocks is). His objections helped Leibniz eventually see that if, as he believed, true unity is indeed an essential feature of substances, then the only real substances in nature—and the building blocks of everything else—are immaterial, soul-like entities: simple spiritual substances that Leibniz would ultimately call "monads." The harmony characterizing the best of all possible worlds is, for the later Leibniz, reduced to a divinely ordained correlation among the perceptions of these atomic minds.

Leibniz knew exactly what to reply to Arnauld's first letter on the *Discourse*. He insists that in making the free choice to create one world rather than another, God does not merely select some initial collection of substances (Adam, plus whatever else was produced directly by God during the six days of creation) and then watch passively and helplessly as the world's series of events necessarily unfolds independently of His will. Rather, an omniscient God, knowing full well what every concept of every individual involves, chooses to actualize one particular set of original substances—that is, the initial state of one possible world—just because of what will follow necessarily from them. In this way, every aspect of creation is envisioned by God and forms a part of His plan.

> We must not think of the intention of God to create a certain man Adam as detached from all the other intentions He has in regard to the children of Adam and of all the human race, as though God first made the decree to create Adam without any relation to his posterity . . . We must think rather that God, choosing not an indeterminate Adam but a particular Adam whose perfect representation is found among the possible beings in the Ideas of God and who is accompanied by certain individual circumstances and among other predicates possesses also that of having in time a certain posterity—God, I say, in choosing him has already had in mind his posterity and chooses them both at the same time.[93]

This difference over divine freedom led Leibniz and Arnauld into an extended discussion about the metaphysics of individuals and the distinction between essential and accidental properties, the nature of necessity, the status of possible versus actual beings, causation, and the nature of bodily and spiritual substances. The letters to Arnauld gave Leibniz the opportunity to explain his objections to various Cartesian positions on mind and matter, and to lay out his view of the weaknesses of Malebranche's theory of occasional causes and, correlatively, the strengths of his own doctrine of preestablished harmony. It is, however, odd that given the dominant theological undercurrents of their intellectual relationship and Leibniz's desire to convert Arnauld to his ecumenical project, one topic never arises. Nowhere in the Leibniz-Arnauld correspondence is there any mention of theodicean strategy or God's choice of the best of all possible worlds.

One reason for this may be that the summary of the *Discourse* that Arnauld read offers only the barest outline of Leibniz's views on this issue. The article titles alone are very general and relatively uninformative. How could Arnauld take issue with the seemingly harmless claim made by the title of article one, that "God does everything in the most desirable way," or article six's title statement that "God does nothing that is not orderly"? Article five's title mentions that in God's conduct, the simplicity of the means counterbalances the richness of effects, but that is as close as Leibniz got in this text to an explanation of what exactly makes this world the best and why it would be worthy of God's choice over all other possible worlds. In the course of their exchanges, Arnauld does raise problems concerning the notion of possible but not actual worlds. "I have no idea of substances that are purely possible, that is to say, that God will never create." All talk of what is merely possible but not actual, Arnauld insists, is reducible to claims about God's omnipotence, what God *could*, but did not, do. "Outside the things that God has created or must create there is . . . only an active and infinite power."[94] But neither Arnauld nor Leibniz brings up, in any of his letters, anything about what moves God to choose one world over another or about how this might resolve the problem of evil.

Arnauld was not unfamiliar with Leibniz's general approach to theodicy, especially if he read the "Confession of a Philosopher" or talked to Leibniz in Paris about such matters. Is it possible that his silence on these aspects of the *Discourse* summary—assuming he was able to fill in the blanks—is due to his general agreement with Leibniz's approach, and in particular with his conception of divine agency? Leibniz does later say that Arnauld "did not seem to be startled" by the early dialogue's account of how "God, having chosen the most perfect of all possible worlds, had been prompted by His wisdom to permit the evil which is bound up with it."[95] And if there *were* a problem, being asked to comment on an outline of a work in progress in which that theory is sketched out would be the right opportunity to bring it up. Is there something about Leibniz's theodicy and depiction of God's activity that, in Arnauld's eyes, saves it from the fatal flaws that he finds in Malebranche's account?

One of the charges Arnauld levels at Malebranche is that it is undignified and inappropriate for God to have to choose the most simple means of acting in creating and sustaining the world, even if that means a sacrifice in overall quality of the product. For an omnipotent being, Arnauld insists, all means are equally easy and available. Leibniz, when composing the *Discourse on Metaphysics*, certainly had Arnauld's *Reflections* in mind, as he had finally read it just a few months earlier. This criticism of Malebranche by Arnauld is probably what led Leibniz to say in the *Discourse* that "nothing costs God anything, just as there is no cost for a philosopher who makes hypotheses in constructing his imaginary world, because God has only to make decrees in order that a real world comes into being."[96] This is just the kind of thing that would please Arnauld and satisfy his demand that any theodicy respect God's omnipotence and freedom. From Arnauld's standpoint, Leibniz may be on better ground here than Malebranche.

Similarly, Leibniz's God, in contrast to Malebranche's, gets to accomplish everything He wants to accomplish. Leibniz's God aims to produce as much perfection as possible through creating a world that is absolutely the best, and He necessarily succeeds in doing so. Unlike

Malebranche's God, who must sacrifice perfection of effect for the sake of simplicity of means and generality of law, Leibniz's God gets to maximize all of His most cherished values: simplicity of laws *and* richness of effect *and* supreme perfection of outcome. He does not have to make any trade-offs. In terms of preserving divine power and liberty, Leibniz's system would seem, on the face of it, to warrant a better reception from Arnauld than Malebranche's received.

Finally, Arnauld must have been content to see that he and Leibniz agreed on the status of evil. Both thinkers refused to see evil as some real imperfection that detracts from the overall goodness of creation. How could Arnauld fail to appreciate Leibniz's almost verbatim approach to the problem, whereby the evils in the world are like dissonances in music that contribute to an overall harmony?

However, these similarities in outlook are only superficial. Leibniz's theodicy could fare no better in Arnauld's eyes than Malebranche's, and for exactly the same reasons. If Arnauld was bothered by the way in which Malebranche's theodicy diminishes God's omnipotence and freedom, and especially by the way God's wisdom "renders Him, in a sense, impotent" to act in certain ways, then he must be equally troubled by the way Leibniz conceives of God's activity. It is true that Malebranche says that God *must* act by general volitions and according to the most simple laws, with His wisdom absolutely determining His will, whereas Leibniz prefers somewhat weaker language, insisting that God's choice of one world over another is only "morally" but not absolutely necessitated. Leibniz says his God could conceivably choose other worlds, but reasons infallibly move Him to choose the best. And Leibniz, being a good compatibilist about free will—recognizing that determination can go hand in hand with freedom, and that a determined will is not necessarily a constrained will—maintains (unlike Malebranche) that God's will can be determined by reasons without this representing a loss of divine liberty.

Arnauld, however, would fail to see a significant difference here. He may have had a fine mind for fine distinctions, but even the moral and nonmetaphysical necessity that obliges Leibniz's God would be too much for him. Leibniz's theodicy must, like Malebranche's, undermine God's omnipotence and freedom. For Leibniz, God's will to create the best, and thus His power to do so, is still determined by His wisdom and goodness. When Leibniz says that "moral necessity . . . constrains the wisest to choose the best," as he does in his *Theodicy*, Arnauld could not possibly be less disturbed than he was by Malebranche's concession of God's "impotence."[97] Once again, wisdom wins out over power, *sagesse* over *toute-puissance*.[98]

Nor would Arnauld be pleased with Leibniz's use of the distinction between God's antecedent will and His consequent will, equivalent as it is to Malebranche's distinction between a simple volition and a practical volition. Leibniz's God wills the salvation of all human beings with only an antecedent, and thus inefficacious, volition. This introduction in God of volitions without effect brought Arnauld's wrath down upon Malebranche, and it ought to do so as well in the case of Leibniz.

Once again, though, there is a deeper problem than just the idea that God's wisdom dominates His will and the threat to divine freedom this represents. Leibniz's whole way of conceiving God and His manner of acting, like that of Malebranche, depicts a deity whose being is structured like that of a practical rational agent, with understanding distinct from will, and this Arnauld cannot accept. It is, as Arnauld insists to Malebranche, to conceive of God in human terms. There is a hint of Arnauld's misgivings on this matter in one of his letters to Leibniz, in which he addresses the claim that God first surveys and evaluates a number of possible worlds before choosing one to create. "I find a great deal of uncertainty in the manner in which we usually represent to ourselves that God acts. We imagine that before purposing to create the world He looked over an infinity of possible things, some of which He chose and rejected the others."[99] Arnauld is bothered not just by the metaphysical issue of Leibniz's appeal to unactualized possibles but also by the theological idea that divine volition is, like human volition, guided by what understanding and intelligence present to it. Leibniz's God has will and wisdom; Arnauld's God is pure will—or, rather, His will *is* His wisdom. Leibniz's God, like Malebranche's God, acts for antecedent reasons; Arnauld's God does not.

The answer to a fundamental theological question is at stake in Arnauld's long, heated, very public dispute with Malebranche concerning ideas, grace, and divine freedom. This question is also not far from his mind in his private correspondence with Leibniz in the mid-1680s. (It must also have been a topic in their discussions in Paris in the early 1670s.) It regards the proper way of conceiving the structure of God's being and depicting how He acts. The God of Malebranche and Leibniz has the faculties of, and behaves like, an agent guided by practical reason. He seeks to achieve ends that He regards as objectively good and chooses means that appear to Him to be the most conducive to those ends. Despite their differences on the finer points of theodicy, Malebranche and Leibniz agree that God is, above all else, a rational being, just like us. Arnauld, on the other hand, objects to precisely this point. He rejects the model of practical reasoning applied to God. It is, he insists, a blasphemous anthropomorphization of the Christian deity.

In the seventeenth century, there was nothing novel about conceiving of God in terms of practical rationality. Malebranche and Leibniz were heirs to a long philosophical and theological tradition that extended back through early Scholasticism. Aquinas, for example, insisted that God always "acts for an end," with the divine will "always having for its object a good." Aquinas's God is a rational God, contrary to "those who say that all things depend on the simple will of God, without any reason."[100] Similarly, William of Ockham, the great fourteenth-century English philosopher, described God as "a rational creator" because His actions are guided by His ideas and understanding of what is good.[101] Thus, the quarrel over God's modus operandi among these seventeenth-century figures is a continuation of discussions in medieval thought about whether it is possible to bridge the infinite divide between the eternal and the created, and to speak as though what can be said of human beings can also be said of God.

The debate also transcends the theological domain and taps into a series of philosophical problems as old as Plato. These include the nature of truth, the possibility of knowledge, and the objectivity of values. And given the close relationship between the philosophical, the theological, and the political in the period, the three-way skirmish in the realm of ideas between Leibniz, Arnauld, and Malebranche also had implications for how one might conceive the nature of political power and the relationship between right and might.

7

The Eternal Truths

In one of Plato's early dialogues, Socrates is walking to the Athenian assembly to stand trial on the charge of corrupting the youth of the city-state. On the way, he runs into his young friend Euthyphro, who is also off to the courts, in his case to pursue charges he has brought against his own father for murder. Euthyphro insists that because his father has killed a man, prosecuting him is the right and pious thing to do. Socrates is concerned that Euthyphro might be proceeding rashly and without full knowledge of the moral character of the action he is about to undertake. To determine whether Euthyphro is justified in believing that prosecuting his father is a pious action, Socrates challenges him to state exactly what piety is; for if he does not know what piety itself is, then he cannot be certain that what he is doing is pious. The arrogant Euthyphro, convinced that he can satisfy Socrates' request, confidently responds that the pious is defined simply as what the gods love. "What is pleasing to the gods is pious, and what is not pleasing to them is impious."

Socrates cannot accept the claim that something is pious just because the gods love it. He suggests that, on the contrary, the gods, because they are generally rational beings, will love something only because they appreciate some feature of the thing, some property of it that makes it worthy of their affection. The gods do not capriciously direct their love toward one thing or another; rather, they love something only because there is some reason why they *should* love it. Thus, Socrates insists, piety, far from being determined by the gods' favor, should be defined by that property or set of properties that all pious things share and that makes them pious, and that therefore causes them to be loved by the gods. As he eventually gets Euthyphro himself to admit, it is not that something is pious because the gods love it; rather, the gods love something only because they see that it is pious.

The philosophical issue in the dialogue's debate over whether something is pious because it is loved by the gods or the gods love something because it is in itself pious has come to be known as the Euthyphro Problem. Are our most important values objectively grounded in the natures of things or are they subjectively based in the predilections of some authority? To put it in terms more familiar to the Western religious tradition: Does God make or do something because it is good, or is something good just because God does it? The Bible says that on each day of creation God surveyed what He had done and "saw that it was good." But did God choose to create what He did because He perceived it to be inherently good? Or was what God created good simply because God created it—with the implication that had God created something entirely different, then *that* would have been good instead?

Central questions of philosophy, theology, morality, and politics depend on how one resolves the dilemma. If Euthyphro is right and something is good simply because God loves it, then goodness, along with many other values, is an ultimately arbitrary and subjective matter. Whatever God loves, by that fact alone, is pious or good. There can be no measure of piety or goodness independent of God's will or favor that might objectively and rationally incline His love one way or another. This is because nothing is in itself good or right (or true or just or pious or beautiful), but a thing becomes such only when God's preference so determines it. In the Socratic view, by contrast, because what is pious or good is so independently of what God (or any rational agent) loves or desires or thinks, there is a universal, objective standard of goodness that explains or establishes why certain things are good. These good things are what reasonable beings (including God) favor.

In the history of philosophy, few thinkers have followed Euthyphro down the path of absolute divine voluntarism. Even medieval philosophers, for the most part deeply pious theologians who were concerned above all with explaining and defending God's glory and power, usually stop short of saying that God's will alone is the source of all values and standards, of all goodness, beauty, and truth. The typical philosopher in the High Middle Ages—such as Aquinas—stresses the objective wisdom and intelligence of God's ways, with the divine reason, informed by eternal and uncreated values, having primacy over and providing motivation for the divine will.[1] What God does He does because He sees that it is good to do; it is not good just because He chooses to do it.

Such values independent of God's will inevitably set boundaries to God's power. For practically all philosophical theologians of the medieval period, while there are infinitely many things that God can do, there also are many things that He cannot do. These thinkers generally agreed that there are some a priori limitations upon God—moral, metaphysical, or at least logical limitations set by objective, independent, and eternal canons of goodness, rationality, or truth—and a good deal of their philosophizing (and disputing) consists of trying to figure out what precisely these are.

Aquinas put the problem well: "All commonly confess that God is omnipotent. But the definition of omnipotence seems difficult to assign. For when it is said that God can do all things, it can be doubted what is comprehended in the extension [of 'all things']."[2]

What exactly can God do? Obviously, God *can* do everything that He actually *does* do. God's power certainly extends to all the ordinary events that take place in the world. These contingent facts constitute the divinely instituted regular course of nature, and thereby express a part of what some medieval theologians called God's *ordained* power. This is the order of things to which God binds Himself at creation, and it includes the lawful behavior of physical bodies and the common events that take place in human souls. God's power also extends to any extraordinary events that may occur. Miracles, understood as violations of the natural order, are also produced by God. Thus, just because a state of affairs is contrary to the laws of nature, it does not follow that God cannot bring it about. If there are limits to God's power, they are not at the boundary of what is natural.

Nor are they at the boundary of what is actual. Just because something has never happened and never will happen, it does not therefore exceed God's power to make it happen. There are many possibilities that will never be realized—naturally or miraculously—but that are nonetheless well within God's abilities. God could have instituted in the beginning an entirely different order of things; in Leibnizian terms, God could have created a different possible world altogether. Such considerations of what God *might* do or *could have* done are referred to as God's *absolute* power or will.[3] If God's ordained power is God's power as expressed in His governance of the world and the laws and order of things He has actually established, then God's absolute power represents what it is theoretically possible for Him to do, regardless of the order He has already created.

However, this distinction between God's absolute power and the settled framework of His ordained power—while effective in showing that what God can do is not limited to what He actually does—does not really address the Euthyphro Problem. Not only does it still leave open the question of what exactly *is* theoretically possible for God to do, but even those thinkers who stress God's omnipotence and free-dom and who defend His independence from what He has in fact done by pointing out what He might do or could have done are usu-ally not willing to concede that there are no limits whatsoever to what God can do. God's absolute power is, for most medieval philosophers, never truly absolute; there are some things that not even God can do. Or, in the striking terms of St. Jerome, "although God can do all things, He cannot raise up a virgin after she has fallen."[4]

Some see the limitations on God's power as derived from His very divinity.[5] In principle, there is no reason why an omnipotent God could not send a perfectly virtuous person to eternal punishment in hell. But this, some philosophers claimed, is something that God's moral nature necessarily prevents Him from doing. As the point is ex-pressed by one eleventh-century thinker, "God could according to His power, but not according to His justice."[6]

Even those philosophers who do not want to concede that God is prevented by His own nature from certain actions acknowledge that there are still some things that are beyond God's omnipotence, some things that He cannot change or affect by His will. Thus, the eternal and immutable laws of morality are often offered as examples of what is resistant to divine fiat. God cannot change the nature of justice and make what is just unjust. What is right and good is such indepen-dently of God's will. God commands us not to perform certain actions because they are wrong, and there is nothing God could do to make them right. There may, some argue, also be metaphysical constraints on God that are in the eternal essences of things: God cannot make a human that is not a rational being, fire that is not hot, or a horse that does not possess all of the essential properties of a horse.

There is even greater consensus that God cannot violate the prin-ciples of mathematics. God cannot make one plus one equal three, or a triangle whose interior angles are more or less than 180 degrees. Above all, almost everyone agrees that while God can do whatever is possible, He cannot do what is logically impossible. God cannot make a square circle, nor can He will that a proposition and its negation are both true at the same time. As Aquinas states the matter, "God is called omnipotent" not because He can do all things whatsoever but "because He can do all things that are possible absolutely," that is, as long as the terms involved do not, when put together, represent a contradiction, "such as, a man is an ass."[7] Likewise, Ockham insists that "an omnipotent being can bring about everything doable that does not involve a contradiction."[8] For Aquinas, Ockham, and others, the truths of mathematics and especially those of logic are not created by God, and they are as objectively binding upon Him—upon His thinking and His acting—as they are upon human beings. This provides them with a convenient solution to another one of the classic paradoxes of omnipotence: the question of whether or not God can nullify His own existence. They answer that because it is logically impossible for a necessarily existing being such as God not to exist, and because God cannot do what is logically impossible, there is therefore no problem in saying that God, although an omnipotent being, cannot bring about His own nonexistence.

Some medievals are often said to have flirted with the idea that God is not bound even by the principle of noncontradiction. Peter Damian, for example, writing in the mid-eleventh century, was among the first seriously to address the question of how one is to understand claims about what God can and cannot do. And he is sometimes interpreted as suggesting that God is not bound even by the laws of logic. On one reading of his *On Divine Omnipotence*, Damian claims that God can in fact do what is logically impossible. Nature may not be able to bring it about that "contraries coincide in the same subject" (such as a body that is both hot and cold), but, he says in the relevant but highly ambiguous text, "on no account should [such lack of means] be applied to the divine majesty."[9] If this is Damian's view, however, he is certainly an exception. So radical a view of divine omnipotence—with God's will and power absolutely unrestricted, circumscribed not even by the boundaries of logical possibility—seems to have been beyond the intellectual horizon of most philosophers in the Middle Ages.

And then came Descartes.

The "father of modern philosophy," the brilliant inventor of analytic geometry and fervent promoter of mathematical physics and the new mechanistic science of nature, was a more robust defender of God's grandeur and omnipotence than anyone before him, and he went where his medieval philosophical ancestors feared to tread. He agreed with Euthyphro.

Readers of Descartes's first published writings, in the 1630s, as well as the six chapters of his popular *Meditations* of 1641, would have had no clue that their author departs from the standard view on divine power. Descartes appears in these works to recognize that there are at least logical limits to what God can do. When considering the skeptical question of whether God has in fact created, outside the mind, an external world, Descartes notes that such a world is at least possible, for "I have never judged that something could not be made by Him except on the grounds that there would be a contradiction in my perceiving it distinctly."[10] Descartes's God seems to be limited even by His own moral nature. The *Meditations* is devoted to showing that human beings can acquire true knowledge of things, as long as they use their rational faculties properly and give their assent only to what they clearly and distinctly perceive with the intellect rather than relying on the misleading testimony of the senses. This, Descartes argues, is because those faculties have been provided by God, an all-powerful, all-perfect being who is incapable of malevolent behavior. Such a God would never give His creatures a cognitive faculty that is systematically deceptive and conducive to falsehoods. As long as that faculty is used correctly, it will provide true and reliable beliefs. On this account, God's moral character apparently prevents Him from the mere possibility of having bad intentions. "It is impossible that God should ever deceive me. For in every case of trickery or deception some imperfection is to be found; and although the ability to deceive appears to be an indication of cleverness or power, the will to deceive is undoubtedly evidence of malice or weakness, and so cannot apply to God."[11]

Nonetheless, some years before composing the *Meditations*, Descartes had arrived at a much more extreme understanding of divine power. In a series of letters to Mersenne in the spring of 1630, he reveals to the Minim friar an opinion that he fears will be a disturbing vision to many.

> The mathematical truths that you call eternal have been laid down by God and depend on Him entirely no less than the rest of His creatures. Indeed, to say that these truths are independent of God is to talk of Him as if He were Jupiter or Saturn and to subject him to the Styx and the Fates.[12]

God created the visible universe (including the principles that govern it, such as the laws of physics) and the souls over which He stands in judgment; on this, Descartes and his predecessors were in agreement. As for the "eternal verities," the earlier philosophers who believed them to be independent of and binding upon God also regarded them as uncreated. Descartes, however, rejects such a distinction between created world and uncreated truths. He insists that these truths, too, are created things. For Descartes, even necessary and unchanging truths are ultimately, like empirical truths, contingent upon an act of the divine will. God made it true that one plus one equals two, but He could just as well have made it true instead that one plus one equals three. Similarly, "[God] was free to make it not true that all the radii of the circle are equal—just as free as He was not to create the world."[13]

Descartes does not deny that these are a special class of truths, different from empirical truths about bodies and minds that actually exist in the world. He says that mathematical truths, although established by God, nonetheless remain eternal and necessary because of the eternity and immutability of the will that creates and sustains them.

> It will be said that if God had established these truths He could change them as a king changes his laws. To this the answer is: Yes He can, if His will can change. "But I understand them to be eternal and unchangeable."—I make the same judgment about God.[14]

Descartes apparently wants to maintain a distinction between necessary and contingent truths. But, contrary to the traditional view, the eternity and necessity of the eternal truths are not things that belong to them intrinsically, independently of what God (eternally) decides.

What Descartes says to Mersenne about mathematical truths applies to all the so-called eternal truths, including metaphysical and moral principles, to all values whatsoever. It applies even to the laws of logic.

> Our mind is finite and so created as to be able to conceive as possible the things that God has wished in fact to be possible, but not be able to conceive as possible things which God could have made possible, but that He has nevertheless wished to make impossible . . . [This] shows us that God cannot have been determined to make it true that contradictories cannot be true together, and therefore that He could have done the opposite . . . I agree

that there are contradictions that are so evident that we cannot put them before our minds without judging them entirely impossible . . . But if we would know the immensity of His power we should not put these thoughts before our minds.[15]

God can make a mountain without a valley, a triangle whose interior angles are more or less than 180 degrees, and an extended space without body (a metaphysical impossibility for Descartes, for whom extension is the essence of matter). God can even make two logically inconsistent propositions (such as "Descartes is French" and "Descartes is not French") be true at the same time and thus violate the law of noncontradiction; or make one and the same proposition both true and false at the same time and thus violate the law of excluded middle. As Descartes puts it, "[God] could have made it false that . . . contradictories could not be true together."[16]

The upshot is that whatever is true is true only because God has made it so, and—as Euthyphro would agree—nothing is good unless God makes it good. "It is impossible to imagine that anything is thought of in the divine intellect as good or true, or worthy of belief or action or omission, prior to the decision of the divine will to make it so."[17] If God knows that something is true or good, it is because He wills it to be true or good; He does not believe it because He sees that it is true nor will it because He sees that it is good. Absolutely nothing is true or good independently of His will.

> God did not will the creation of the world in time because He saw it would be better this way than if He had created it from eternity; nor did He will that the three angles of a triangle should be equal to two right angles because He recognized that it could not be otherwise, and so on. On the contrary, it is because He willed to create the world in time that it is better this way than if

He had created it from eternity; and it is because He willed that the three angles of a triangle should necessarily equal two right angles that this is true . . . If some reason for something's being good had existed prior to His preordination, this would have determined God to prefer those things that it was best to do. But on the contrary, just because He resolved to prefer those things that are now to be done, for this very reason, in the words of Genesis, "they are very good"; in other words, the reason for their goodness depends on the fact that He exercised His will to make them so.[18]

Descartes sees this doctrine as the natural consequence of a proper understanding of the divine nature. God's simplicity means that God is not a composite being, made up of parts, and thus there is no real distinction between His attributes. In particular, God's understanding is not separate from His will. "In God willing and knowing are a single thing in such a way that by the very fact of willing something He knows it and it is only for this reason that such a thing is true."[19] God's will cannot be directed by His wisdom, by what He knows and judges, because this would imply a distinction between two faculties and a priority of one over the other. For God to know that one plus one equals two is identical with God willing that one plus one equal two. To Mersenne, Descartes wrote that "you ask what God did in order to produce [these truths]. I reply that from all eternity He willed and understood them to be, and by that very fact He created them. Or, if you would reserve the word 'created' for the existence of things, then He established them and made them. In God, willing, understanding and creating are all the same thing without one being prior to the other even conceptually."[20]

Descartes also regards the creation of the eternal truths as the only position that is consistent with God's omnipotence and greatness.

"The power of God," he insists, "cannot have any limits": not epistemic or moral limits, and—what his medieval predecessors were not
willing to concede—not even logical limits. "I do not think that we
should ever say of anything that it cannot be brought about by God.
For since every basis of truth and goodness depends on his omnipotence, I would not dare say that God cannot make a mountain without a valley, or bring it about that one and two are not three. I merely
say that He has given me such a mind that I cannot conceive a mountain without a valley, or a sum of one and two that is not three; such
things involve a contradiction in my conception."[21]

For Descartes, then, divine omnipotence requires not only that
God enjoy complete independence of being and power but also the
total dependence of everything else upon Him. This means that He is
the cause not only of the existence of things but also of their essences.
This, in fact, is precisely how God creates the eternal truths. By establishing the essential nature of the triangle to be what it is—and He
could have made it different from how it in fact is, although we cannot possibly conceive it otherwise than having the properties it does—
He thereby causes there to be certain truths about triangles, even if
it should happen that no triangles ever actually exist. Replying to
Mersenne, he writes, "You ask me by what kind of causality God established the eternal truths. I reply: by the same kind of causality as
He created all things, that is to say, as their efficient and total cause.
For it is certain that He is the author of the essence of created things
no less than of their existence; and this essence is nothing other than
the eternal truths."[22]

It follows from all this that Descartes's God must be an absolutely
free and arbitrary God, guided or limited by no laws, principles, standards, or values that are independent of His will. The Cartesian God is
bound by no objective canons of rationality or morality. At the basis of
all creation lies a completely indifferent will. When God creates the
truths, He does so "freely and indifferently."[23] It is, Descartes writes,

"self-contradictory to suppose that the will of God was not indifferent from eternity with respect to everything that has happened or will ever happen."[24] Such a God is not rationally determined to make the choices He makes. He does not do what He does for objective reasons, because all such reasons—moral, metaphysical, and logical—are the effect of His will. In this respect, God's mode of activity is completely different from human action, which operates on the basis of practical reasoning in conformity with independent values and standards. "The supreme indifference to be found in God is the supreme indication of His omnipotence," Descartes says, whereas human beings rarely act out of indifference but rather tend to pursue those things that they, through the understanding, perceive to be good.[25]

Descartes was well aware of the originality—even the audacity—of his position. He encouraged Mersenne "not to hesitate to assert and proclaim everywhere that it is God who has laid down these laws in nature just as a king lays down laws in his kingdom," but he also asked that Mersenne "not mention my name."[26] While he eventually softened this cautious stance and explained the doctrine in letters to others—including a young French cleric named Antoine Arnauld—and even in some of his published writings, his hesitations were justified. The doctrine became so controversial in the second half of the seventeenth century that even his most devoted followers hesitated to accept it.[27]

Never has a philosopher's brilliance been so wasted on mundane matters as was Leibniz's in the mid-1680s. In the employ of the new duke of Hanover, Ernst August, Leibniz was given the assignment of writing the history of the House of Brunswick-Lüneburg. The project, which turned out to be an enormous undertaking, one that he would never complete, did give him a good excuse for extensive travel—and time away from Hanover—as he sought out records and documents in far-flung collections. But much to Leibniz's frustration, it also meant fewer opportunities for his philosophical and mathematical pursuits.

> It cannot be said how extraordinarily distracted I am. I dig things out of the archives, I inspect old papers, I search for unknown manuscripts. From these I try to throw light on the history of Brunswick. I send and receive a great number of letters. I truly have so many new results in mathematics, so many philosophical ideas, so many other scholarly observations that I would not want to lose, that I often hesitate, wavering between tasks, and feel almost like that line from Ovid: "Wealth impoverishes me."

He had to keep his pursuit of these "new results" a secret from his employer. "All these labors of mine, if you exclude the historical, are almost clandestine, for you know that at the Court something far different is sought and expected."[28]

Still, the ever-active, hyperproductive Leibniz, who needed very little sleep, found the time to continue working on ideas formulated during his stay in Paris. He concentrated especially on topics in metaphysics and natural science during these extremely important years in his philosophical and scientific development. In various writings, he struggled for the right expression of his views, aiming above all to correct the dominant program in philosophy and physics that had been established by Descartes and his followers. It was during this period that Leibniz first took aim at Malebranche's misguided defense of Descartes's account of the laws of nature. At the same time, he continued to argue that his own preestablished harmony was superior—both philosophically and theologically—to Malebranche's occasionalism.

There was, however, one particular legacy of Descartes's philosophy on which Leibniz and Malebranche found common ground. On the basis of their shared fundamental assumptions about God's nature and rational behavior, and especially the belief that a wise God always acts to maximize certain objective values—either by choosing what is best or by acting in ways most expressive of His attributes—the two agreed that Descartes's position on the eternal truths was simply wrong, and even dangerous.

Leibniz was a lifelong foe of divine voluntarism.[29] In his mind, the flaws of Descartes's doctrine ran deep. Not only did it offer a false picture of God's nature and of the way in which He operates, Leibniz thought, but it also threatened religious piety and even everyday morality. Writing in the mid-1680s, he notes that "I am far removed from the opinion of those who maintain that there are no principles of goodness or perfection in the nature of things, or in the ideas that God has about them, and who say that the works of God are good only through the formal reason that God has made them."[30] To claim, as Descartes does, that "the principles of goodness and beauty are arbitrary" is, Leibniz argues, ultimately to deprive the works of God of any true goodness or beauty. These qualities would be nothing but an extrinsic, merely accidental feature of God's work, derived only from the fact that God has brought them about; such value properties could just as well have belonged to some other works, had God chosen to create them instead.

Leibniz insists that the view that "the eternal truths of metaphysics and geometry, and consequently the principles of goodness, of justice, and of perfection are effects only of the will of God" undermines the necessity and objectivity of all epistemic, moral, and aesthetic standards and judgments. What is good and right and true and just and beautiful could just as well have been otherwise, and there would be no compelling reason why God did not in fact make it otherwise.

The moral character of God Himself is threatened by the voluntarist position. "In saying, therefore, that things are not good according to any standard of goodness, but simply by the will of God, it seems to me that one destroys, without realizing it, all the love of God and all His glory; for why praise Him for what He has done if He would be equally praiseworthy in doing the contrary? Where will be His justice and His wisdom if He has only a certain despotic power, if arbitrary will takes the place of reasonableness, and if in accord with the definition of tyrants, justice consists in that which is pleasing to the most powerful?"[31] Almost twenty years later, in his "Reflections on the Common Concept of Justice," Leibniz reaffirms his position with a resounding rejection of Euthyphro's view:

> It is generally agreed that whatever God wills is good and just. But there remains the question whether it is good and just because God wills it or whether God wills it because it is good and just; in other words, whether justice and goodness are arbitrary or whether they belong to the necessary and eternal truths about the nature of things, as do numbers and proportions . . . As a matter of fact, [the arbitrary view] would destroy the justice of God. For why praise Him for acting justly if the concept of justice adds nothing to His act. And to say *stat pro ratione voluntas*—"Let my will stand for the reason"—is definitely the motto of a tyrant.[32]

Unlike Descartes's "despotic" God, Leibniz's rational God chooses nothing from caprice or indifference; rather, He does things only for reasons. And the reasons that move God are objective and independent of His will. "Every act of willing," Leibniz says, "presupposes some reason for the willing, and this reason, of course, must precede the act."

Leibniz's fear is that the Cartesian position on the eternal truths makes it impossible to offer a theodicean justification of God's ways that provides a coherent and satisfactory solution to the problem of evil. If whatever God does is good just because God does it, then a defense of God's justice and goodness is meaningless. "Indifference with regard to good and evil would indicate a lack of goodness or of wisdom . . . If justice was established arbitrarily and without any cause, if God came upon it by a kind of hazard, as when one draws lots, His goodness and His wisdom are not manifested in it, and there is nothing at all to attach Him to it."[33] It would make no more sense to ask why God does what is good than to ask why the Devil does what is evil, since whatever the Devil does is, by the fact of his doing it, evil.

As Leibniz sees it, if God chooses one world over any other, it is because He recognizes that that world is, objectively and in its own right, better than all other possible worlds; this is what supplies God with a sufficient reason for choosing that world. The actual world was created by God because He saw that it is the best of all possible worlds; it is not the best of all possible worlds just because God created it.

Despite his unquestionable Cartesian credentials and a tendency to exaggerate the differences between his own solution to the problem of evil and that of Leibniz, Malebranche unequivocally departed from his philosophical mentor's views on the eternal truths and is in agreement with his Lutheran colleague on this central theodicean issue.

> If eternal laws and truths depended on God, if they had been established by a free volition of the Creator, in short, if the Reason we consult [according to the Vision in God doctrine] were not necessary and independent, it seems evident to me that there would no longer be any true science and that we might be mistaken in claiming that the arithmetic or geometry of the Chinese is like our own. For in the final analysis, if it were not absolutely

necessary that twice four be eight, or that the three angles of a triangle be equal to two right angles, what assur-
ance would we have that these kinds of truths are not like
those that are found only in certain universities, or that
last only for a certain time?[34]

Again, the concern is not just with mathematics. Piety is what it is, regardless of what anyone (including God) wants it to be. Goodness,
beauty, and other universal norms are independent of the desires, preferences, and inclinations of all agents, human and divine. God cannot
make what is unjust into what is just, nor can He, through His will
alone, reverse all of the values that inform our judgments about what
is true and false and good and bad. In the *Dialogues on Metaphysics*,
Theodore, fearful of the ethical consequences of the Cartesian doctrine, sounds the alarm: "Everything is inverted if we claim that God
is above Reason and has no rule in His plans other than His mere will.
This false principle spreads such blanket darkness that it confounds the
good with the evil, the true with the false, and creates out of everything a chaos in which the mind no longer knows anything." There
are moments when this character's concerns, while expressed in more
picturesque terms, echo those of Leibniz. If Descartes is right, then
claims about God's moral nature are empty and there is no point in
praising God for what He has done, because He would be equally
praiseworthy had He done just the opposite.

According to this principle, the universe is perfect because God willed it. Monsters are works as perfect as others according to the plans of God. It is good to have eyes
in our head, but they would have been as wisely placed
anywhere else, had God so placed them. However we in-
vert the world, whatever chaos we make out of it, it will
always be equally admirable, since its entire beauty consists in its conformity with the divine will, which is not

obliged to conform to order . . . All the beauty of the
universe must therefore disappear in view of that great
principle that God is above the Reason that enlightens all
minds, and that His wholly arbitrary will is the sole rule
of His actions.[35]

Malebranche's God creates the world and all the laws that govern
its ordinary and extraordinary causal relationships, including the behaviors of bodies and minds, the power of angels to affect events, and
the distribution of grace. God's selection of one set of mundane or
salvific laws over all others was not arbitrary but was guided, even determined, by objective reasons. God was rationally moved to establish
the simplest laws of all, even at the cost of allowing a host of evils into
the world. But because it was possible for God not to create any world
at all, the laws of physics and many other principles governing things
are fundamentally contingent on God's will.

Standing above all those laws, however, and serving as their true
measure is an uncreated, supreme wisdom, Order itself. This, as we
have seen, comprises the ultimate truths of mathematics, metaphysics,
and morality that are grounded in the eternal ideas of things. The laws
that God creates with and for the world must be consistent with Order. Because Order specifies that one kind of being is nobler than another—for example, that the human soul is of greater value than any
body—it restricts the kinds of subsidiary laws that God can institute
("God cannot subject a mind to a body and make it serve the latter").
But not only do the immutable, necessary dictates of Order surpass
the laws of nature and grace; they also transcend the divine will and
represent the absolute limitations on divine power. "God cannot possibly will that the mind should be subject to the body because the wisdom according to which God wills all that He wills clearly shows me
that this would be contrary to Order."[36]

The eternal truths depend on the divine understanding in that they
are just the necessary relations found within and among the ideas in

God's wisdom. They are coeternal with God; if God did not exist, then neither would the eternal idea of a triangle (the essence of the triangle); nor would the truths about triangles derivable from it exist, all of which God knows eternally. But these ideas or essences of things, while deriving their reality (a kind of borrowed eternity) from God's knowing them, do not depend on the divine will in the way in which created things do. God does not invent the truths of logic, mathematics, metaphysics, morality, or theology; He discovers them in His wisdom. And what He finds there is an objective body of knowledge that is resistant to, even binding upon, His volitions.

The God of Leibniz and Malebranche is an intelligible God. His way of acting is scrutable to human reason. True, their God is, unlike human beings, omnipotent, endowed with infinite power. But there are well-defined limits to that power. These two philosophers, like so many before them, agree that God certainly cannot do what involves a logical contradiction. But they also agree that neither can He make the values of things different from what they, in fact, are. The rationalist God's will is bounded by uncreated logical, mathematical, metaphysical, and moral truths—truths that He cannot violate or change, not even in theory. Put another way, this God operates just as human beings operate: through practical reason, confronted with objective values that are not of His making and that normatively serve Him in making the choices that He makes. In Leibniz's words, "as to order and justice, I believe that there are universal rules that must hold with respect to God and with respect to intelligent creatures."[37]

The relationship between wisdom and will in the rationalist God mirrors their relationship in human beings. God knows and wills things in the same way that we do. The wisdom that moves Malebranche's God is—through the Vision in God doctrine—literally identical with the wisdom that informs our reasoning. "God is not only wise, but wisdom; not only knowing, but knowledge; not only enlightened, but the light that illumines His own self and indeed all intellects . . . I am certain that God sees exactly the same thing I see, the same truth."[38] Descartes's God, by contrast, is, in the deepest sense, unintelligible. What appear as necessary, objective, and independent truths to us do not so appear to God, on whose will they ultimately depend. In the Cartesian scheme, God's relationship to truths and values is radically different from ours. With the divine rationalism of Leibniz and Malebranche, there is a commensurability between the human and the divine; with the divine voluntarism of Descartes, we cannot even conceive of what divine wisdom is like.

On July 25, 1641, a student named Charles Wallon de Beaupuis stood before the learned gentlemen of the Sorbonne and defended a series of philosophical, mathematical, and physical theses. Among these are the claim that "one should seek the Sovereign good for its own sake, and all other goods only for the sake of the Sovereign good," the proposition that "the planets borrow their light from the sun; but as for the stars, this is uncertain," and a pair of theses stating that to imagine that there are "real eternal essences outside of God is to suffer from a waking dream" and that "the possibility of things is nothing other than the immense virtue of God."[39]

At one point during the proceedings, Wallon de Beaupuis made the further observation that "Being [Ens] pertains synonymously to God and creatures, both with respect to substance and with respect to accident." God and His properties exist in the same sense in which a created being and its properties exist. The young man thereby took up the defense of a thesis much in discussion among his Parisian contemporaries: the so-called doctrine of univocity, or the view that the same terms ordinarily used to characterize human reality and its various activities can also be used "univocally"—with no significant change of meaning—to characterize God's being and attributes.[40] One can speak, for example, of God's knowledge or wisdom and human knowledge or wisdom in the same basic terms, with the caveat that God's knowledge is, if not qualitatively then at least quantitatively, different from that of humans. Because God is an infinite, eternal being and humans are only finite, the extent of His knowledge far surpasses the cognitive abilities of His creatures. But what it is for God to know a truth is substantially the same as what it is for a human being to know a truth. Or, as Malebranche and Leibniz later argued, when God knows and wills the good, what happens is not essentially different from what takes place when a human being knows and wills the good.

With this thesis, Wallon de Beaupuis entered highly contested territory. Throughout the Middle Ages, philosophical theologians debated at length and with great vehemence the question of whether *being* and other terms could be predicated univocally of God and creatures, or only equivocally.[41] Those who favored the doctrine of equivocity insisted that the metaphysical distance between the infinite and the finite is too great for there to be any shared meaning when ordinary categories are applied to both God and His creatures. Although reference can be made to God's understanding or God's will just as well as to a human being's understanding or will, it must be borne in mind that the terms *understanding* and *will* are being used equivocally, because God's understanding and other faculties can be nothing like what they are in humans, and thus nothing of the divine can be known by considering the human.

Apparently, there was at least one partisan of equivocity in the audience at the Sorbonne that day, and he took umbrage with Wallon de Beaupuis's thesis. Léonor de la Barde, an Oratorian and a canon at the Cathedral of Nôtre Dame, was, according to an early historical account of the event,

> a very learned man and a subtle theologian . . . [He] attacked this proposition and strongly pushed the respondent. The presiding officer [or sponsor of the disputation], seeing [the respondent] stymied by the strength of the objection, came to his aid. But he soon found himself so hard-pressed and so convinced by the reasons

put forth by the disputant, that he saw that he had no choice but to render glory to the truth. He preferred to admit that he had nothing to respond than to seek out false feints or evasions, that ordinarily are never lacking to a Professor on such an occasion, and that he in particular would have excelled at finding. "I believe, Monsieur, that you are right," he said to Monsieur de La Barde, "and I promise you that henceforth I abandon my opinion in order to follow yours."[42]

The man who came to Wallon de Beaupuis's aid at this juncture in the disputation was the young Antoine Arnauld, newly ordained as a priest and starting to make his mark on the local philosophical scene. In 1639, Arnauld began a two-year stint teaching philosophy at the Collège de Mans, a school in Paris associated with the Sorbonne, to fulfill the pedagogical requirement for membership in that illustrious society. According to the theology faculty's regulations, Arnauld, like other candidates, was supposed to have done his teaching before beginning work on his *License*, the degree that would confer upon him the status of "Doctor of Theology" that Arnauld had begun studying for in 1638. For unknown reasons, Arnauld did not satisfy his teaching obligation until after entering this final stage in his professional education. This technicality may have provided his later enemies just the excuse they were looking for to deny him membership in the Sorbonne.

Arnauld drafted the "Philosophical Conclusions" that Wallon de Beaupuis, his student, was defending. In the medieval and early modern educational system in France and elsewhere, it was standard for degree candidates to cut their academic teeth by publicly taking on objections to theses composed by their teachers—ordinarily theses those teachers wanted to see defended. This suggests that at this early point in his career, Arnauld had no difficulty accepting the doctrine of univocity. While Arnauld had been impressed by what he read just a few months earlier in the manuscript of Descartes's *Meditations*, and while he was taken by what he saw as the new philosophy's many advantages over the old Aristotelian system, in the summer of 1641 he had not yet been exposed to the account of the creation of the eternal truths. Descartes's idiosyncratic expression of the doctrine of equivocity—based on the numerical identification of understanding and will in God, which is entirely unlike the relationship between the two faculties in a human being—appears in the philosopher's replies to the "Objections" collected by Mersenne and published together with the *Meditations*, but not until later that year, as well as in his letters, which were not available in print until 1657. Nor was Arnauld aware yet of Descartes's forthright insistence that "of all the individual attributes which, by a defect of our intellect, we assign to God in a piecemeal fashion, corresponding to the way in which we perceive them in ourselves, none belong to God and to ourselves in the manner that in the Schools is called 'univocal.' "[43] There was thus no reason why Arnauld, only beginning his philosophical and theological career, and certainly not yet fully committed to Cartesianism,[44] should not, in preparing Wallon de Beaupuis's theses, naturally have followed the standard Augustinian and Thomistic line on the uncreated nature of the eternal truths and, consequently, on the general resemblance between God's way of knowing and willing and our own.

However, Arnauld did not have to wait for any lessons from Descartes on this matter. Whatever De la Barde said from the audience on that summer day—his exact arguments are lost—must have been very convincing. Arnauld, a stubborn man even in his youth, was not one to change his mind easily and concede the point of an opponent. Moreover, the concession was not merely the respectful but temporary indulgence of a superior's judgment. Six years later, on February 9, 1647, Wallon de Beaupuis again defended a thesis under Arnauld's supervision, this time for his bachelor's degree. Now among the claims was the following: "Nothing pertains in a univocal manner to God and to creatures."[45]

There is no text in which Arnauld openly declares himself for or against the Cartesian doctrine of the creation of the eternal truths. And despite much prodding from others curious about his views on the matter, especially given his general fealty to Descartes's philosophy, he never explicitly shows his hand.[46] Leibniz tried to draw Arnauld out on this issue in their correspondence. In an early letter of May 1686, Arnauld expresses his concern about what he sees as the consequences of Leibniz's view of truth and the spontaneity of substances ("That the individual concept of each person involves once and for all everything that will ever happen to him"). He is worried, as we have seen, about some of the things that are thereby objectively embedded in the concept of an individual and whose occurrence is, should God create that individual, thus entirely independent of God's will. Adam's actual existence may be the result of a "free decree" of God. But, Arnauld fears, if Leibniz is right, then once God has decided to create Adam, everything that happens to Adam happens with a "fatalistic necessity." If Adam exists, then it is certain that Adam will sin and there is nothing God can do about it, just because sin is an immutable part of his essence.

In his notes for a response to this letter, Leibniz takes Arnauld's comments to be evidence that he rejects God's creation of the eternal essences of things, presumably because Arnauld does seem to accept that the individual concept of Adam includes, independently of God's will, if not all of Adam's posterity then at least some minimal set of essential properties that make Adam "what he is in himself." "I see that Monsieur Arnauld has not remembered, or at least, has not adhered, to the position of the Cartesians who maintain that God, by His will, establishes the eternal truths . . . But I share their opinion no more than Monsieur Arnauld."[47] In the letter he sent to Arnauld in July, he seems slightly less certain of Arnauld's stance on this issue, but still senses that he and Arnauld are in agreement. "The most abstract specific concepts embrace only necessary or eternal truths that do not depend upon the decrees of God (whatever the Cartesians may say about this, whom it seems you have not followed at this point)."[48] In his subsequent reply, Arnauld passes over this remark without comment and moves on to other troubling questions.

Much of what Arnauld says in his writings against Malebranche, however, and especially on matters that bear a close relation to the question of the eternal truths, points in a very clear direction. Like Descartes, Arnauld claims that there is no real distinction between divine will and understanding. "His will is His wisdom." Thus, God's knowing something is equivalent to His willing it. Arnauld also insists that God's freedom and omnipotence require that He act with "a liberty of indifference" in creating things outside Himself, an indifference that can be explained only if there are no values or reasons independent of His will. "It is the divine will that determines itself, freely and indifferently, toward all things to which it does not bear a necessary relation, that is, to all things that are not God."[49] Arnauld's rejection of the notion that God's choices are guided and motivated by reasons independent of the will, "as if His will, in order to will nothing other than what is good, had need of being regulated by something other than itself," would seem to commit him to the Euthyphro-like position that something is right or good or reasonable only because God has willed it.[50] God does not choose something because it is wise; rather, whatever God chooses is wise only because "everything that He wills is . . . essentially wise as soon as He wills it."[51]

Arnauld consistently denies that God acts "arbitrarily" or "capriciously," and he insists in several contexts that whatever God does is done "reasonably."[52] But these are ambiguous claims. An act of will can be capricious if it is not moved by logically antecedent reasons. Given everything Arnauld says about the relationship between wisdom and will in God, and in the light of the kinds of criticisms he levels against Malebranche's conception of divine agency, it is not clear how he can avoid the conclusion that God *is* capricious or arbitrary in this sense. If the problem with the Oratorian's (and Leibniz's) God is that any objective and independent reasons that allegedly guide the divine will must undermine God's freedom, then Arnauld cannot allow for such reasons.

On the other hand, by *capricious* or *arbitrary* Arnauld may mean "unrelated to any reasons whatsoever." He can then argue that his God is *not* capricious in this broad sense. While the will of Arnauld's God is not moved by antecedent, determining reasons—just because there are no such reasons outside God's will—there are nonetheless reasons that are a *consequence* of His will, just because they are created by it. God's will is a rule or reason unto itself. Just as whatever God wills "is wise as soon as He wills it," so God's performing some action or causing some event is what makes that action or event a reasonable thing to do. These are ex post facto reasons, created by the divine act of willing itself, and they allow Arnauld to continue to speak of God's will as *raisonnable*. God's volitions and actions are reasonable not because they are guided by reasons, as would be the case were He an agent whose actions were governed by practical rationality, but because they make reasons.

A rnauld was not shy about expressing his opinions. This makes his reticence on the matter of absolute divine voluntarism, which everyone else was talking about, all the more curious. Still, his uncharacteristic reserve cannot hide one very compelling fact. There is every reason why Arnauld *should* have followed Euthyphro and Descartes toward an extreme divine voluntarism. Such a doctrine clearly lends support to the Jansenist account of salvation and of God's free and unmotivated distribution of grace. But it also serves well to ground Arnauld's more general attack on Malebranche, Leibniz, and anyone else tempted to portray God as a rational agent.

Again, it is not that Arnauld's God has His reasons, but that they must remain hidden from us. Arnauld's project involves a wholesale rejection of the anthropomorphizing of God's ways that depicts His attributes and His actions within the structure of practical rationality. He accomplishes this by essentially doing away with the entire edifice of divine reasons itself. All the norms of rationality—logical, mathematical, and moral—now have their foundation only in the indifference of divine choice. Arnauld's God—as a being by whom all reasons are created, as a deity who knows truths only because He wills them to be—is beyond rationality altogether.

Where divine rationality goes, however, so goes the project of theodicy. If the divine will is the source of all reasons, if there are no independent, objective, and accessible standards of truth and goodness to which even God's choices are subject or in the light of which God's decisions can be made intelligible, then hope for a rational justification of God's ways in the face of the apparent evils in His creation is doomed.[53] As Leibniz observed, if whatever God does is necessarily just and wise only because God does it, then all theodicean claims are trivial.

There is suffering among the innocent, prosperity among the wicked, and eternal damnation of innumerable souls. Where is the justice in that? How can it possibly be argued that this is the best of all possible worlds? Arnauld's reply to the challenge posed by the problem of evil can be only this: Such is God's will. There is, quite simply, nothing more to be said on the matter. This is not to be understood as the commonplace demand that one should have faith in God, that He is following some order of justice, albeit one that is well beyond the reach of our understanding. It is not a claim that we should put our trust in God's infinite but incomprehensible goodness and know that He will never truly act unjustly (in some meaningful sense of the term). Rather, what Arnauld is saying—contrary to Malebranche and Leibniz—is that our formal concepts of justice and goodness and reasonableness have no application whatsoever when it comes to God's actions. And this means that to engage in theodicean speculation is a foolish endeavor based on a failure to understand God's absolute transcendence of all rational and moral categories.

Such a position is of little comfort in the face of the world's seemingly endless obstacles to our happiness and well-being. It goes well beyond any lesson that Job is supposed to take away from his tribulations. True, he is finally told by God Himself not to presume to understand or question His ways, for these cannot but exceed the reach of a puny creature such as a human being.

> *Where were you when I laid the earth's foundations?*
> *Tell me, if you know and understand.*
> *Who settled its dimensions? Surely you should know.*
> *Who stretched his measuring-line over it?*
> *On what do its supporting pillars rest?*
> *Who set its cornerstone in place? . . .*
> *Who put wisdom in depths of darkness and veiled understanding in*
>   *secrecy?*
> *Who is wise enough to marshal the rain-clouds and empty the cisterns*
>   *of heaven, when the dusty soil sets hard as iron, and the clods of*
>   *earth cling together? (Job 38:4–6, 36–38)*

But nowhere in this story is it ever suggested that God transcends wisdom itself or that it is meaningless to speak of God's goodness. On the contrary, when God throws Job's challenge back in his face, He only reinforces the justice and reason of His ways: "Dare you deny that I am just or put me in the wrong that you may be right?" (Job 40:8).

The philosophical confrontation with evil has thus led to a kind of theological schism. A theodicy requires a portrait of God. Among a trio of philosophers who began as friends in Paris in the mid-1670s, but whose relationships became contentious as the century waned, we find the culmination of two radically different traditions of depicting God's nature and His relationship to creation. On the one hand, there is the rational God of Malebranche and Leibniz; on the other hand, the voluntarist God of Arnauld. The rational God acts as we act, with reasons and a conception of what is good; the voluntarist God operates through sheer will alone, and thus transcends all rational and moral canons.[54]

This philosophical divide is not unlike a certain political dualism in the period. Defenders of royal absolutism regarded the king as above the law, mainly because his will was the source of all law (and his might the source of the law's normativity). What is just and right in the state is so only because the king has declared it to be so; had the king's will been otherwise, then society's norms would be different. The king's power is, according to this theory, not absolutely absolute because he must ultimately answer to God. As Bishop Bossuet, Arnauld's friend and defender, argued, "kings, although their power comes from on high, should not regard themselves as masters of that power to use it at their pleasure . . . they must employ it with fear and self-restraint, as a thing coming from God and of which God will demand an account."[55] But, God aside, for the political absolutist there are no natural or worldly standards of justice and reasonableness to which the king is responsible in declaring the law; whatever order the king issues is, by that declarative act alone, right. Or, as the arch-defender of political voluntarism Richard Nixon so revealingly put it, "when the president does it, that means it is not illegal."

A constitutional monarchy, by contrast, involves normative constraints upon what the sovereign may command. These constraints are imposed by principles that, relative to the king's will, are independent and objective and enshrined in the state's constitution. The values expressed by these principles are not created by the king; on the contrary, they stand as absolute limitations upon his power. The king may not order what, according to the constitution, is unjust. Even if the person who holds the kingship does so independently of the constitution itself—by heredity, for example—his authority does not extend beyond the boundaries set by the highest law of the land.

This is not to say that the choice of one God over another is necessarily also a political act. It is true that Leibniz thought that the example of divine justice, conceived as the charity of the wise, served also to legitimate a similar understanding of human justice; God's rationally just behavior, consisting in "the reasonable advancement of the good of others," is the proper model for our just behavior, and the principles of His kingdom are to be emulated in our earthly realm. "God is the monarch of the most perfect republic composed of all spirits," he says in article thirty-six of the *Discourse*, "and the happiness of this city of God is His principal purpose." The felicity and prosperity of the individuals belonging to His empire are of the highest concern to God, making Him "the most just and the most debonair of monarchs." But one does need to exercise caution when drawing parallels between theological positions and political persuasions. The English poet John Milton, who upheld a voluntarist conception of God and thus was an absolutist with respect to the divine realm, was a resolute republican when it came to human affairs. And while there is no reason to think that either Arnauld or Malebranche wavered in his commitment to the absolute power of the French king, the two men found themselves on opposite sides of the divide on the matter of God's rationality. In the seventeenth century, answers to the question of whether God acts with wisdom or with an absolute will transcended politics and nationality.

They also seem to have transcended religion. Whether or not one believed God to be guided by objective and independent moral principles certainly had implications for how one conceived of the distribution of grace and the true path to eternal salvation, as we have seen; and Arnauld's Jansenism must have made the voluntarist position practically irresistible to him. But the Catholic Malebranche and the Lutheran Leibniz could share a commitment to a rationalist God, while two Catholics such as Arnauld and Malebranche could have a serious falling-out over the issue.

Nor does the choice of one God or the other reflect any kind of divergence between conservative and progressive views in intellectual matters. Leibniz, Malebranche, and Arnauld were all enthusiastic partisans of the new science, whether in its Cartesian guise or (for Leibniz) some other model; their disagreements in matters of natural philosophy—above all, physics—had nothing to do with the question of the rationality or arbitrariness of the divine will. It is clear from the case of Descartes, who thought he could derive the laws of nature from a consideration of God's attributes, that voluntarism did not necessarily mean obscurantism.

The adoption of a God for these early modern thinkers, in short, represented a fundamental theological orientation, one that did not necessarily follow from or imply any other allegiances they may have had—political, religious, or scientific. Leibniz and Malebranche focused on wisdom and goodness as God's defining attributes; for them, God was above all a moral person. Arnauld elevated omnipotence to the supreme position; what mattered for him was sui generis divine power.

At the same time, the choice was more than just an isolated commitment of theology; it represented a broad philosophical vision of things. To choose a God was, in fact, to choose a world, even an entire universe. Standing before the God of reason and the God of will, a philosopher faces a set of questions about the nature of reality itself. Do we inhabit a cosmos that is fundamentally intelligible because its creation is grounded in a rational decision informed by certain absolute values? Is the world's existence the result of a reasonable act of creation and the expression of an infinite wisdom? Or, on the other hand, is the universe ultimately a nonrational, even arbitrary piece of work—a position that the seventeenth-century Cambridge Platonist Henry More labeled the "belch of hell" and "horrid blasphemy"?[56] Does the origin of things lie in an indifferent action—an apparently capricious exercise of causal power—by a Creator who cannot possibly be motivated by reasons because His will finds no reasons independent of itself? In short, does the universe exist by *ratio* or by *voluntas*, by wisdom or power?

In the final decades of the seventeenth century, a thinker had to be careful about which answer he pursued to this question. Leibniz, Malebranche, and Arnauld (as well as Bayle and other interested parties) recognized that there was yet another philosophical possibility on the horizon. Bred in the freethinking, tolerant environment of Amsterdam and defended by an excommunicated Jew, this third option was, in Leibniz's words, an "impious and irreligious hypothesis" that few regarded without horror. But it was also a position to which both rationalism and voluntarism, if taken too far and without due caution to their deeper implications, drew uncomfortably close.

8

The Specter of Spinoza

Leibniz left Paris on October 4, 1676—a Sunday morning—never to see the city again. While he could not put off his departure any longer, he was in no rush to get to Hanover. He still had a good deal of unfinished philosophical business to attend to before taking up his duties at court. In fact, judging from the sheer number of unpublished manuscripts, incomplete notes, aborted drafts, and revised papers left after his death, the rest of Leibniz's life was nothing but unfinished philosophical business. He decided to take advantage of his impending voyage to pursue one or two things. Despite the impatience of the duke to have him in residence, Leibniz took the long way home.

His first stop was England, where he went directly to see his friend Henry Oldenburg in London. Oldenburg showed Leibniz some of Newton's papers, which he copied, and they talked about philosophical and scientific matters. Leibniz also made the acquaintance of a number of German diplomats and aristocrats residing in the English capital, one of whom, Prince Ruprecht von der Pfalz, offered him transport on his yacht to the next stop on his itinerary. Thus, in early November, Leibniz was on a boat crossing the North Sea on his way to the Netherlands.

After landing in Rotterdam, Leibniz quickly set out for Amsterdam. By the middle of the seventeenth century, this flourishing port on the Amstel River had eclipsed Antwerp as the center of northern European trade and was key to the young Dutch Republic's rapid rise as a major commercial and military power. It was also the most open, cosmopolitan, and liberal city on the Continent. It had a rich intellectual and cultural life and was unsurpassed for its extraordinary mix of nonconformists, freethinkers, political radicals, and religious dissenters. Leibniz met with some of the city's most interesting and independent philosophical characters, including the diverse members of the Cartesian circle who gathered regularly to discuss metaphysical, political, and religious matters. From Amsterdam, he went on to Haarlem, Leiden, and Delft, where he met the scientist Antonij van Leeuwenhoek, the great microscopist. Finally, in the third week of November, Leibniz landed not at his ultimate destination—much to the consternation of his employer—but at the doorstep of the person who was most likely the reason for this detour through the Low Countries: Baruch de Spinoza.[1]

Spinoza was just a few days shy of his forty-third birthday when Leibniz arrived in The Hague; because of his ongoing respiratory problems, exacerbated by the glass dust from the lens grinding he had taken up to support himself, he would die within the year.

By this time the most notorious philosopher in all of Europe, Spinoza had published only two books, one of which did not even have his name on it. They were enough, though, to secure his reputation as a radical, even "dangerous" thinker. His critical exposition of the principles of Descartes's philosophy appeared in 1663, and as a result Spinoza was regarded as an important if unorthodox adherent of Cartesianism. This meant that the enemies of the new philosophy—and there were many, especially in the Netherlands—directed their ire at Spinoza himself. The notion that he was a member of any respectable (or at least recognizable) philosophical school, Cartesianism included, was dispelled when the scandalous *Theological-Political Treatise* was published—anonymously, with a false city and publisher on the title page—in 1670.

The *Treatise*—with its rigorous depiction of the Bible as not of divine origin but a mere work of human literature; its attack on sectarian religion as organized superstition and a danger to the well-being of the state; its argument for the toleration of philosophical thinking; and its debunking of miracles, revelation, and divine providence as products of the imagination—was widely and vociferously condemned by ecclesiastic and political authorities in and beyond the Republic. It was regarded as the work of an atheist and a libertine, a "godless [book] . . . forged in hell" and full of "abominations and abhorrent heresies" that no right-thinking person could possibly countenance. "In my opinion," wrote Régnier de Mansveld, a professor at the University of Utrecht, "that Treatise ought to be buried forever in an eternal oblivion."[2] The outcry was so strong that Spinoza abandoned his plan to publish his philosophical masterpiece, the *Ethics*; it did not appear in print until an edition was put out by his friends soon after his death.

Spinoza was born in Amsterdam in 1632, the middle son in a prominent family of moderate means in the city's Portuguese-Jewish community.[3] As a boy—known to his fellow Portuguese as Bento—he had been one of the star pupils in the congregation's Talmud Torah school. He was intellectually gifted, and this could not have gone unnoticed by the congregation's rabbis. But he never made it into the upper levels of the curriculum, those that included advanced study of

Talmud. At the age of seventeen, he was forced to cut short his formal schooling to help run the family's importing business. While he seems not to have been a very good businessman, Spinoza continued to run the firm with his brother Gabriel after their father's death, and to all appearances was an upstanding figure in the community.

All this changed on July 27, 1656, when Spinoza was issued the harshest writ of *herem*, or ostracism, ever pronounced by the Sephardic community of Amsterdam.

> The sirs of the *ma'amad* [the congregation's lay governing board] having long known of the evil opinions and acts of Baruch de Espinoza, have endeavored by various means and promises to turn him from his evil ways. But having failed to make him mend his wicked ways, and, on the contrary, daily receiving more and more serious information about the abominable heresies which he practiced and taught and about his monstrous deeds, and having for this numerous trustworthy witnesses who have deposed and born witness to this effect in the presence of the said Espinoza, they became convinced of the truth of this matter; and after all of this has been investigated in the presence of the honorable *hakhamim* [rabbis] they have decided, with their consent, that the said Espinoza should be banned and expelled from the people of Israel. By decree of the angels and by the command of the holy men, we ban, expel, curse and damn Baruch de Espinoza, with the consent of God, Blessed be He, and with the consent of the entire holy congregation, and in front of these holy scrolls with the six hundred and thirteen precepts which are written therein; cursing him with the excommunication with which Joshua banned Jericho and with the curse with which Elisha cursed the

boys and with all the castigations which are written in
the Book of the Law. Cursed be he by day and cursed be
he by night; cursed be he when he lies down and cursed
be he when he rises up. Cursed be he when he goes out
and cursed be he when he comes in. The Lord will not
spare him, but then the anger of the Lord and his jeal-
ousy shall smoke against that man, and all the curses
that are written in this book shall lie upon him, and
the Lord shall blot out his name from under heaven.
And the Lord shall separate him unto evil out of all
the tribes of Israel, according to all the curses of the
covenant that are written in this book of the law. But
you that cleave unto the Lord your God are alive every
one of you this day.

The Portuguese document concludes with the warning that "no one
should communicate with him, not even in writing, nor accord him
any favor nor stay with him under the same roof nor [come] within
four cubits in his vicinity; nor shall he read any treatise composed or
written by him."[4] The ban was never rescinded.

We do not know for certain what Spinoza's "monstrous deeds" and
"abominable heresies" were alleged to have been. The *herem* itself does
not specify anything in particular; and there is no extant documentary
evidence from the period that fills the gap. Most likely, he was giving
utterance to just those radical ideas on God, freedom, and religion
that he later expressed in his philosophical writings.[5]

In the *Ethics*, which he began working on sometime in the early
1660s, Spinoza denies the traditional God of Abrahamic religions as
a pernicious anthropomorphic fiction. God, he insists, is not endowed with any of the psychological or moral characteristics necessary
for a providential being. God does not will, judge, command, or de-
liberate. Nor is God good, wise, and just. Spinoza's God is not a

personal God to whom one would pray or seek solace in times of trouble; it is not a God that can be the object of reverential awe or worshipful submission. For Spinoza, God is nothing but nature—*Deus sive Natura*, "God or Nature," in his famous phrase—the infinite, necessarily existing, eternal, and active substance of the universe. There is nothing good or bad, perfect or imperfect about God or Nature; it just *is*.

Whatever else that exists is "in" God in the sense of being within nature (or a "mode" of its substance). There is nothing supernatural for Spinoza; whatever is or happens is a part of nature, and it comes about with an absolute necessity and as a result of nature's laws and processes. Even human beings and their states of mind—their volitions, passions, thoughts, and desires—are determined by natural causality; there is no freedom of the will and no uncaused spontaneity anywhere in nature, not even in the human psyche. With this metaphysics, Spinoza also eliminates both the divine creation of the world, because nature (God) is a self-caused and eternal system, and the possibility of true miracles, because there can be no supernaturally caused exceptions to the necessary order of nature.

Spinoza, moreover, denies that human beings are endowed with an immortal soul. There is an eternal aspect of the human mind—namely, the adequate ideas or truths that the virtuous person pursuing knowledge acquires in his lifetime. Because these ideas are, like all truths, eternal, they do not come to an end with the death of the person. But this eternity of the mind, which is enjoyed and confers benefits in this world, must not be confused with the personal immortality of the soul in some world to come, a superstitious doctrine that Spinoza believes only fosters the harmful passions of hope (for eternal reward) and fear (of eternal punishment) and thus gives rise to our willing submission to ecclesiastic authorities who claim to know the path to salvation. The life of freedom and happiness, as Spinoza envisions it, is guided by reason and knowledge; it is a life in which the power of the passions and the "bondage" to which they lead are diminished, and a person is an active agent pursuing true, not illusory, goods.

L ike so many thinkers of his time, Leibniz had some harsh things to say about Spinoza. Writing to Thomasius in Leipzig, who had attacked the *Theological-Political Treatise* as "a godless work," Leibniz commends his old teacher for "treating this intolerably impudent work on the liberty of philosophers as it deserves."[6] A professor at Utrecht, Johann Georg Graevius, called the *Treatise* "a most pestilential book . . . which opens wide the window to atheism"; Leibniz's letter to him says exactly what Leibniz thinks Graevius wants to hear: "I have read Spinoza's book. I deplore that a man of such evident erudition should have fallen so low . . . Writings of this type tend to subvert the Christian religion, whose edifice has been consolidated by the precious blood, sweat, and prodigious sacrifices of the martyrs."[7] Even in his introductory letter to Arnauld in 1671, Leibniz waves his anti-Spinozist credentials by referring to the *Treatise* as "the terrifying work" and "the horrible book."[8]

And yet, here Leibniz was in The Hague, going out of his way to meet the author of such an abomination. This was an encounter he anticipated with great eagerness. Leibniz had been thinking about Spinoza's ideas for some time, and not always as negatively as his letter to Graevius would suggest. Well after reading the *Treatise*, and just a month before his letter to Arnauld, Leibniz wrote to Spinoza himself. In his very cordial note, he praises Spinoza's "remarkable skill in optics" and encloses a paper on the refraction of light rays through a lens, "A Note on Advanced Optics," on which he would like Spinoza to comment.[9] He is clearly using the mathematical question as a pretext for opening up a correspondence with a man whose views on religion he may abhor but whose philosophical perspicuity he admires greatly. Spinoza's reply is short but holds out hope of a continued exchange on optical matters; he also offers to send Leibniz a copy of the

Theological-Political Treatise, in case he has not yet read it. Unfortunately, no other letters between the two have survived, although the conversation on optics may have continued, and possibly even expanded into the metaphysical and theological questions on which Leibniz was no doubt keen to engage Spinoza.

Two years later, when in Paris, Leibniz befriended a young fellow German, Ehrenfried Walther von Tschirnhaus. Tschirnhaus himself had just spent some time in Amsterdam. Leibniz learned that while he was there, Tschirnhaus got to know some members of Spinoza's close circle of friends and patrons, who met frequently to discuss his ideas. When Tschirnhaus left the Netherlands, first for London and then for Paris, he carried with him a manuscript copy of Spinoza's *Ethics*— given to him by one of Spinoza's friends or possibly even by Spinoza himself, but under the condition that he not show it to anyone.

Leibniz was anxious to see it. In the fall of 1675, a mutual acquaintance of Tschirnhaus and Spinoza, Georg Hermann Schuller, wrote to The Hague to tell Spinoza that Tschirnhaus had met Leibniz and would like to show him his copy of the *Ethics*.

> He [Tschirnhaus] has met a man named Leibniz of remarkable learning, most skilled in the various sciences and free from the common theological prejudices. He has established a close friendship with him, based on the fact that like him he is working on the problem of the perfecting of the intellect, and indeed he considers there is nothing better or more important than this. In ethics, he says, Leibniz is most practiced, and speaks solely from the dictates of reason uninfluenced by emotion. He adds that in physics and especially in metaphysical studies of God and the Soul he is most skilled, and he finally concludes that he is a person most worthy of having your writings communicated to him, if [your] consent is first given; for he thinks that the Author will derive considerable advan-

tage therefrom, as he undertakes to show at some length, if this should please you. If not, have no doubt that he will honorably keep them secret in accordance with his promise, just as in fact he has made not the slightest mention of them.

As though Schuller has not already said enough to favorably dispose Spinoza toward Leibniz and allow Tschirnhaus to show the latter the manuscript, he adds that "this same Leibniz thinks highly of the *Theological-Political Treatise*, on which subject he once wrote you a letter, if you remember."[10]

Spinoza was well aware of the reception his book was receiving in Germany and France; he may have been suspicious about Leibniz's motives, or simply cautious (the motto on his signet ring was *Caute*: "Be cautious"). Either way, Spinoza refused to give his consent to Tschirnhaus's request.

> I believe I know Leibniz, of whom he writes, through correspondence, but I do not understand why he, a councilor of Frankfurt, has gone to France. As far as I can judge from his letter, he seemed to me a person of liberal mind and well versed in every science. Still, I think it imprudent to entrust my writings to him so hastily. I should first like to know what he is doing in France, and to hear our friend Tschirnhaus's opinion of him after a longer acquaintance and a closer knowledge of his character.[11]

Tschirnhaus probably did not show the *Ethics* to Leibniz. He did, however, tell Leibniz all about its contents. "Tschirnhaus has told me many things about the book manuscript of Spinoza," Leibniz wrote from Paris in 1676. "Spinoza's book will be about God, the mind, happiness or the idea of the perfect human being, the improvement of the mind, the improvement of the body, etc."[12]

A few months later, Leibniz was on his way to the Netherlands. By this time, he had studied closely what he was able to of Spinoza's philosophy, and he was now thinking about what to say to him when they met. In transit, he prepared some written notes, including an argument "that a most perfect being [i.e., God] exists," which he later showed to Spinoza, who apparently approved of it. "I presented this argument to M. Spinosa [sic] when I was at The Hague, who thought it to be solid."[13]

The encounter between the two men—so different in so many ways, with their coming from such diverse ethnic, social, political, and religious worlds—went well. In later years, Leibniz was fond of recalling details. "The famous Jew Spinoza had an olive complexion and something Spanish about his face. He was a philosopher by profession and led a tranquil and private life, passing his time in polishing lenses, to make telescopes and microscopes."[14] Their extensive conversation lasted at least several days and ranged over a variety of topics. Leibniz was particularly interested in Spinoza's metaphysics of God. Writing to his friend the *abbé* Jean Gallois in 1677, just after Spinoza's death, Leibniz says that

> Spinosa [sic] died this winter. I saw him while passing through Holland, and I spoke with him several times and at great length. He has a strange metaphysics, full of paradoxes. Among other things, he believes that the world and God are but a single substantial thing, that God is the substance of all things, and that creatures are only modes or accidents. But I noticed that some of his purported demonstrations, that he showed me, are not exactly right. It is not as easy as one thinks to provide true demonstrations in metaphysics.[15]

Leibniz was clearly fascinated, even somewhat obsessed by Spinoza's philosophy. The influence of the man he called "that discerning

Jew" is evident throughout his writings. In his extensive notes on Spinoza's posthumous works, including the published version of the *Ethics*, he found "a lot of good thoughts," but also many things that are "wild and absurd," even dangerous.[16] At one point in his life, he even thought of himself as a "Spinozist." In an unpublished piece written thirty years after their meeting, Leibniz says, "I went a little too far in another time and I began to lean to the side of the Spinozists, who grant nothing but an infinite power of God."[17] But Leibniz realized very early that on the most fundamental elements of his philosophy—the nature of God, His rationality, and His choice of the best, all present in Leibniz's thinking even before he went to Paris—there is no room for compromise.

Spinoza's God does not choose the best of all possible worlds. Spinoza's God, in fact, does not choose anything whatsoever. Spinoza's identification of God with the eternal, infinite, necessarily existing substance of Nature itself—with the most general natures of things (Thought and Extension) and the universal causal principles and laws embedded in these—means that whatever exists within Nature (and this is everything possible) "follows from" or is caused by God or Nature with an absolute, inevitable necessity. Nothing whatsoever could possibly have been otherwise: not the universe itself, nor any individual thing or event within it. "All things, I say, are in God, and all things that happen, happen only through the laws of God's infinite nature and follow . . . from the necessity of his essence."[18]

The metaphysics of God in the *Ethics*, motivated as it is by an extreme antianthropomorphism, rules out any depiction of God that involves Him considering alternative possibilities, acting for purposes, making choices based on reasons, and assessing outcomes. "There are those who feign God, like man, consisting of a body and a mind, and subject to passions. But how far they wander from the true knowledge of God, is sufficiently established by what has already been demon-strated."[19] All talk of God's purposes, intentions, goals, preferences, or aims is just a fiction propagated by manipulative ecclesiastics. "All the prejudices I here undertake to expose depend on this one: that men commonly suppose that all natural things act, as men do, on account of an end; indeed, they maintain as certain that God himself directs all things to some certain end, for they say that God has made all things for man, and man that he might worship God."[20]

God is not some goal-oriented planner who then judges things by how well they conform to his purposes. Things happen only because of Nature and its laws. "Nature has no end set before it . . . All things proceed by a certain eternal necessity of nature." To believe otherwise is to fall prey to the same superstitions that lie at the heart of the or-ganized religions.

> [People] find—both in themselves and outside them-selves—many means that are very helpful in seeking their own advantage, e.g., eyes for seeing, teeth for chewing, plants and animals for food, the sun for light, the sea for supporting fish . . . Hence, they consider all natural things as means to their own advantage. And knowing that they had found these means, not provided them for themselves, they had reason to believe that there was someone else who had prepared those means for their use. For after they considered things as means, they could not believe that the things had made themselves; but from the means they were accustomed to prepare for themselves, they had to infer that there was a ruler, or a number of rulers of nature, endowed with human free-dom, who had taken care of all things for them, and made all things for their use. And because they had never heard anything about the temperament of these rulers,

they had to judge it from their own. Hence, they maintained that the gods direct all things for the use of men in order to bind men to them and be held by men in the highest honor. So it has happened that each of them has thought up from his own temperament different ways of worshipping God, so that God might love them above all the rest, and direct the whole of Nature according to the needs of their blind desire and insatiable greed. Thus this prejudice was changed into superstition, and struck deep roots in their minds.[21]

In a letter to one of his more troublesome correspondents, the merchant Willem van Blijenburgh, Spinoza emphasizes the absurdity of conceiving of God in this way. The language of traditional theology, he says, represents God "as a perfect man" and claims that "God desires something, that God is displeased with the deeds of the impious and pleased with those of the pious." In all philosophical rigor, however, "we clearly understand that to ascribe to God those attributes that make a man perfect would be as wrong as to ascribe to a man the attributes that make perfect an elephant or an ass."[22] Some years later, in a letter to the Dutchman Hugo Boxel, Spinoza resorts to sarcasm to make his point:

> When you say that you do not see what sort of God I have if I deny him the actions of seeing, hearing, attending, willing, etc. and that he possesses those faculties in an eminent degree, I suspect that you believe that there is no greater perfection than can be explicated by the aforementioned attributes. I am not surprised, for I believe that a triangle, if it could speak, would likewise say that God is eminently triangular, and a circle that God's nature is eminently circular.[23]

A judging God who has plans and acts purposively is a God to be obeyed and placated. Opportunistic preachers are then able to play on our hopes and fears in the face of such a God. They prescribe ways of acting that are calculated to allow us to avoid being punished by that deity and to earn His rewards. But, Spinoza insists, to see God or Nature as acting for the sake of ends—to find purpose in Nature—is to misconstrue Nature, to "turn it upside down" by putting the effect (the end result) before the true cause. In Spinoza's view, the traditional religious conception of God leads only to superstition, not enlightenment.

Like the belief in miracles, the projection of purposiveness and practical reason onto God or Nature is due only to ignorance of the true causes of phenomena.

> If a stone has fallen from a room onto someone's head and killed him, they will show, in the following way, that the stone fell in order to kill the man. For if it did not fall to that end, God willing it, how could so many circumstances have concurred by chance (for often many circumstances do concur at once)? Perhaps you will answer that it happened because the wind was blowing hard and the man was walking that way. But they will persist: why was the wind blowing hard at that time? why was the man walking that way at that time? If you answer again that the wind arose then because on the preceding day, while the weather was still calm, the sea began to toss, and that the man had been invited by a friend, they will press on—for there is no end to the questions that can be asked: but why was the sea tossing? why was the man invited at just that time? And so they will not stop asking for the causes of causes until you take refuge in the will of God, i.e., the sanctuary of ignorance.[24]

God as Nature is not endowed with will, much less with freedom of the will. God may be the cause of all things, even the *free* cause of all things, but this is only because whatever is, is in Nature and is therefore brought about by Nature; and because Nature is all there is, there is nothing outside Nature to constrain it to do one thing rather than another.

> There can be nothing outside [God] by which he is determined or compelled to act. Therefore, God acts from the laws of his nature alone, and is compelled by no one . . . From this it follows, first, that there is no cause, either extrinsically or intrinsically, which prompts God to action, except the perfection of his nature . . . It follows, secondly, that God alone is a free cause. For God alone exists only from the necessity of his nature . . . and acts from the necessity of his nature.[25]

For this reason, Spinoza makes it clear that while neither option is acceptable, if he were forced to choose he would favor the voluntarist God rather than the traditional rationalist one. "I confess that this opinion, which subjects all things to a certain indifferent will of God, and makes all things depend on His good pleasure, is nearer the truth than that of those who maintain that God does all things for the sake of the good. For they seem to place something outside God, which does not depend on God, to which God attends, as a model, in what He does, and at which He aims, as at a certain goal. This is simply to subject God to fate. Nothing more absurd can be maintained about God, whom we have shown to be the first and only free cause."[26]

In the end, though, Spinoza's God is neither an arbitrary nor a rational deity. The existence of God or Nature itself is absolutely necessary—it cannot not exist; and whatever happens in nature—everything that has been or will be—is caused by God or Nature, not by choice but by necessity, and thus comes about through natural principles with a geometric inevitability.

> I think I have shown clearly enough . . . that from God's supreme power, or infinite nature, infinitely many things in infinitely many modes, i.e., all things, have necessarily flowed, or always followed, by the same necessity and in the same way as from the nature of a triangle it follows, from eternity to eternity, that its three angles are equal to two right angles.[27]

To say that the things that follow from God's nature might not have been, or could have been otherwise, is to say that God's nature itself might have been different, which, Spinoza insists, is absurd, because God or Nature necessarily exists as it is. "Things could have been produced by God in no other way, and in no other order than they have been produced."[28]

For Spinoza, this is not the best of all possible worlds; it is the only possible world.

It may be that Leibniz never dreamed that he of all people would have to mount a rearguard defense against the charge of Spinozism. So much of his philosophical theology is constructed in direct opposition to the God of "the Jew of Voorburg." And yet it is an accusation that has haunted his system continually, from the criticisms on freedom raised by Arnauld and Bayle in the seventeenth century to recent scholarship.

Leibniz recognized and even flirted with the potential necessitarian dangers in his own views. Writing to the legal scholar Magnus Wedderkopf in 1671, Leibniz explains that "the ultimate reason" for the divine will is the divine intellect, "for God wills the things He understands to be the best and most harmonious and selects them, as it were, from an infinite number of all possibilities." He concedes that "because God is the most perfect mind it is impossible for Him not to be affected by the most perfect harmony, and thus to be necessitated to do the best by the very ideality of things."[29]

The question is whether it is logically conceivable that God, an absolutely perfect being, not pursue the most perfect course and will the existence of the best of all possible worlds. Could God, given what He essentially and necessarily is, possibly choose otherwise? In 1671, Leibniz is certain that the answer to this question is no; moreover, this is a position he maintains throughout his later writings on the topic.[30] But then it appears that the existence of the best of all possible worlds and everything in it is no less necessary than the existence of Spinoza's Nature. Creation must ultimately be the result not of God's choice but of God's being, so there really are no other possible worlds.

Leibniz expended much intellectual energy throughout the rest of his philosophical career in finding some way to avoid this shocking Spinozistic denouement. Perhaps it was his confrontation with Spinoza—first, through Tschirnhaus's lessons in Paris, and then face-to-face with the man himself—that truly awakened him to the alarming possibilities implicit in his own ideas about God's choice of "the best."

During at least one of the meetings in The Hague, Leibniz seems to have turned the discussion to the question of whether there are any possible worlds not actually created by God.[31] Spinoza would have immediately explained that there are not. Gaping at the yawning metaphysical chasm opening up before him, Leibniz very soon thereafter came upon what would become an essential part of his response to the charge that, according to his own principles, the existence of the world is absolutely necessary. It appears in the notes he made while reading the *Ethics* a year later, just after its publication. Commenting on Spinoza's proposition that "the world could not have been produced in any other way than it has been produced, for it follows from the immutable nature of God," Leibniz replies that "on the hypothesis that the divine will chooses the best or works in the most perfect way, certainly only this world could have been produced, but if the nature of the world is considered in itself, a different world could have been produced."[32] Relative to God's nature and will, no other world is possible. God must choose the best, this particular world is the best, and so God cannot but choose it.[33] However, this does not mean that there is not an infinity of other conceivable worlds that, taken on their own terms, are perfectly possible in themselves insofar as there is nothing internally inconsistent about them. God, because of what He is, might not be able to choose them, but that does not keep them from being worlds that are logically possible in their own right.

> Those things [which God does not will] . . . remain possible, even if they are not chosen by God. It is possible indeed for even that to exist which God does not will to exist, because it would be able to exist of its own nature if God willed that it exist. But God cannot will that it exist. I agree; yet it remains possible in its own nature, even if it is not possible in respect to the divine will. For we have defined possible in its own nature as that which does not imply a contradiction in itself even if its coexistence with God can be said in some way to imply a contradiction.[34]

Leibniz admits that "when I found myself very close to the opinions of those who hold everything to be absolutely necessary"—that is, Spinoza—this solution is what "pulled me back from the precipice."[35] The presence of alternative possibilities, while none of them are compatible with God's nature, is nonetheless sufficient, at least to Leibniz, for preserving the reality of God's choice. He says that this means that God's willing the best of all possible worlds is not metaphysically or logically necessary but only morally necessary, even if God could not conceivably choose otherwise. God's creation of the best avoids the geometric determinism of Spinoza's philosophy because Leibniz's God is an agent who does what He does because it is the one alternative among many that He ought to do according to reason, according to a choice that is influenced by a judgment of what is good. The choice may be infallible and inevitable, it may be a "moral absurdity" to think that a perfectly good and wise God might do otherwise, but it nonetheless remains a choice.

Perhaps emboldened by the ingenuity of this approach, Leibniz sometimes seems to want to retreat even from the idea that God cannot possibly choose anything but the best. He speaks of "reasons that impel" or "prompt" or "incline without necessitating," and he compares the rational considerations that morally move the divine will with weights that, by causing an imbalance, physically move bodies. God's choosing the best may not, he occasionally suggests, be necessary at all. "God does not fail to choose the best, but He is not constrained to do so: nay, more, there is no necessity in the object of God's choice, for another sequence of things is equally possible. For that very reason the choice is free and independent of necessity, because it is made between several possibles, and the will is determined only by the prepondering goodness of the object."[36]

Leibniz insists, in fact, that it is the Cartesian God, Arnauld's God, whose will is independent of all determining reasons, who most closely resembles the Spinozist deity. It is an odd claim, because Spinoza's God wills nothing at all. But writing to Gerhard Wolter Molanus around 1679, Leibniz offers his standard criticism that "Descartes's God, or perfect being, is not a God like the one we imagine or hope for, that is, a God just and wise, doing everything possible for the good of creatures." He adds that "Descartes's God is something approaching the God of Spinoza . . . Descartes's God has neither will nor understanding, since according to Descartes He does not have the good as the object of the will, nor the true as the object of the understanding."[37] Leibniz means that Descartes, by eliminating rational choice in God, essentially eliminates divine choice altogether. A God who does not will for the sake of reasons and to achieve what is good is not really endowed with intellect and will at all—just like the God of the *Ethics*.

The fear of God—of Spinoza's God—has clearly possessed him. Leibniz cannot allow that God might be anything but a person, an agent who acts as we act. Soon after his conversations over the *Ethics* with Tschirnhaus in Paris, Leibniz notes that "God is not as some represent him—something metaphysical, imaginary, incapable of thought, will, or action, so that it would be the same as if you were to say that God is nature, fate, fortune, necessity, the world. Rather, God is a certain substance, a person, a mind."[38] Thirty-five years later, near the end of his life, Leibniz wrote in the *Theodicy* that according to Spinoza, "all things exist through the necessity of the divine nature, without any act of choice by God," adding that "we will not waste time here in refuting an opinion so bad, and indeed so inexplicable."[39] A bad and inexplicable opinion, perhaps, but one that Leibniz went to a great deal of trouble to avoid.

While Leibniz was trying to keep from falling into a fatalistic vortex, Malebranche and Arnauld were wrestling with their own Spinozistic demons.

No one in the period was accused of Spinozism more often and for a greater variety of reasons than Malebranche. It was a charge against which he continually had to defend himself, much to his great chagrin and increasing annoyance. His doctrine of the Vision in God, that we see in God the eternal mathematical extension of bodies, seemed to many to imply that extension itself, the matter of the universe, is eternal and uncreated and literally in God, thus turning Malebranche's deity into the material substance of bodies and making Him look suspiciously like Spinoza's Nature.[40]

Malebranche's theory of occasionalism, with its elimination of any causal activity from the natural world—whose objects are reduced to mere "occasions" for the exercise of God's unique efficacious power—

appeared to some of Malebranche's critics to rob creatures of any real substantiality, so that God alone is the true substance of nature. Leibniz insists that "the doctrine of occasional causes that some defend is fraught with dangerous consequences . . . So far is this doctrine from increasing the glory of God by removing the idol of nature that it seems rather, like Spinoza, to make out of God the nature of the world itself, by causing created things to disappear into mere modifications of the one divine substance, since that which does not act, which lacks active force . . . can in no way be a substance."[41]

Spinozism was often regarded in the second half of the seventeenth century to be nothing but an extreme version of Descartes's philosophy, its metaphysical principles taken to their ultimate logical conclusion. As the most prominent representative of Cartesianism at the time, Malebranche took the brunt of the attacks from the anti-Cartesians, especially those in France and the Netherlands. Thus, Noel Aubert de Versé—an erstwhile Catholic who, as a Calvinist convert, wrote a refutation of Spinoza in 1684—insists that Malebranche, just because of his commitment to Descartes, is a Spinozist in spite of himself. "Father Malebranche, who defines God the way Spinoza does . . . cannot avoid falling in a precipice that is scarcely two fingers' distance from that of Spinoza, to wit, that the universe is only an emanation of God."[42] This kind of attack gave Malebranche further motivation not only to distance himself from any general kind of atheistic materialism, but also to try to drive a wedge between true Cartesian principles and the philosophy of the infamous Jew. Like Leibniz, Malebranche, as he responded to critics over the years, seems always to have had at least one eye on Spinoza.

Malebranche calls Spinoza "that unholy man of our time . . . a true atheist."[43] He admits in 1713 that while he read a part of Spinoza's *Ethics* "some time ago," he was "soon disgusted, not only by the horrifying consequences, but by the falsity of the author's alleged demonstrations." Spinoza's God, he insists, is "a monster . . . an appalling and ridiculous chimera."[44] The heretic's irreligious system is "highly obscure and full of equivocations,"[45] undoubtedly making it all the more maddening that he—not only a pious Catholic priest but also a skilled philosopher—should be forced to defend himself from such calumnies.

By contrast with Leibniz, Malebranche is, as we have seen, prepared honestly to embrace the latent necessitarianism in his strongly rationalist conception of God's choice to create one world over any other. Leibniz's God faces reasons that "incline without necessitating"; Malebranche's God is "rendered impotent" by His wisdom, unable to act in any way but that which is most worthy of His attributes. In the end, neither God can truly choose any world other than the one He has chosen. But Malebranche has made his peace with this. What allows him to do so is his belief that God's more fundamental decision to create in the first place is completely arbitrary, unmotivated and undetermined by anything. This affords Malebranche an effective firebreak against Spinozistic necessity in the existence of the world.

This is not good enough for Arnauld. He sees here a real threat to God's freedom and to the contingency of creation. Any kind of determinism operating on the divine will and rendering it incapable of choosing otherwise is, for the uncompromising Jansenist, an open invitation to Spinoza and his absolutely necessary universe.

Writing to Louis–Paul du Vaucel in 1691, Arnauld says, "I have not read any of the books of Spinosa [sic]. But I know that these are very evil books . . . He is a pure atheist, who believes in no other God than nature. It is perfectly within one's natural right not to read such books, unless it is to refute them, and unless one has the talent to do so."[46] Arnauld's denial of any direct acquaintance with Spinoza's writings cannot be taken at face value. Some years before his letter to Du Vaucel, Arnauld certainly did read at least one of Spinoza's works, the *Theological-Political Treatise*. A copy of the embattled book was sent to him by another friend, Johann van Neercassel, archbishop of Utrecht, in 1678. Arnauld read the treatise, which he called "one of the most evil books in the world," and subsequently lobbied to have it banned in France. He is reported also to have composed *un petit écrit contre Spinosa*, but this has been lost.[47]

While Arnauld may have declined to open the *Ethics* or any of Spinoza's other posthumously published writings—not even for the purpose of "refuting" them—he was clearly familiar with what he often calls their "blasphemous" and "abominable" contents. One can read his long debate with Malebranche, and even his comments on Leibniz's metaphysics, as part of an extended crusade against Spinozism. Arnauld, more forcefully than anyone else, argues that Malebranche's introduction of an "intelligible extension, infinite, and uncreated" in God is tantamount to making God material and reducing finite things to nothing more than modes of His substance. This, he cries, is Spinozism. And his critique of Malebranche's solution to the problem of evil, especially the idea that God acts only by general volitions and never by particular volitions, is grounded in a fear that Malebranche's philosophy, like that of Spinoza, thoroughly undermines any meaningful understanding of divine providence.

Spinoza himself is never explicitly mentioned in the *Philosophical and Theological Reflections*, in which Arnauld directly attacks Malebranche's theodicy; nor does Spinoza's name come up in the correspondence with Leibniz in the 1680s, when Arnauld is assailing Leibniz on the apparent necessity of all things, given God's choice to create one Adam rather than another. This is curious. Arnauld was not one to let slip an opportunity to wound an opponent's reputation with a malicious label or to hesitate to suggest guilt by ideological association. Moreover, the ever-vigilant Arnauld, eager to defend the true Catholic faith against its enemies, is quick to see Spinozism wherever he turns. Does he not see it here, where it matters most to him—in the defense of God's freedom and the utter contingency of His choices?

In fact, he does. His name may be absent from these writings, but Spinoza is present, as the Devil whom Arnauld tries to keep at bay as he confronts the deity of Leibniz and Malebranche. He is there in the "necessity more than fatal" that Arnauld believes is implied by Leibniz's conception of God's choice of the world; and he is there in the "constraint" and "obligation" under which Malebranche's God operates and that destroy His liberty of indifference. Arnauld can see no significant difference between a God the effects of whose will are determined by independent considerations of wisdom, justice, and goodness, and a God from whose nature everything follows with an absolute inevitability. Neither is capable of doing otherwise than as He does, and both are no less bound than Zeus is by the fates. While Arnauld had a fine mind for fine distinctions, and analytical skills capable of discriminations where lesser thinkers lumped things together, he could not admit that Leibniz and Malebranche were any better off here than the radical thinker from Amsterdam from whom they were so concerned to distance themselves. For Arnauld, the rationalist's God is ultimately no different from Spinoza's God.

Epilogue

This debate at the end of the seventeenth century was a true battle of the Gods. What was at stake was nothing less than the meaning of existence, the understanding of why things are as they are. The choice was clear: either the universe is ultimately an arbitrary product, the effect of an indifferent will guided by no objective values and subject to no independent canons of reason or goodness; or it is the result of wisdom, intelligible to its core and informed by a rationality and a sense of value that are, in essence, not very different from our own; or (to mention the most terrifying possibility of all) it simply *is*, necessary through its causes and transparent to the investigations of metaphysics and science but essentially devoid of any meaning or value whatsoever.

It was also a battle among giants. Two Catholic priests and a Lutheran counselor to royalty. One was the most skilled and famous theological controversialist of his time; another was the most accomplished representative of the period's dominant philosophy; the third was the most naturally brilliant polymath of the century.

Arnauld was never one to give up a fight. From his early polemical writings as a combative young cleric to his final defense of his beloved Port-Royal, he was a tenacious, even ferocious opponent. Malebranche and Leibniz knew this when they first engaged him; they were also conscious of the power and penetration of the intellect with which they were dealing, which is why they kept coming back for more. But they also believed that Arnauld's was essentially a lost cause, and not only because Jansenism would never fully recover from the onslaught of church and state.

These rationalists saw a basic philosophical incoherence in the view according to which both God is a supremely moral being and His will alone is what determines right and wrong and good and bad. God, they perceived, cannot be moral if what God commands is right only because God commands it, or if what God chooses is good just because God chooses it. An arbitrary God who is unmotivated by objective standards of reason and right is not a moral God. Socrates had insisted that Euthyphro's position, a kind of ethical religious fundamentalism, leads necessarily to divine caprice and amorality. Leibniz and Malebranche agreed. They argued that the view adopted by Arnauld, the most radical of all Cartesian doctrines, trivializes any attempt to characterize God in moral terms. To say that what is right is so only because God commands it, to insist that God's laws are not grounded in anything independent of God's will, is to empty the notions of divine justice, goodness, and wisdom of any substantive content.

The point is well taken. But perhaps the peace-loving Malebranche (averse as he was to confrontation) and the ecumenical-minded Leibniz (always seeking reconciliation) knew not to expect any kind of concession from a man with the unwavering commitment and fearsome temper of an Arnauld. Jansenists in seventeenth-century France were given to extremes. They never compromised.

. . .

The antecedents of the dialogue between Leibniz, Arnauld, and Malebranche lie in discussions of God's absolute and ordained power in the Middle Ages and in debates in Jewish and Christian philosophy over the rationality of His commandments; its deep ancestry extends back to Plato. In many respects, then, it was an old argument. But their conversation was also firmly embedded in the world of the seventeenth century. With an urgency in addressing problems of justice in the distribution of God's grace and His election of the saved—and, in the light of these, a need to reexamine the nature of divine and human freedom—it was a characteristic intellectual affair of post-Reformation Europe. And with its focus on questions about the laws of nature, the intelligibility of phenomena, and the metaphysical foundations of physics, it also firmly belonged to the milieu of the Scientific Revolution.

But all that was more than three hundred years ago. Philosophy has long since divorced itself from theology, and the universes of Descartes, Leibniz, and Newton belong to the history of science. With the disappearance of its intellectual, religious, and historical contexts, a struggle over questions about God's justice between two Catholic priests and a Lutheran polymath in the waning decades of the Sun King's reign may appear today to be of only antiquarian interest. One might even look at this particular debate over theodicy and divine power as nothing but a leftover of late medieval thought, one last product of a God-centered mentality that would soon be replaced by the deism of Voltaire and the modern naturalism of Hume and other Enlightenment thinkers. But among the dangers of conventional textbook categories and of imposing upon intellectual history such artificial (and often anachronistic) boundaries as medieval versus modern and theological versus philosophical is that they can obscure important philosophical legacies.

Of course, people who believe in a providential God still do (and should) wrestle with the problem of evil—particularly in the shadow of the enormous atrocities that have been perpetrated within the last seventy years; and the theodicean strategies offered by Leibniz ("Consider the larger picture; it all fits together into a plan that, on the whole, is the best") and Arnauld ("One cannot hope to fathom the divine will; it is a law unto itself") continue to provide answers and perhaps even comfort to religiously minded individuals.

But there is an even more important—because more universal—legacy of the early modern debate over divine rationality. It lies in the sphere of moral thought and concerns the foundations of the ethical judgments we make about people, events, and actions.

Divine voluntarism survives among those who believe that moral values and principles derive only from God's will. The view is not simply that God is needed to enforce such values and to motivate human ethical behavior with the promise of reward and the threat of punishment; it is the stronger claim that without God as their source, the values simply would not exist. Religious moral fundamentalism is the latter-day offspring of Euthyphro's position. Why is it morally wrong to kill or steal or lie? Because God says so; and if God had never uttered a word about such actions, or if he had decreed differently, they would not be wrong (or so the position implies). Moral claims, on this account, achieve a degree of objectivity and universality because they are established by an infinite, necessarily existing agent whose eternal act of will governs all of creation; it is always and everywhere wrong for one human being to kill another, the argument runs, because God's immutable decree applies always and everywhere. However, all such claims, while objectively valid for God's creatures, ultimately can represent nothing but His own subjective preferences.

To nonbelievers, and even to believers (as Leibniz and Malebranche showed), divine moral voluntarism faces some troubling objections. Why, for example, does God's commanding an action make it the *moral* thing to do (as opposed to simply being the pious or religiously observant thing to do)? The voluntarist cannot reply, as Leibniz would, that God is a supremely moral being who would never command us to do anything except what is in itself good and right, since that is to presume that there is a standard of goodness and rightness independent of God's will, which is inconsistent with the position's central thesis. Moreover, it is very difficult indeed to accept the idea that if God does not exist, then neither does morality. Can it really be the case that, as Ivan Karamazov put it, if there is no God then everything is permitted?

In contrast, moral rationalism grounds judgments about what is good or bad or right or wrong without any reference to the individual preferences, choices, or desires of agents. For the rationalist, moral principles are discovered, not created; their truth is independent of what anyone—divine or human—wants or believes. Moreover, it is reason—impersonal, dispassionate, universal reason, not sentiment or divine revelation—that discovers them. The true, albeit secular, heir to the rationalism of Leibniz and Malebranche is, in other words, Kant. According to Kantian ethics, the moral law is reason's law, and it has nothing to do with subjective inclinations. Reason alone can see whether an action is right or wrong—mainly by determining through an a priori logical procedure whether it is the kind of action that can in principle be commanded of everyone without exception. And Kant certainly did not intend the moral law to apply only to human beings, with God somehow above it. The moral law (or "categorical imperative")—"Always act so that you, as a rational moral agent, could will that the maxim of your action should become a universal law governing the behavior of all rational moral agents"—holds for *all* rational beings: human, divine, or otherwise. The values embedded in the law (primarily a respect for the dignity and autonomy of other rational beings) and in the moral judgments that follow from it represent objective, rational standards—just like the principles that guide Leibniz's God in His choice of the best of all possible worlds and the Order that, for Malebranche, governs divine agency. To the extent that one believes that there is a universal rationality and objectivity to moral and other value judgments, and that the foundations of ethics have nothing to do with what God may or may not want, one has rejected the voluntarist paradigm and followed in certain seventeenth-century footsteps.

I t is about time that I started feeling like an old man of eighty," Arnauld wrote to Nicole in 1692.[1] Arnaulds tended to live a long time. Those few lucky enough to survive childhood could generally look forward to enjoying another eight or more decades in this best of all possible worlds. Antoine's brother Robert Arnauld d'Andilly died when he was eighty-six; another brother, Henri Arnauld, archbishop of Angers, was almost ninety-five when he died. For years, Arnauld successfully avoided the machinations of those who eagerly wished to see him expire in prison. But even he, the youngest and most formidable in that family of formidable personalities, eventually had to come to terms with the natural decline of his considerable powers.

The final years of his life were not easy. The rigors of exile took their toll on his physical energy, and the endless battles in which he engaged exhausted his spirit. In November of 1693, nine months before his death, he told Du Vaucel that "I do not feel well, and I am hardly in any condition to work. Besides, my eyesight has grown so weak over the last two years that, in order to preserve it, I must read very little and hardly write a thing. Thus, do not count on me for anything that requires a particular application, at least as long as I do not have any better health than I do at present."[2] Still, he rallied and fought to the end with all the intellectual vigor he could muster. Among his final writings are further attacks on Jesuit moral theory, short pieces on grace and liberty, and even a number of letters to Malebranche renewing, after a relatively quiet period, their philosophical and theological debate. His last work was yet another missive for

Malebranche, composed on July 25, 1694, in which he takes stock of their long, acrimonious fight and accuses Malebranche of always having treated him with a condescending tone and a lack of personal consideration. A few weeks later, Arnauld died, his friend Pasquier Quesnel reports, "with his pen in hand."[3]

While he no doubt mourned the passing of a great adversary, Malebranche also appreciated the peace that came with the end of a long and very public feud. Still, Arnauld's death did not mean that the conversation itself had to come to an end. When Quesnel finally published Arnauld's last four letters to Malebranche in 1698, Malebranche took it upon himself in the following year to compose a response, although he did not publish it until 1705. Apparently, he did not share Leibniz's scruples against taking advantage of someone's death to have the last word. He especially wanted to set the record straight because he believed that Arnauld had always misrepresented his views.

Despite having had some of his writings placed on the Vatican's Index in 1690, Malebranche continued to enjoy an illustrious international reputation in the philosophical and scientific worlds. Over the years, he refined his metaphysical and theological system in a series of treatises, dialogues, and epistolary responses to his critics. His works were popular and were studied not only in the schools and academies of Paris but "throughout the provinces . . . with admirers and supporters in small villages," according to Father André.[4] Malebranche also had friends in higher places, French partisans who did not care what Rome thought; in 1699, they elected him to the Académie Royale des Sciences, primarily for his work on the laws of motion.

Like Arnauld, Malebranche never enjoyed robust health. He lived a good deal longer than he probably expected. He was a large man, about six feet tall, but with a "weak complexion," according to one acquaintance. His spinal problems were a constant source of pain throughout his life. He was also plagued by ongoing digestive trouble, Father André says, so much so that "for almost twenty years, he could barely keep down the food in his stomach." "There was hardly a part of his body which did not ail him, but he dealt with it all with such great resignation to the will of God that one never heard him complain."[5]

In 1696, Malebranche suffered a long and severe illness. His fevers were so violent, his condition so weakened, that his friends and doctors were all but certain that he was about to die. He recovered, however, thanks to "his pious and philosophical meditations."[6] The literary fruit of his near-death experience and his consequent reflections on his own mortality were the *Dialogues on Death*. In this very personal composition, Malebranche takes on the fear of dying. It is an irrational fear, he insists, the product of an unhealthy attachment to the transitory goods of this world instead of the true, eternal goods of the spirit. The way to approach death "without horror and dread" is to give up the love of the body and have faith in God's justice and a firm conviction in the immortality of the soul. "Death is terrible only for sinners. The just, on the other hand, desire it, for it is the moment when God will provide to each person the recompense or the punishment due for his works."[7]

In mid-June 1715 it was time for Malebranche to put these Augustinian consolatory thoughts to the test. Once again he fell seriously ill, this time as he was visiting a friend in Villeneuve St. Georges. Almost twenty years older than when he last faced death, he no longer had the strength, or perhaps the will, to fight it off. After a few days, when it seemed safe to transport him, Father Malebranche was taken back to the Oratory in Paris, where he died on October 13.

The year after Malebranche was elected to the Académie Royale des Sciences, the same honor was finally accorded to Leibniz, as a "foreign member." One month later, the Elector of Brandenburg, thinking that his own people were in need of a similar learned body, summoned Leibniz from Hanover to help found the Berlin Society of Sciences and serve as its first president. It was an extraordinary tribute, not just to Leibniz's learning but to his skills as a courtier as well.

Meanwhile, he continued his service to the duke of Hanover and his extensive traveling, ostensibly in pursuit of research for the family history but more likely to satisfy an irrepressibly peripatetic spirit. From early 1711 through the winter of 1712, Leibniz was, again to the annoyance of the duke, constantly on the move. He spent time in Hanover, Berlin, Leipzig, Karlsbad, Torgau, Wolfenbüttel, Dresden, Prague, and, for an extended stay, Vienna, where he took up the task of establishing his own Society of Sciences for the Hapsburg emperor. He never gave up on his grand ecumenical project. Leibniz remained hopeful about the reunion of at least the Protestant faiths, and found encouragement in the fact that the new king of England and head of the Anglican Church, George I (the former Georg Ludwig, Elector of Hanover), was a Lutheran.

Even in old age, and despite a heavy load of administrative work and historical research, Leibniz continued to develop and clarify his philosophical ideas in essays, letters, and articles for learned journals. He kept up with events in the Republic of Letters, and he made extensive comments just after Malebranche's death in his copy of one of the Oratorian's last writings, the *Dialogue Between a Christian Philosopher and a Chinese Philosopher.*

A fair amount of Leibniz's energy in his final years was taken up by the ongoing dispute with Newton over who was the first to invent the calculus. The Royal Society, of which both men were members, had ruled in Newton's favor. Leibniz was deeply hurt by this, and by the strong and often personal attacks directed at him by Newton's English followers. In his correspondence with Samuel Clarke, a Newtonian, Leibniz took the opportunity to defend his views on space, the void, preestablished harmony, freedom of the will, and, above all, the way in which God's choice is always directed by wisdom. Clarke had argued that unless God is arbitrary in the exercise of His will, He will have no real power of choice at all. Leibniz replied, as he had to so many others, that God always chooses for the best, and that to insist otherwise is to deprive God's choices of their wisdom.

Leibniz had not been to England since passing through on his way home from Paris in 1676. When, in the fall of 1716, his old friend Princess Caroline (later to be queen of England) expressed her fervent wish that he join her there, he had to decline. She was eager to enjoy, once again, the pleasure of Leibniz's company, but there was also some hope that he might be able to take up the position of court historiographer and do for her family what he was doing for the House of Brunswick-Lüneburg. However, Leibniz had more than enough work to occupy him on the Continent, and there was little chance that his German employer would allow him yet another extended sabbatical. By this time, Leibniz, who had earlier decided that his history would be able to cover only the period from 768 to 1024, had now given up hope of finishing even this much of the project, particularly as he began seriously to feel the effects of age.

He had long suffered from very painful attacks of gout and arthritis, but for the most part had been able to weather them. Writing to his friend Nicolas Rémond in March 1716, Leibniz says that "my little troubles are quite tolerable, and even without pain, as long as I stay at rest. They did not keep me from taking a trip to Brunswick . . . and if they do not become worse, they will not keep me from taking even grander voyages."[8] Just a few months later, he could hardly pick up a pen.

By early November, Leibniz was confined to bed. He did not think it was anything serious, nothing a little rest would not cure. After a couple of days, when his condition grew worse, a doctor was finally called. There was little he could do except to try to relieve some of Leibniz's discomfort. Always the optimist, Leibniz did not see any need for the pastor to be summoned; he thought there would be time for that later. There was not, and he died that evening, November 14, 1716, at the age of seventy.

Notes

Bibliography

Acknowledgments

Index

Notes

Abbreviations Used

Works by Leibniz

A   *Sämtliche Schriften und Briefe*. Ed. Deutsche Akademie der Wissenschaften. Multiple vols. in 7 series (Darmstadt/Leipzig/Berlin: Akademie Verlag, 1923).

AG   *Philosophical Essays*. Ed. and trans. Roger Ariew and Daniel Garber (Indianapolis: Hackett, 1989).

Couturat *Opuscules et fragments inédits de Leibniz*. Ed. Louis Couturat (Paris: Presses Universitaires de France, 1903; reprinted Hildesheim: Georg Olms, 1961).

DS   *Deutsche Schriften*, 2 vols. Ed. G. E. Guhrauer (Berlin, 1838–40).

FdC   *Nouvelles lettres et opuscules inédits de Leibniz*. Ed. Louis Alexandre Foucher de Careil (Paris: Ladrange, 1854; reprinted Hildesheim: Georg Olms, 1975).

GM   *Mathematische Schriften*. 7 vols. Ed. C. I. Gerhardt (Berlin: A. Asher; Halle: H. W. Schmidt, 1849–63).

GP   *Philosophische Schriften*. 7 vols. Ed. C. I. Gerhardt (Berlin: Weidmann, 1875–90; reprinted Hildesheim: Georg Olms, 1978).

Grua   *Textes inédits d'après de la bibliothèque provinciale de Hanovre*. 2 vols. Ed. Gaston Grua (Paris: Presses Universitaires de France, 1948).

H   *Theodicy: Essays on the Goodness of God, the Freedom of Man, and the Ori-*

gin of Evil. Ed. Austin Farrar, trans. E. M. Huggard (La Salle, Ill.: Open Court, 1985).

Klopp   *Die Werke von Leibniz. Reihe 1: Historisch-politische und staatswissenschaftliche Schriften*. 11 vols. Ed. Onno Klopp (Hanover: Klindworth, 1864–84).

L   *Philosophical Papers and Letters*. Ed. and trans. Leroy Loemker, 2nd ed. (Dordrecht: D. Reidel, 1969).

M   *Discourse on Metaphysics/Correspondence with Arnauld/Monadology*. Ed. and trans. George Montgomery (La Salle, Ill.: Open Court, 1980).

RP   *Political Writings*. Ed. Patrick Riley (Cambridge: Cambridge University Press, 1972).

Works by Malebranche

JS   *Dialogues on Metaphysics and on Religion*. Ed. Nicholas Jolley, trans. David Scott (Cambridge: Cambridge University Press, 1997).

LO   *The Search After Truth*. Trans. Thomas M. Lennon and Paul J. Olscamp (Columbus: Ohio State University Press, 1980).

OC   *Oeuvres complètes de Malebranche*. 20 vols. Ed. André Robinet (Paris: J. Vrin, 1958–76).

R   *Treatise on Nature and Grace*. Trans. Patrick Riley (Oxford: Oxford University Press, 1992).

TNG   *Traité de la nature et de la grace*.

Works by Arnauld

OA   *Oeuvres de Messire Antoine Arnauld, docteur de la maison et société de Sorbonne*. 43 vols. (Lausanne: Sigismond d'Arnay, 1775).

TP   *Textes philosophiques*. Ed. Denis Moreau (Paris: Presses Universitaires de France, 2001).

Works by Descartes

AT   *Oeuvres de Descartes*. 12 vols. Ed. Charles Adam and Paul Tannery (Paris: J. Vrin, 1974–83).

CSM   *The Philosophical Writings of Descartes*. 2 vols. Ed. and trans. John Cottingham, Robert Stoothoff, and Dugald Murdoch (Cambridge: Cambridge University Press, 1985).

CSMK   *The Philosophical Writings of Descartes*, vol. 3 (correspondence). Ed. and trans. John Cottingham, Robert Stoothoff, Dugald Murdoch, and Anthony Kenny (Cambridge: Cambridge University Press, 1991).

Works by Spinoza

S   *The Letters*. Trans. Samuel Shirley (Indianapolis: Hackett, 1995).

G   *Spinoza Opera*. 5 vols. Ed. Carl Gebhardt (Heidelberg: Carl Winters Universitätsverlag, 1925; reprinted 1972).

C   *The Collected Works of Spinoza*, vol. 1. Trans. Edwin Curley (Princeton, N.J.: Princeton University Press, 1985).

Other Works

MLRP   *Malebranche et Leibniz: Relations personelles.* Ed. André Robinet (Paris: J. Vrin, 1955).

OD   Pierre Bayle, *Oeuvres diverses* (The Hague, 1727–31; reprinted in 6 vols., Hildesheim: Georg Olms, 1964–82).

HCD   Pierre Bayle, *Historical and Critical Dictionary.* Ed. and trans. Richard H. Popkin (Indianapolis: Bobbs-Merrill, 1965).

1: Leibniz in Paris

1. This was the year of the Dutch revolt against Spain and, thus, the beginning of the Eighty Years War.
2. For Leibniz's biography, see E. J. Aiton, *Leibniz: A Biography* (Bristol and Boston: Adam Hilger, 1985); and Maria Rosa Antognazza, *Leibniz: A Biography* (Cambridge: Cambridge University Press, 2008).
3. See George MacDonald Ross, "Leibniz and the Nuremberg Alchemical Society," *Studia Leibnitiana* 6 (1974): 222–48 (p. 222).
4. Letter to Nicolas Rémond, January 10, 1714, G III.605.
5. RP 121ff.
6. A I.3.272.
7. G IV.105–110; A VI.1.508–512.
8. A I.7.638.
9. Johann Christian von Boineberg to the king of France, January 20, 1672, A I.1.249–54.
10. For a study of this phase of Paris's history, see Colin Jones, *Paris: The Biography of a City* (New York: Viking, 2005), chap. 5.
11. Klopp II.125. The letter was written on March 18, the day before Leibniz's departure.
12. Letter of November 1672, Klopp II.140.
13. Letter to Melchior Friedrich von Schönborn, January 1676, A I.1.397. In fact, Leibniz will later say that his French is better than his Latin: "I understand enough Latin to read what others have written, but I am not sufficiently comfortable with it for distinctly explaining my own thoughts" (Letter to Molanus, ca. 1678, GP I.286).
14. Letter to Johann Friedrich, duke of Hanover, January 21, 1675, A I.1.491–92.
15. A I.1.452.
16. Letter to Johann Friedrich, duke of Hanover, January 21, 1675, A I.1.492.
17. See the letter to Thomasius of April 30, 1669, A II.1.14–24.
18. Klopp IV.452–54.

19. Letter to Christian von Mecklenburg, March 1675, A I.1.476.
20. FdC V.359.
21. Letter to Christian von Mecklenburg, March 1675, A I.1.476.
22. Letter to Melchior Friedrich von Schönborn, March 10, 1673, AI.1.316.
23. Compare, for example, Christia Mercer, *Leibniz's Metaphysics: Its Origins and Development* (Cambridge and New York: Cambridge University Press, 2001), who argues that Leibniz's "basic metaphysical commitments" were already in place by 1671, with Catherine Wilson, *Leibniz's Metaphysics: A Historical and Comparative Study* (Princeton, N.J.: Princeton University Press, 1989), who offers a more long-term developmental picture.

2: Philosophy on the Left Bank

1. Françisque Bouillier, *Histoire de la philosophie Cartésienne*, 2 vols. (Paris: Delagrave, 1868), II.469.
2. For an account of these events, see Adrien Baillet, *La vie de Monsieur Descartes* (Paris: Daniel Horthemels, 1691; reprint: 2 vols., New York and London: Garland, 1987), vol. 2, pp. 439–43.
3. For a fuller discussion of these modes of explanation, see Steven Nadler, "Doctrines of Explanation in Late Scholasticism and in the Mechanical Philosophy," in D. Garber and M. Ayers (eds.), *The Cambridge History of Seventeenth-Century Philosophy*, 2 vols. (Cambridge: Cambridge University Press, 1998), II.513–52, especially pp. 514–18.
4. Act III, third intermission, lines 58–66.
5. *Principles of Philosophy*, preface to the French edition, AT IXb.8.
6. See *Principles of Philosophy*, IV.20–23.
7. Not all partisans of the mechanical philosophy were Cartesian dualists; Leibniz explicitly rejected Cartesian dualism, while John Locke, committed to mechanistic explanations in science, was skeptical about such metaphysical questions.
8. Impenetrability is somewhat problematic as a basic property of Cartesian geometric bodies; see Daniel Garber, *Descartes's Metaphysical Physics* (Chicago: University of Chicago Press, 1990), pp. 144–48.
9. See, for example, "Fourth Objections" and "Fourth Replies" (appended to the *Meditations*), AT VII.217–18, 248–56; and the "Sixth Replies," AT VII.433–34. Questions about the Eucharist dominated the controversies around Cartesian philosophy throughout the seventeenth century; see Tad Schmaltz, *Radical Cartesianism: The French Reception of Descartes* (Cambridge: Cambridge University Press, 2002); and Jean-Robert Armogathe, *Theologia Cartesiana* (The Hague: Martinus Nijhoff, 1977).
10. See the "Fourth Replies," AT VII.248–56; CSM II.173–78.
11. AT III.340.

12. It has been argued that this is also what doomed Galileo with Rome; see Pietro Redondi, *Galileo Heretic* (Princeton, N.J.: Princeton University Press, 1989).

13. Bouillier, *Histoire de la philosophie Cartésienne*, I.441.

14. Pierre Jurieu, *La Politique du clergé de France*, 2nd ed. (Cologne: Pierre Martean, 1681), p. 107. For a discussion of Jansenism and Cartesianism, see Steven Nadler, "Cartesianism and Port Royal," *The Monist* 71 (1988): 573–84.

15. Bouillier, *Histoire de la philosophie Cartésienne*, I.430.

16. See *Theodicy*, §376.

17. These remarks come from Huet's memoirs, and are quoted in Pierre-Daniel Huet, *Against Cartesian Philosophy*, ed. and trans. Thomas M. Lennon (Amherst, N.Y.: Humanity Books, 2005), pp. 23–24.

18. For a study of Foucher's confrontation with Cartesian philosophy, see Richard A. Watson, *The Downfall of Cartesianism* (The Hague: Martinus Nijhoff, 1966). On Leibniz and Foucher, see Stuart Brown, "The Leibniz-Foucher Alliance and Its Philosophical Bases," in Paul Lodge (ed.), *Leibniz and His Correspondents* (Cambridge: Cambridge University Press, 2004).

19. Letter to Molanus (?), ca. 1679, A II.1.500; AG 241.

20. Letter to Molanus (?), A II.1.499; AG 240.

21. *Discourse on Metaphysics*, §18, GP IV.444; M 32–33.

22. A II.1.15.

23. "A New System of Nature," GP IV.478.

24. GM I.83.

25. Descartes did nonetheless believe that bodies have a force for acting on or resisting other bodies, which he measured in terms of the mass of the body multiplied by its speed (*Principles of Philosophy* II.43, 45).

26. *Discourse on Metaphysics*, §§17–21. See also the 1686 paper, "A Brief Demonstration of a Notable Error of Descartes," GM VI.117–19.

27. Letter to Arnauld, November 28/December 8, 1686, GP II.77.

28. *Discourse on Metaphysics*, §18, GP IV.444; M 33.

29. *Discourse on Metaphysics*, §12, GP IV.436; M 18.

30. Letter to Arnauld, November 28/December 8, 1686, GP II.77–78.

31. Letter to Molanus (?), ca. 1679, A II.1.499; AG 240.

32. "A New System of Nature," GP IV.485; AG 144.

33. Postscript of a letter to Basnage de Beauval, of 1696, GP IV.498.

34. "A New System of Nature," GP IV.484; AG 143–44.

35. For a discussion of this development, see Daniel Garber, "Leibniz and the Foundations of Physics: The Middle Years," in Kathleen Okruhlik and Gregory Brown (eds.), *The Natural Philosophy of Leibniz* (Dordrecht: Reidel, 1985), pp. 27–129. There is a good deal of contention among scholars as to whether or not Leibniz did have a transitional stage incorporating true corporeal substances on the Aristotelian model or had the monadological picture in mind from the start; see Mercer, *Leibniz's Metaphysics*, for an extended defense of the latter

view; see also Robert M. Adams, *Leibniz: Determinist, Theist, Idealist* (Oxford: Oxford University Press, 1994).

36. For example, in the essay "On Body and Force, Against the Cartesians," of 1702. Cartesianism, on the wane in England and elsewhere, was soon on its way out even in France, to be supplanted by Newtonianism.

37. Yves Marie André, *La Vie de R. P. Malebranche* (Paris, 1886; reprint Geneva: Slatkine, 1970), p. 5.

38. Ibid., p. 12.

39. *Dialogues on Metaphysics*, III.4, OC XII.65; JS 33.

40. *Search After Truth*, III.2.vi, OC I.439; LO 231. For a study of Malebranche's theory of Vision in God, see Steven Nadler, *Malebranche and Ideas* (Oxford: Oxford University Press, 1992).

41. See Steven Nadler, "Malebranche on Causation," in Steven Nadler (ed.), *The Cambridge Companion to Malebranche* (Cambridge and New York: Cambridge University Press, 2000), pp. 112–38.

42. Most notably, among the Arabic followers of Al-Ashari; see Majid Fakhry, *Islamic Occasionalism and Its Critique by Averroës and Avicenna* (London: Allen and Unwin, 1958).

43. *Search After Truth*, VI.2.iii, OC II.316; LO 450.

44. Ibid.

45. *Dialogues on Metaphysics*, VII.7, OC XII.157; JS 112; VII.10, OC XII.160; JS 115.

46. *Dialogues on Metaphysics*, VII.10–11, OC XII.160–62; JS 115–17.

47. *Search After Truth*, VI.2.iii, OC II.309; LO 446.

48. "Préface contre le livre de Foucher," OC II.496.

49. For an analysis of the Malebranche-Leibniz relationship in Paris, see MLRP 23–40.

50. The later dating is provided for the letters exchanged just after the meeting by the editors of the Akademie edition (A II.1.254–59). Robinet, on the other hand, provides the earlier dating (MLRP 41–48). Robinet believes that Malebranche's student Jean Prestet was also at the meeting (25–26).

51. A II.1.254.

52. Leibniz himself, however, agreed that the material world is a plenum and that a vacuum is impossible.

3: Le Grand Arnauld

1. Klopp II.139.

2. On Arnauld's biography, see Emile Jacques, *Les Années d'exil d'Antoine Arnauld* (Louvain: Publications Universitaires de Louvain, 1976).

3. For a magisterial history of Port-Royal and the controversies concerning Jansenism, see Charles Augustin Sainte-Beuve, *Port-Royal*, 7 vols. (Paris: La

Connaissance, 1928). See also Alexander Sedgwick, *Jansenism in Seventeenth-Century France: Voices from the Wilderness* (Charlottesville: University Press of Virginia, 1977), and *The Travails of Conscience: The Arnauld Family and the Ancien Régime* (Cambridge, Mass.: Harvard University Press, 1998).

4. Cornelius Jansen, *Augustinus*, IX.470. For the best summary of Jansen's work, see Nigel Abercrombie, *The Origins of Jansenism* (Oxford: Clarendon Press, 1936), pp. 125–58. For a deeper analysis, see Jean Laporte, *La Doctrine de Port-Royal*, vol. 2, part I: *Les Vérités de la grace* (Paris: Presses Universitaires de France, 1923).

5. Letter X, in Blaise Pascal, *The Provincial Letters* (Harmondsworth: Penguin, 1967), pp. 160–61.

6. Sedgwick, *Travails of Conscience*, p. 60.

7. OA I.30–31.

8. Nicolas Fontaine, *Mémoires pour servir à l'histoire de Port-Royal*, 2 vols. (Utrecht, 1736); republished as *Mémoires ou histoire des Solitaires de Port-Royal* (Paris: Honoré Champion, 2001), p. 354.

9. See Abercrombie, *Origins of Jansenism*, pp. 187–90.

10. *Mémoires sur la destruction de l'abbaye de Port-Royal des Champs*, 2 vols. (Utrecht, 1759), I.16.

11. Quoted in Sedgwick, *Travails of Conscience*, p. 126.

12. *Mémoires*, p. 522.

13. For a study of Jansenism during the Fronde, see Sedgwick, *Jansenism in Seventeenth-Century France*, chap. 3.

14. OA I.250.

15. OA XLIII.174.

16. The pain experienced by the nuns is described in *Divers actes, lettres, et relations des religieuses de Port-Royal du Saint-Sacrament touchant au sujet de la signature du formulaire*, 3 vols. (Utrecht, 1735).

17. Jansen's view was that freedom requires only an absence of external constraint.

18. *Humanae libertatis notio*, OA X.614–24; also found at TP 241.

19. See also OA III.662–63. For a deeper and more nuanced analysis of Arnauld's views on freedom, see Laporte, *La Doctrine de Port-Royal*, II.1; Elmar Kremer, "Grace and Free Will in Arnauld," in Elmar Kremer (ed.), *The Great Arnauld and Some of His Philosophical Correspondents* (Toronto: University of Toronto Press, 1994), pp. 219–39; and Robert C. Sleigh, Jr., "Arnauld on Efficacious Grace and Free Choice," in Elmar Kremer (ed.), *Interpreting Arnauld* (Toronto: University of Toronto Press, 1996), pp. 164–75.

20. AT VII.214; CSM II.150.

21. AT VII.196–218; CSM II.138–53.

22. AT III.331.

23. AT III.334.

24. AT V.192.

25. AT VII.218; CSM II.154.

26. For a discussion of Arnauld as a defender of Descartes, particularly on the issue of the Eucharist, see Steven Nadler, "Arnauld, Descartes and Transubstantiation: Reconciling Cartesian Metaphysics and Real Presence," *Journal of the History of Ideas* 49 (1988): 229–46.

27. *Difficultés proposes à M. Steyaert*, §94, OA IX.306.

28. The piece is in Victor Cousin, "De la persécution du Cartésianisme en France," *Fragments Philosophiques, Oeuvres* (Brussels, 1841), II.181–91. Arnauld is also the coauthor (with Pierre Nicole) of the famous *La Logique, ou l'art de penser*, the so-called "Port-Royal Logic" (1661), a treatise on mind, language, and reasoning thoroughly permeated by Cartesian principles. Arnauld and Nicole also co-wrote the "Port-Royal Grammar," used as a textbook in the schools run by Port-Royal.

29. The letter is in A II.1.169–81; and translated excerpts in L 148–50.

30. A II.1.175. For Leibniz's early work on transubstantiation, see Christia Mercer, *Leibniz's Metaphysics*, pp. 82–89.

31. For the reception of Spinoza's work, see Steven Nadler, *Spinoza: A Life* (Cambridge: Cambridge University Press, 1999), chap. 11.

32. A II.1.155.

33. See Boineberg's letter to Leibniz of November 1671, A I.1.245.

34. OA XLIII.154.

35. A I.1.487.

36. Letter to Johann Friedrich, Spring 1679 (?), A II.1.488.

37. A I.1.175.

38. A I.1.451.

39. Klopp II.139.

40. Jacques, *Les Années d'exil d'Antoine Arnauld*, p. 34.

41. OA II.255.

42. A II.1.231.

43. A I.3.283–85.

44. A I.3.285–86.

45. A I.4.352.

46. A II.1.488.

47. A II.1.477–78.

48. OC VII.451.

49. OA XXXIX.3.

50. OA XXXIX.69.

51. OC VII.451.

52. Letter to Tschirnhaus, OC XVIII.345. Father André, who knew Malebranche personally, supports Arnauld's and Leibniz's warmer account of the relationship between Arnauld and Malebranche: they were, he says, "fort bons amis" (*La Vie de R. P. Malebranche*, p. 78). See also Robinet's note on this, OC VI.ii–iii: "On peut donc estimer que les relations entre Malebranche et Arnauld furent d'abord amicales, allant même jusqu'à une certaine connivence philosophique."

53. This is purely speculative. There is no documentary evidence of any three-way meetings between Leibniz, Arnauld, and Malebranche. However, I find it hard to believe that such philosophical gatherings did not take place, given their mutual interests and personal contacts.

4: Theodicy

1. GP IV.477; L 453.
2. L 457.
3. For general studies of Bayle's life and thought, see Elisabeth Labrousse, *Pierre Bayle*, 2 vols. (The Hague: Martinus Nijhoff, 1963–64); Paul Dibon (ed.), *Pierre Bayle: Le Philosophe de Rotterdam* (Amsterdam: Elsevier, 1959); and Howard Robinson, *Bayle the Skeptic* (New York: Columbia University Press, 1931).
4. See André Robinet, "L'aphilosophie de P. Bayle devant les philosophies de Malebranche et Leibniz," in Dibon, *Pierre Bayle: Le Philosophe de Rotterdam*, pp. 48–61.
5. OD 263.
6. Article "Rorarius," remark H.
7. "Rorarius," remark L, in HCD 247.
8. GP IV.565; L 581.
9. GP IV.520; L 494.
10. "Rorarius," remark L.
11. "Reply to the Thoughts on the System of Preestablished Harmony contained in the Second Edition of M. Bayle's Critical Dictionary, Article Rorarius," GP IV.554–71; L 574–85.
12. The principle of divine omniscience is sometimes stated as the idea not that God knows everything but that God knows everything that is in principle knowable. This is meant to leave open the possibility that there are many things God does not know (e.g., the free actions of human beings) without undermining His omniscience, because these unknown events are supposed to be in principle unknowable.
13. Quoted by the fourth-century Church father Lactantius, *De Ira Dei*, trans. M. F. McDonald (Washington, D.C.: The Catholic University of America Press, 1965), pp. 92 (translation slightly modified).
14. *Summa Theologiae*, Part I, Q. 49, art. 2.
15. *Summa Theologiae*, Parts I–II, Q. 79, art. 2.
16. See, for example, Augustine, *Confessions*, VII.13–14.
17. *Guide of the Perplexed*, III.12; trans. Shlomo Pines, 2 vols. (Chicago: University of Chicago Press, 1963), vol. 2, p. 442.
18. *Guide of the Perplexed*, III.12, vol. 2, p. 444.
19. The first use of the term appears in a short Latin piece from around 1697 (Grua I.370).

20. This thesis has been persuasively argued for by Donald Rutherford, *Leibniz and the Rational Order of Nature* (Cambridge: Cambridge University Press, 1995).

21. HCD 144.

22. HCD 151.

23. See the letter to Des Bosses of September 3, 1708, GP II.356.

24. GP IV.555; L 575.

25. GP IV.567; L 582.

26. In 1707, just after Bayle's death, Leibniz wrote (but did not publish) a preliminary note ("des pensées"), the short "Theodicy, or Apology for the Justice of God Through the Idea of It That He Has Given Us" (Grua II.495–98).

27. Grua II.495.

28. Leibniz's name did not appear on the cover until the 1716 Latin edition, published just after his death.

29. *Theodicy*, §29, GP VI.67; H 91.

30. *Theodicy*, §4, GP VI.51; H 75.

31. *Theodicy*, GP VI.29; H 53.

32. *Theodicy*, §43, GP VI.74–75; H 98.

33. *Theodicy*, GP VI.34; H 58.

34. *Theodicy*, GP VI.35–36; H 59–60.

35. *Theodicy*, §§107–108, GP VI.162–63; H 182.

36. Strictly speaking, for Leibniz it is not possible for two worlds to differ only in a single detail. If one thing is different between two worlds, then every other substance must be different as well. This is because in Leibniz's philosophy, within any one world "all is connected" and there are "no purely extrinsic denominations," and thus the differences in that thing will be reflected in concomitant differences in all the other substances. For the same reason, it does not make sense to speak of one and the same thing existing in two worlds, because each thing expresses or is a reflection of the particular world to which it belongs.

37. *Theodicy*, §225, H 267–68.

38. *Summa Theologiae*, Part I, Q. 25, art. 6. For a discussion of this issue, particularly in relation to the later Thomist thinker Francisco Suárez, see Emanuela Scribano, "False Enemies: Malebranche, Leibniz and the Best of All Possible Worlds," *Oxford Studies in Early Modern Philosophy* 1 (2003): 165–82; and Robert M. Adams, "Must God Create the Best?" *The Philosophical Review* 81 (1972): 317–32.

39. *Theodicy*, §8, H 128.

40. Ibid.

41. *Theodicy*, §16, H 131.

42. Again, there can be no comparison of how an individual might fare in different possible worlds, because any particular individual is world-bound— that is, he is unique to the world in which he exists. This is because the concept of that individual is determined by his relations to all other substances in the world he inhabits—that is, by the world itself. Thus, if the question is about the fortunes of

individual S in world A, one should speak about how an individual very much like (but not identical to) S fares comparatively in world B.

43. *Theodicy*, §212, GP VI.245; H 260.

44. *Theodicy*, §9, GP VI.107–108; H 128–29.

45. Of course, having less evil than the actual world is only a sufficient condition for being less than the best world; it is not a necessary condition. There are many possible worlds that have more evil than the actual world, and many worlds that have the same amount of evil as the actual world, all of which are less than the best. Worlds can differ one from another in many aspects, and thus fall short of optimality for many reasons, some having nothing to do with quantity or quality of evil.

46. *Theodicy*, §10, GP VI.108; H 129.

47. *Theodicy*, §134, GP VI.187–88; H 206.

48. *Theodicy*, §12, GP VI.109; H 130.

49. "On the Radical Origination of Things," GP VII.306–307; L 488–89.

50. See *Theodicy*, §13 and §263, where he discusses Maimonides's quantitative response.

51. Leibniz remains troubled by the problem this poses not for God's wisdom or goodness but for His justice, and therefore sometimes argues that ultimately the suffering of the virtuous in this life will be compensated for in the afterlife; see *Monadology*, §§87–90. In §89, he even claims that divine justice plays itself out in this life, because "sins will bring their own penalty with them through the order of nature . . . and in the same way good actions will attain their rewards . . . although this cannot, and ought not, always take place without delay." And in "On the Radical Origination of Things," he insists that "as for the afflictions, especially of good men, however, we must take it as certain that these lead to their greater good" (GP VI.307; L 490).

52. Because evil itself is really nothing but an absence of good, strictly speaking it cannot make a "positive" contribution to the contents of the world. Rather, this contribution is made by the lesser degrees of goodness (represented, for example, by ignorance and vice) in things.

53. *Theodicy*, §9, GP VI.108; H 129.

54. *Theodicy*, §265, GP VI.275; H 290.

55. *Theodicy*, §119, GP VI.171; H 190.

56. *Confessio Philosophi*, A VI.3.121.

57. *Theodicy*, §145, GP VI.196; H 214. See also *Discourse on Metaphysics*, §5: "It is sufficient to have this confidence in God, that he has done everything for the best and that nothing will be able to injure those who love him. To know in particular, however, the reasons that have moved him to choose this order of the universe, to permit sin, to dispense his salutary grace in a certain manner—this passes the capacity of a finite mind, above all when such a mind has not come into the joy of the vision of God" (GP IV.430; M 8).

58. See "On the Radical Origination of Things," GP VII.306; L 489: "The world is

not only the most perfect naturally or if you prefer, metaphysically—in other words, that that series of things has been produced that actually presents the greatest amount of reality—but also that it is the most perfect morally, because moral perfection is truly natural in minds themselves."

59. For a good discussion of this point, see George MacDonald Ross, "Leibniz and the Concept of Metaphysical Perfection," *Studia Leibnitiana*, Sonderheft 21 (1992): 143–52; and Rutherford, *Leibniz and the Rational Order of Nature*, pp. 24–26.

60. *Discourse on Metaphysics*, §5, GP IV.430; M 8.

61. *Discourse on Metaphysics*, §6, GP IV.431; M 11.

62. Letter to Malebranche, June 22/July 2, 1679, GP I.331; L 211.

63. I am thus opting for the reading whereby Leibniz's God gets to maximize both major values, simplicity (of laws) and richness and quantity (of reality), rather than the reading whereby the two values are in tension and God must sacrifice absolute maximization for the sake of relative maximization (whereby there may be worlds with greater reality, but only because they have less simple laws). Scholarly opinion is divided on this matter. Rutherford, for example, adopts the former reading (it is a major theme in his *Leibniz and the Rational Order of Nature*), while Bertrand Russell (*A Critical Exposition of the Philosophy of Leibniz*, 2nd ed. [London: George Allen and Unwin, 1937]), Nicholas Rescher (*Leibniz: An Introduction to His Philosophy* [Lanham, Md.: University Press of America, 1979]), and Catherine Wilson ("Leibnizian Optimism," *Journal of Philosophy* 80 (1983): 765–83) adopt the latter reading.

64. *Confessio Philosophi*, A VI.3.116.

65. Grua, I.12.

66. "De Existentia," A VI.3.588.

67. See *Discourse on Metaphysics*, §6.

68. "On the Radical Origination of Things," GP VII.306.

69. For example, *Theodicy*, §10.

70. See *Principles of Nature and Grace*, §10, where he clearly states that the best of all possible worlds contains "the greatest happiness and goodness in created things that the universe could allow." For an argument that the best world maximizes happiness, see Rutherford, *Leibniz and the Rational Order of Nature*, chap. 3.

71. *Theodicy*, §241, GP VI.261; H 276. In this case, "consider the whole" means something like: Look beyond the narrow confines of this temporary existence and take into account a person's long-term (i.e., eternal) fate.

72. *Theodicy*, §§22–23, GP VI.115–16; H 137.

5: The Kingdoms of Nature and Grace

1. DS II.66–67.

2. According to Robinet, what Leibniz discovered in the years immediately after

Paris (where he regarded Malebranche as a straightforward Cartesian) was the Oratorian's "originality"; see MLRP 77–86.

3. MLRP 129. It was not true; Arnauld was in the Low Countries.

4. There are many more letters involving third parties, in which Leibniz or Malebranche shows interest in the activities of the other.

5. MLRP 103. The book was a gift to Leibniz from Princess Elizabeth of the Palatinate, well known as Descartes's philosophically acute correspondent in the 1640s, now Abbess of Hervorde.

6. MLRP 89.

7. May and June [?], 1679, MLRP 116–17. Robinet notes that it is likely but uncertain that Malebranche was the intended recipient of the second letter.

8. Quoted in the preface by Jacques Brunschwig (ed.), *Essais de Théodicée* (Paris: Garnier-Flammarion, 1969), p. 16.

9. The story is related by Robinet, MLRP 77–78.

10. MLRP 417.

11. §208.

12. The first edition of the work was published before Bayle started the *Nouvelles*.

13. OC VIII–IX.1156.

14. *Première apologie pour M. Jansenius*, OA XV–XVI.184–85; 246.

15. OC V.xliv.

16. See the letter quoted at ibid.

17. *Dialogues on Metaphysics*, IX.9, OC XII.211; JS 160–61.

18. TNG I.12, OC V.27; R 116.

19. TNG I.27, OC V.40; R 122.

20. TNG I.3, OC V.15; R 113.

21. *Méditations chrétiennes*, VII.2, OC X.69.

22. TNG I.13, OC V.28; R 116.

23. TNG I.15, OC V.30; R 117.

24. *Dialogues on Metaphysics*, XII.11, OC XII.293; JS 230.

25. *Dialogues on Metaphysics*, XIII.3, OC XII.310; JS 245.

26. There is some debate among scholars as to whether Malebranche's God maximizes the simplicity of laws at the expense of the world's perfection, or reconciles simplicity of laws and perfection of world, compromising on both. While I opt for the former reading, Denis Moreau argues for the latter; see "Malebranche on Disorder and Physical Evil: Manicheanism or Philosophical Courage?" in Elmar Kremer and Michael Latzer (eds.), *The Problem of Evil in Early Modern Philosophy* (Toronto: University of Toronto Press, 2001), pp. 81–100.

27. OC IX.1085.

28. *Dialogues on Metaphysics*, XIII.8, OC XII.318; JS 252. See also *Réponse aux Reflexions [d'Arnauld]*, OC IX.768.

29. For a study of the history of the notion of "general will" and of Malebranche's role therein, see Patrick Riley, *The General Will Before Rousseau: The Transforma-*

tion of the Divine into the Civic (Princeton, N.J.: Princeton University Press, 1986), especially chap. 1–3.

30. Malebranche's clearest statement on general versus particular volitions is at TNG, Elucidation I.

31. TNG I.57. While miracles are "arbitrary" in the sense that they are violations of the laws of nature, they are not arbitrary in the stronger sense that there is no reason for them; Malebranche insists that miracles are necessitated either by higher-level laws unknown to us or by what he calls "Order," the eternal truths that transcend the laws altogether and provide the reasons for them (see TNG II.45; and *Dialogues on Metaphysics*, VIII.3).

32. See *Traité de Morale*, XXV. For a study of the importance of law—natural, social, and salvific—in Malebranche's philosophy, see Marie-Frédérique Pellegrin, *Le Système de la loi de Nicolas Malebranche* (Paris: J. Vrin, 2006).

33. TNG I.18, OC V.32; R 118.

34. Ibid.

35. TNG I.59, OC V.63; R 137.

36. *Dialogues on Metaphysics*, IX.9, OC XII.212; JS 161.

37. *Search After Truth*, Elucidation 15, OC III.218; LO 665.

38. TNG I.20.addition, OC V.34.

39. *Dialogues on Metaphysics*, IX.11, OC XII.215–16; JS 164.

40. TNG I.14, OC V.29; R 116–17.

41. Malebranche actually distinguishes between the grace of Jesus Christ, or "the grace of feeling" (or "the grace of the Redeemer"), and the grace of the Creator, or "the grace of enlightenment." The grace of Jesus Christ is at work to counterbalance the pleasures of concupiscence and in the conversion of postlapsarian human beings toward God; see TNG III.18–24.

42. TNG I.38, OC V.47; R 127.

43. TNG I.45, OC V.51; R 130.

44. TNG I.44, OC V.50–51; R 129.

45. Malebranche insists that the grace of the Redeemer is always efficacious "by itself," in the sense that it always brings about its immediate effect, namely, a pleasure or delight; it does not, however, always have enough of an effect to counteract concupiscence and result in conversion; see TNG III.20.

46. See OC VIII.655.

47. TNG II.17.addition, OC V.78–83.

48. Letter to the Marquis d'Allemans, OC XVIII.447.

49. Quoted at OC V.xxxiii.

50. §204, GP IV.238; H 254.

51. §206, GP IV.240; H 256.

52. §208, GP IV.241; H 257.

53. MLRP 417.

54. MLRP 418.

55. *Dialogues on Metaphysics*, XIII.8, OC XII.318; JS 252.

56. If Rutherford is right that Leibniz's God maximizes not just the simplicity of the laws but also the goodness and the happiness of creatures to an absolute degree, then this would represent a significant difference with Malebranche; see *Leibniz and the Rational Order of Nature*.

57. See Donald Rutherford, "Malebranche's Theodicy," in Nadler (ed.), *The Cambridge Companion to Malebranche*, pp. 165–89, 173. For further discussion of the differences between Leibniz and Malebranche, see also his "Natures, Laws and Miracles: The Roots of Leibniz's Critique of Occasionalism," in Steven Nadler (ed.), *Causation in Early Modern Philosophy: Cartesianism, Occasionalism, and Preestablished Harmony* (University Park: Penn State Press, 1993), 135–58, esp. pp. 152–57 for the issue of theodicy.

58. For a brief comparison of Leibniz and Malebranche on some of these issues, see Patrick Riley's introduction to his translation of the *Treatise on Nature and Grace*, R 34–38.

59. This is from Malebranche's reply to Arnauld's *Reflections philosophiques et théologiques*, OC VIII.765. Malebranche's view on the reality of evil is, according to Denis Moreau, a "rupture" with all other thinkers on the problem of evil, and is what constitutes "l'originalité malebranchiste"; see *Deux Cartésiens: La Polémique Arnauld-Malebranche* (Paris: J. Vrin, 1999), pp. 93–95, 112.

60. IX.9, OC XII.212; JS 161.

61. *Dialogue Between a Christian Philosopher and a Chinese Philosopher* (*Entretien d'un philosophe Chrétien et d'un philosophe Chinois*), OC XV.53.

62. TNG I.22.addition, OC V.36.

63. *Discourse on Metaphysics*, §3.

64. TNG I.38–39.addition, OC V.47. Sleigh stresses this significant difference between the two; see *Leibniz and Arnauld: A Commentary on Their Correspondence* (New Haven, Conn.: Yale University Press, 1990), p. 45. Denis Moreau makes a similar point in a different way when he notes that Malebranche's God is limited by considerations of theology, whereas Leibniz's God is limited by considerations of cosmology; see "Malebranche on Disorder and Physical Evil," p. 86.

65. See Charles Larmore, *Modernité et morale* (Paris: Presses Universitaires de France, 1993), chap. 5.

66. GP I.330; L 210–11.

67. *Theodicy*, §8, GP VI.107; H 128.

68. See Leibniz's fourth letter to Samuel Clarke, GP VII.372; L 687. This is only one of many occasions where Leibniz employs this argument for his law.

69. Leibniz's Fifth Paper (for Clarke), G VII.393; L 699 (translation modified).

70. *Theodicy*, §337, GP VI.315; H 328.

71. Quoted by Leibniz at *Theodicy*, §227, GP VI.253; H 268.

72. *Theodicy*, §191, GP VI.230; H 246–47.

73. *Theodicy*, §45, GP VI.1127–28; H 148.

74. OC IV.30–31. For a discussion of this, see André Robinet, *Système et existence dans l'oeuvre de Malebranche* (Paris: J. Vrin, 1965), p. 22.

75. *Search After Truth*, Elucidation 8, OC III.85–86; LO 586–87.
76. See *Dialogues on Metaphysics*, VIII.13.
77. TNG II.45.
78. This is from the reply to Arnauld's *Reflections philosophiques et théologiques*, OC VIII.752–53.
79. *Dialogues on Metaphysics*, IX.3, OC XII.201; JS 152.
80. TNG, Third Elucidation, OC V.180.
81. *Doutes sur le système physique des causes occasionnelles*, esp. chap. 4.
82. See, for example, Catherine Wilson, "Leibnizian Optimism." Wilson argues that Leibniz took from Malebranche his "conception of God as a divine strategian," and that Malebranche's views represent the "origins" of Leibnizian optimism (p. 767).
83. A VI.3.124; S 49.
84. A II.1.117; S 3.

6: "Touch the Mountains and They Smoke"

1. Jacques, *Les années d'exil d'Antoine Arnauld*, p. 106.
2. OC XVIII.95.
3. For a résumé of the debate over the chronology of events leading up to the dinner at the Marquis de Roucy, see Ginette Dreyfus's discussion at OC V.xxiv, n. 8.
4. The series of documents related to this event are in OC XVIII.147–56, and OA XXXVIII.425–29.
5. OC XVIII.151.
6. Father André's account is excerpted at OC XVIII.156.
7. OA XXXVIII.426.
8. OC V.xxvi–xxvii.
9. The text of the letter is at OA XXXVIII.426.
10. OC XVIII.72–73.
11. OA XXXVIII.428.
12. OA XXXVIII.427; OC XVIII.xxix.
13. Letter to De Roucy, OA XXXVIII.427.
14. OC XVIII.200.
15. Ibid.
16. OC XVIII.202.
17. There are many levels to the Arnauld-Malebranche debate. For a study of some of these, see Denis Moreau, *Deux Cartésiens*; Aloyse-Raymond Ndiaye, *La Philosophie d'Antoine Arnauld* (Paris: J. Vrin, 1991); and Steven Nadler, *Arnauld and the Cartesian Philosophy of Ideas* (Princeton, N.J.: Princeton University Press, 1989).
18. Both Arnauld and Malebranche are "unorthodox" Cartesians—Malebranche

certainly more so—for the modifications they introduce into Descartes's meta-physics and epistemology. See Ferdinand Alquié, *Le Cartésianisme de Malebranche* (Paris: J. Vrin, 1974); Steven Nadler, "Occasionalism and the Question of Ar-nauld's Cartesianism," in Roger Ariew and Marjorie Grene (eds.), *Descartes and His Contemporaries* (Chicago: University of Chicago Press, 1995), pp. 129–44; and Ndiaye, *La Philosophie d'Antoine Arnauld,* part III.

19. The work is in OA XXXVIII.

20. I examine these aspects of the Arnauld-Malebranche debate in greater detail in *Arnauld and the Cartesian Philosophy of Ideas,* and *Malebranche and Ideas.*

21. *Défense de M. Arnauld,* OA XXXVIII.390.

22. This point is made most effectively by Denis Moreau, in *Deux Cartésiens.*

23. And yet, Malebranche sometimes hedges on this and insists that "although we are all joined to the order or wisdom of God, we do not know all its rules" (*Search,* Elucidation 15, OC III.220; LO 666).

24. On the other hand, Arnauld's insistence that grace is given without any regard to merit and in an ad hoc, even capricious manner is, for Malebranche, Cal-vinism.

25. *Reflections,* OA XXXIX.628–29.

26. *Reflections,* OA XXXIX.572–73.

27. *Reflections,* OA XXXIX.162.

28. *Reflections,* OA XXXIX.193.

29. *Reflections,* OA XXXIX.205.

30. *Reflections,* OA XXXIX.225.

31. *Reflections,* OA XXXIX.205–206.

32. *Reflections,* OA XXXIX.197.

33. *Reflections,* OA XXXIX.238.

34. *Reflections,* OA XXXIX.312.

35. *Reflections,* OA XXXIX.303.

36. I argue elsewhere that Arnauld misreads Malebranche on the nature of God's volitions; see "Occasionalism and General Will in Malebranche," *Journal of the History of Philosophy* 31 (1993): 31–47.

37. *Reflections,* OA XXXIX.586.

38. *Reflections,* OA XXXIX.292.

39. *Reflections,* OA XXXIX.350.

40. *Reflections,* OA XXXIX.245.

41. *Reflections,* OA XXXIX.244–45.

42. *Reflections,* OA XXXIX.195.

43. *Reflections,* OA XXXIX.410.

44. *Reflections,* OA XXXIX.595.

45. *Reflections,* OA XXXIX.631.

46. *Reflections,* OA XXXIX.491.

47. *Reflections,* OA XXXIX.631.

48. Second letter to Malebranche, OA XXXIX.30.

49. *Reflections*, OA XXXIX.431.
50. *Reflections*, OA XXXIX.449.
51. In addition to the passage cited above, see TNG, OC V.180, 185.
52. *Reflections*, OA XXXIX.600. According to Arnauld, it also generates a problem of consistency for Malebranche because Malebranche does want to say that God *is* indifferent in the initial choice to create a world outside Himself.
53. *Reflections*, OA XXXIX.598–99.
54. *Reflections*, OA XXXIX.599. As Robert C. Sleigh, Jr., points out, this concern (worded in almost exactly the same way) reappears less than two years later in his criticisms of Leibniz; see *Leibniz and Arnauld: A Commentary on Their Correspondence*, pp. 45–47.
55. *Reflections*, OA XXXIX.599.
56. *Reflections*, OA XXXIX.578.
57. *Reflections*, OA XXXIX.599. As Vincent Carraud suggests, however, it is "a strangely Cartesian" Aquinas whom Arnauld is framing here; see "Arnauld: A Cartesian Theologian? Omnipotence, Freedom of Indifference, and the Creation of the Eternal Truths," in Elmar Kremer (ed.), *Interpreting Arnauld* (Toronto: University of Toronto Press, 1996), pp. 91–110, esp. 99–100.
58. *Reflections*, II.26, OA XXXIX.599–600.
59. *Reflections*, II.3, OA XXXIX.433. Carraud notes that this is Arnauld's refusal "to submit God to causality, that is, to submit His will to rationality in the form of a principle of reason" ("Arnauld: A Cartesian Theologian?"). See also Thomas Lennon, "Occasionalism, Jansenism, and Skepticism: Divine Providence and the Order of Grace," *Irish Theological Quarterly* 45 (1978): 185–90; Lennon recognizes that contrary to Malebranche's "rationally constrained" God, for Arnauld "divine self-determination [is] utterly unconstrained and thus mysterious" (p. 186).
60. I do not believe that scholars have fully appreciated how radical Arnauld's conception of God is; see my "Arnauld's God," *Journal of the History of Philosophy* (forthcoming).
61. OC VI.11.
62. Ibid.
63. Letter to Pierre Nicole, January 1684, OA II.378–79.
64. These and other sentiments are expressed in the letters collected in OC XVIII.
65. "An Examination of Père Malebranche's Opinion of Seeing All Things in God," not published until after Locke's death in 1704.
66. OD I.533a.
67. *Pensées diverses sur le comète*, written in 1680, OD III.139.
68. *Réponse aux questions d'un provincial*, OD III.825–26.
69. *Entretien de Maxime et de Thémiste*, OD IV.64a.
70. A I.3.321–22.
71. OA II.355.

72. MLRP 149.
73. A II.1.541–42.
74. A II.1.544. Leibniz read the materials from the debate by the middle of this year.
75. Letter to Hessen-Rheinfels, December 29, 1684, A II.1.544.
76. Letter to Hessen-Rheinfels, March 4/14, 1685, A II.1.544–45. See also MLRP 138–39, 194–244.
77. To Tschirnhaus, November 1684, A II.1.542.
78. See Geneviève Rodis-Lewis (ed.), *Lettres de Leibniz à Arnauld* (Paris: Presses Universitaires de France, 1952), p. 5.
79. Jacques, *Les années d'exil d'Antoine Arnauld*, 441.
80. Ibid., 439 n. 111. For a good discussion of Hessen-Rheinfels's role in the Leibniz-Arnauld correspondence, see Sleigh, *Leibniz and Arnauld*, chap. 2.
81. GP II.11; M 67.
82. *Discourse on Metaphysics*, §§1–7.
83. *Theodicy*, Preface, GP VI.43; H 67.
84. That Arnauld actually read the piece is suggested by Leibniz's claim that "Arnauld did not seem to be startled by it" (*Theodicy*, §211, GP VI.244; H 260), although, as Sleigh says, perhaps Arnauld was not startled because he did not read it (*Leibniz and Arnauld*, 18).
85. Leibniz to Ernst, December 23, 1685, A I.4.393.
86. Arnauld to Ernst, March 13, 1686, GP II.15; M 73.
87. Arnauld to Ernst, March 13, 1686, GP II.15–16; M 74.
88. Leibniz to Ernst, April 12, 1686, GP II.16; M 74–75.
89. Leibniz to Ernst, April 12, 1686, GP II.22; M 82–83.
90. Psalm 144, line 5.
91. Leibniz to Ernst, April 12, 1686, GP II.24; M 85–86.
92. Arnauld to Leibniz, May 13, 1686, GP II.25–6; M 88–89.
93. Leibniz to Ernst, April 12, 1686, GP II.19; M 78.
94. Arnauld to Leibniz, May 13, 1686, GP II.31–32; M 97.
95. *Theodicy*, §211, GP VI.244; H 260.
96. *Discourse on Metaphysics*, §5, GP IV.430–31; M 9.
97. *Theodicy*, §367, GP VI.333; H 345.
98. I agree with Sleigh's judgment here: "Had Arnauld grasped the full scope of the principle of sufficient reason in Leibniz's philosophy, in particular its application to God's will in every single act of that will, even creation, Arnauld would have been convinced that Leibniz's scheme fared no better than Malebranche's with respect to a proper account of God's freedom in creation. The fact is that Arnauld saw . . . the idea that there must be some reason for God's decision to create, other than simple appeal to his will, as the real culprit" (*Leibniz and Arnauld*, pp. 46–47).
99. Arnauld to Leibniz, May 13, 1686, GP II.31; M 96.
100. See *Summa Contra Gentiles*, II.23–24.

101. *Commentary on the First Book of Sentences*, "Ordinatio," in Gerard Etzkorn and Francis Kelley (eds.), vol. 4 of *Opera Theologica* (New York: St. Bonaventure University Press, 1979), pp. 492, 504, 506.

7: The Eternal Truths

1. At the same time, Aquinas also insists on an identity of will and wisdom in God: "In God, power, essence, will, intellect, wisdom, and justice are one and the same" (*Summa Theologiae*, Ia, Q. 25, art. 5, rep. 1).
2. *Summa Theologiae*, Ia, Q. 25, a 3.
3. For a discussion of the issue of "ordained" versus "absolute" power, see Francis Oakley, *Omnipotence, Covenant, and Order: An Excursion in the History of Ideas from Abelard to Leibniz* (Ithaca, N.Y.: Cornell University Press, 1984); and William Courtenay, *Covenant and Causality in Medieval Thought* (London: Variorum Reprints, 1984), chap. 4, "The Dialectic of Divine Omnipotence." One of the issues examined by Courtenay is whether miracles fall under God's ordained power or God's absolute power, as well as how the distinction evolves from being a way of considering possibilities that had been open to God at creation to being a way of thinking of potential divine actions.
4. Letter 12, in F. A. Wright (ed.), *Select Letters of St. Jerome* (London: Heinemann, 1933), p. 62.
5. What is in question here is not simply a matter of what God will not ever do but what, because of His nature, He truly cannot do. Thus, it really is a limitation upon God's absolute power, upon what God, being what He is, theoretically can do.
6. From the school of Anselm of Laon, quoted in Courtenay, "The Dialectic of Divine Omnipotence," p. 4. Again, while this looks like merely a distinction between God's absolute power ("according to His power") and His ordained power ("according to His justice"), I do not think that is the real issue here. I believe that what is being claimed is that even God's absolute power is limited by His justice, and that the ordained power is represented by what divine justice has in fact decreed (with God's absolute power represented by other orders of things that that justice might have or could have decreed but did not).
7. *Summa Theologiae*, Ia, Q. 25, art. 3.
8. "Ordinatio," I, d. 20, q. 1, in *Opera Theologica*, vol. 4, p. 36.
9. This is a highly contested reading of Damian's thought, first offered by J. A. Endres in "Die Dialektiker und ihre Gegner im 11. Jahrhundert," *Philosophisches Jahrbuch* 19 (1906): 20–33. More recent scholars have argued effectively against this reading; see, for example, Peter Remnant, "Peter Damian: Could God Change the Past?" *Canadian Journal of Philosophy* 8 (1978): 259–68. However, it still appears from time to time in the scholarly literature; see, for example, Oakley, *Omnipotence, Covenant, and Order*, pp. 43–44; and Marilyn McCord Adams,

William Ockham, 2 vols. (Notre Dame, Ind.: University of Notre Dame Press, 1987), vol. 2, p. 1153.

10. AT VII.72; CSM II.50.
11. Fourth Meditation, AT VII.53; CSM II.37.
12. To Mersenne, April 15, 1630, AT I.145; CSMK III.23.
13. To Mersenne, May 27, 1630, AT I.152; CSMK III.25.
14. To Mersenne, April 15, 1630, AT I.145–46; CSMK III.23.
15. To Mesland, May 2, 1644, AT IV.118–19; CSMK III.235.
16. There is a good deal of controversy in the scholarly literature over whether or not the principles of logic are included in the doctrine of the created truths; compare, for example, Amos Funkenstein, "Descartes, Eternal Truths, and the Divine Omnipotence," in Stephen Gaukroger (ed.), *Descartes: Philosophy, Mathematics and Physics* (Sussex: Harvester Press, 1980), pp. 181–95, and Harry Frankfurt, "Descartes on the Creation of the Eternal Truths," *The Philosophical Review* 86 (1977): 36–57.
17. "Sixth Replies," AT VII.432; CSM II.291.
18. "Sixth Replies," AT VII.432, 435–36; CSM II.291, 294.
19. To Mersenne, May 6, 1630, AT I.149; CSMK III.24.
20. To Mersenne, May 27, 1630, AT I.152–53; CSMK III.25–26.
21. For Arnauld, July 29, 1648, AT V.224; CSMK III.358–59.
22. To Mersenne, May 27, 1630, AT I.151–52; CSMK III.25.
23. To Mesland, May 2, 1644, AT IV.118; CSMK III.235.
24. "Sixth Replies," AT VII.431–32; CSM II.291.
25. "Sixth Replies," AT VII.432–33; CSM II.292. As Jean-Luc Marion so eloquently shows, Descartes rejects the Scholastic (Suárezian) doctrine of univocity (or analogy) applied to the divine understanding and human understanding, whereby terms employed to conceive the human can also be used to conceive the divine; see *Sur la théologie blanche de Descartes* (Paris: Presses Universitaires de France, 1981). For Descartes, "no essence can belong univocally to both God and His creatures" ("Sixth Replies," AT VII.433; CSM II.292).
26. To Mersenne, April 15, 1630, AT I.145; CSMK III.23.
27. For a study of the legacy of the doctrine among Cartesians, see Tad Schmaltz, *Radical Cartesianism*.
28. Letter to Vincent Placcius, A VI.1.59–60. My thanks to Donald Rutherford for bringing this passage to my attention.
29. Marion rightly cautions against using the label "voluntarism" for Descartes's position, insofar as it suggests a continued distinction between divine faculties, except now with will having priority over understanding—which is incompatible with Descartes's insistence that there is no such distinction in God; see *Sur la théologie blanche de Descartes*, 282–96. However, the term, while misleading in this way, does serve well to highlight the fact that for Descartes, the eternal truths are dependent on God's causal power, even if His willing those truths is identical with His understanding them.

30. *Discourse on Metaphysics*, §2, GP IV.427; M 4.

31. *Discourse on Metaphysics*, §2, GP IV.427–28; M 4–5. Marion argues that in formulating his critique of Descartes's doctrine, Leibniz willfully misreads it to introduce a priority of will and understanding in God; see "De la création des vérités éternelles au principe de la raison. Remarques sur l'anti-Cartésianisme de Spinoza, Malebranche, Leibniz," *XVIIe siècle* 37 (1985): 143–64.

32. "Reflections on the Common Concept of Justice," L 562.

33. *Theodicy*, §175–76, GP VI.218–19; H 236–37.

34. *Search After Truth*, Elucidation 10, OC III.132; LO 615.

35. *Dialogues on Metaphysics*, IX.13, OC XII.220–21; JS 168–69.

36. *Search After Truth*, Elucidation 8, OC III.85; LO 587.

37. A I.13.11.

38. *Dialogues on Metaphysics*, VIII.11, OC XII.188–89; JS 140–41.

39. The *Conclusiones Philosophicae* can be found at OA XXXVIII.1–8.

40. As Denis Moreau observes, "contrary to a certain tradition, in philosophical Paris of the 1640s debates over the univocity of being were far from being forgotten, abandoned, or outdated"; see TP 5.

41. Medieval univocalists include John Duns Scotus ("I say that God is conceived not only in a concept analogous to the concept of a creature, that is, one that is wholly other than that which is predicated of creatures, but even in some concept univocal to Himself and to a creature," *Opus oxoniense* I, Dist. III, Q. 1; Duns Scotus, *Philosophical Writings*, ed. Allan Wolter [Indianapolis: Hackett, 1987], p. 19); and William of Ockham, who insists that unless concepts derivable from creatures were applicable to God, "then in this life we could not arrive at a cognition of God's wisdom . . . through the wisdom of a creature any more than, through the cognition of a stone, we obtain a cognition that God is a stone" (*Reportatio* III, Q. 8; Ockham, *Philosophical Writings*, ed. Philotheus Bohner [Indianapolis: Hackett, 1990], p. 112). Aquinas tried to steer a middle course between univocity and equivocity with his doctrine of analogy: terms predicated of human beings can also be predicated of God in a different but related (analogical) sense.

42. OA XXXVIII.i.

43. Replies to Second Objections, AT IX.108.

44. Arnauld had a few scruples to overcome before committing himself to the Cartesian philosophy; on this, see Steven Nadler, "Arnauld, Descartes, and Transubstantiation: Reconciling Cartesian Metaphysics and Real Presence."

45. OA X.vii–viii. Denis Moreau argues in *Deux Cartésiens* that, in fact, Arnauld's entire campaign against Malebranche, and especially the argument against the Vision in God in *On True and False Ideas*, is directed at the doctrine of univocity.

46. This has led to a debate over whether or not Arnauld adopts the creation of the eternal truths doctrine. See Henri Gouhier, *Cartésianisme et Augustinisme au XVIIème siècle* (Paris: J. Vrin, 1978), p. 156; André Robinet, "Avant Propos," in Ndiaye, *La Philosophie d'Antoine Arnauld*, p. 8; A.-R. Ndiaye, "Le Statut des

vérités éternelles dans la philosophie d'Antoine Arnauld: Cartésianisme ou Augustinisme?" in *Antoine Arnauld (1612–1694): Philosophe, écrivain, théologien, Chroniques de Port-Royal* 44 (Paris: Bibliothèque Mazarine, 1995), 283–96; and Emmanuel Faye, "The Cartesianism of Desgabets and Arnauld and the Problem of the Eternal Truths," *Oxford Studies in Early Modern Philosophy* 2 (2005): 193–209. All of these scholars argue that Arnauld rejects the doctrine. On the other hand, see Moreau, *Deux Cartésiens* (chap. 6) for a persuasive argument that Arnauld agrees with Descartes; see also Jean Laporte, *La Doctrine de Port-Royal*, vol. 2, part 1, *Les Vérités de la grace*, 335.

47. GP II.38; M 106.
48. GP II.49; M 121.
49. *Reflections*, OA XXXIX.599.
50. *Reflections*, OA XXXIX.599–600.
51. *Reflections*, OA XXXIX.578.
52. *Reflections*, OA XXXIX.493.
53. Gilles Olivo makes this point with respect to Descartes; see *Descartes et l'essence de la vérité* (Paris: Presses Universitaires de France, 2005), 355–57.
54. The same basic dispute occurs in intellectual circles in England during this period—for example, there is the confrontation between the extreme divine voluntarism of Hobbes and the divine rationalism of the Cambridge Platonists. For a discussion of the debate as it occurs on the other side of the English Channel, see Stephen M. Fallon, " 'To Act or Not': Milton's Conception of Divine Freedom," *Journal of the History of Ideas* 49 (1988): 425–49.
55. *Political Treatise*, J. H. Robinson, ed., *Readings in European History*, 2 vols. (Boston: Ginn, 1906), 2:274.
56. See Fallon, " 'To Act or Not,' " p. 8.

8: The Specter of Spinoza

1. For a fuller discussion of Leibniz's meeting with Spinoza, see the account in Matthew Stewart, *The Courtier and the Heretic: Leibniz, Spinoza, and the Fate of God in the Modern World* (New York: W. W. Norton and Co., 2006). Their philosophical relationship has been much studied; see Georges Friedmann, *Leibniz et Spinoza,* 2nd ed. (Paris: Gallimard, 1964); *Studia Leibnitiana, Supplementa* 18 (1978); and *Studia Spinozana* 6 (1990), "Spinoza and Leibniz."
2. Jacob Freudenthal, ed., *Die Lebensgeschichte Spinoza's* (Leipzig: Verlag Von Veit, 1899), p. 74.
3. For a full biographical account, see Nadler, *Spinoza: A Life*.
4. The Hebrew text is no longer extant, but the Portuguese version is in the Book of Ordinances (*Livro dos Acordos de Naçao e Ascamot*), in the Municipal Archives of the City of Amsterdam, Archives for the Portuguese Jewish Community in Amsterdam, 334, no. 19, fol. 408.

5. For an extended examination of this question, see Steven Nadler, *Spinoza's Heresy: Immortality and the Jewish Mind* (Oxford: Oxford University Press, 2002).

6. A II.1.66.

7. A I.1.48. For a discussion of the differences among Leibniz's responses to Spinoza's works, see Stewart, *Courtier and the Heretic*, chap. 7.

8. A II.1.171.

9. Ep. 45, G IV.231–34.

10. Ep. 70, G IV.301–303; S 327–28.

11. Ep. 72, G IV.305; S 330–31.

12. Freudenthal, *Die Lebensgeschichte Spinoza's*, 201.

13. A II.1.271–72.

14. Freudenthal, *Die Lebensgeschichte Spinoza's*, p. 220.

15. A II.1.379–80.

16. For example, *Theodicy*, §173, GP VI.217; H 234–35. For Leibniz's commentary on the *Ethics*, see A VI.4b.1764–777.

17. A VI.6.73. There is a great deal of debate concerning the extent to which Leibniz did or did not have a Spinozist period in his intellectual development. For example, Stewart (*Courtier and the Heretic*), following Ludwig Stein (*Leibniz und Spinoza: Ein Beitrag zur Entwicklungsgeschichte der Leibnizischen Philosophie* [Berlin: Georg Reimer, 1890]) argues that he did; Friedmann (*Leibniz et Spinoza*) insists that he did not.

18. *Ethics*, IP15S[VI], G II.60; C 424.

19. *Ethics*, IP15S[I], G II.57; C 421.

20. *Ethics*, I, Appendix, G II.78; C 439–40.

21. *Ethics*, I, Appendix, G II.78–79; C 440–41.

22. Ep. 23, G IV.148; S 166.

23. Ep. 56, G IV.260; S 277.

24. *Ethics*, I, Appendix, G II.80–81; C 443.

25. *Ethics*, IP17, G II.61; C 425.

26. *Ethics*, IP33S2, G II.76; C 438–39.

27. *Ethics*, IP17S1, G II.62; C 426.

28. *Ethics*, IP33, G II.73; C 436.

29. A II.1.117; L 146. Leibniz may be trying to pull back at the last minute when, in the next line, he says that "this in no way detracts from freedom. For it is the highest freedom to be impelled to the best by a right reason." The door to necessitarianism has been opened, however, and it is not clear whether Leibniz can close it simply by substituting reasons that "impel" rather than necessitate.

30. In his comments on some letters from Spinoza to Oldenburg that Oldenburg allowed Leibniz to see when he was in London on the way to The Hague, Leibniz singles out as standing in need of explanation Spinoza's claim that "all things follow from the nature of God with an inevitable necessity." He provides the following gloss: "The world could not have been produced in any other way, since God is not able not to act in the most perfect manner. For since He is perfectly

wise, he chooses the best" (A VI.3.364). For a more extensive discussion of Leibniz's views on this, see Robert M. Adams, *Leibniz: Determinist, Theist, Idealist*, chap. 1.

31. The issue appears in the notes that Leibniz prepared before their meeting; Couturat, 529–30; L 168–69.

32. A VI.4b.1776; L 204.

33. Another strategy adopted by Leibniz is to claim that while the world chosen by God is the best of all possible worlds, it is not necessarily the best of all possible worlds. Therefore, the claim that God chooses this world is not absolutely necessary. See, for example, Grua II.493.

34. Grua I.289.

35. "On Freedom," L 263.

36. *Theodicy*, §45, GP VI.128; H 148.

37. GP IV.299; AG 242.

38. A VI.3.474–75.

39. *Theodicy*, §173, GP VI.217; H 234.

40. This issue is a major theme of the correspondence between Malebranche and Jean-Jacques Dortous de Mairan; see *Correspondance avec J.-J. Dortous de Mairan*, ed. Joseph Moreau (Paris: J. Vrin, 1947), and especially Moreau's introduction, "Malebranche et le Spinozisme," pp. 2–98.

41. "On Nature Itself," GP IV.515; L 507.

42. Quoted in Jean-Christophe Bardout, *Malebranche et la métaphysique* (Paris: Presses Universitaires de France, 1999), p. 228. See also Jonathan Israel, *Radical Enlightenment: Philosophy and the Making of Modernity, 1650–1750* (Oxford: Oxford University Press, 2001), p. 353.

43. *Dialogues on Metaphysics*, VIII.9, OC XII.186; JS 138.

44. *Dialogues on Metaphysics*, IX.2, OC XII.199–200; JS 150.

45. Malebranche's first letter to De Mairan, OC XIX.854.

46. OA III.406.

47. OA X.xv–xvi.

Epilogue

1. OA XLII, letter 47.

2. OA III, letter 983.

3. Quoted in Jacques, *Les Années d'exil d'Antoine Arnauld*, p. 701.

4. André, *La Vie de R. P. Malebranche*, p. 301.

5. Ibid., pp. 419–20.

6. For an account of this illness, see André, *La Vie de R. P. Malebranche*, pp. 264–65.

7. OC XIII.365.

8. GP III.673.

Bibliography

Abercrombie, Nigel. *The Origins of Jansenism* (Oxford: Clarendon Press, 1936).

Adams, Marilyn McCord. *William Ockham*, 2 vols. (Notre Dame, Ind.: University of Notre Dame Press, 1987).

Adams, Robert M. "Must God Create the Best?" *The Philosophical Review* 81 (1972): 317–32.

———. *Leibniz: Determinist, Theist, Idealist* (Oxford: Oxford University Press, 1994).

Aiton, E. J. *Leibniz: A Biography* (Bristol and Boston: Adam Hilger, 1985).

Alquié, Ferdinand. *Le Cartésianisme de Malebranche* (Paris: J. Vrin, 1974).

André, Yves Marie. *La Vie de R. P. Malebranche* (Paris, 1886; reprinted Geneva: Slatkine, 1970).

Antognazza, Maria Rosa. *Leibniz: A Biography* (Cambridge: Cambridge University Press, 2008).

Armogathe, Jean-Robert. *Theologia Cartesiana* (The Hague: Martinus Nijhoff, 1977).

Baillet, Adrien. *La Vie de Monsieur Descartes*, 2 vols. (Paris: Daniel Horthemels, 1691; reprinted New York and London: Garland, 1987).

Bardout, Jean-Christophe. *Malebranche et la métaphysique* (Paris: Presses Universitaires de France, 1999).

Bouillier, Francisque. *Histoire de la philosophie Cartésienne*, 2 vols. (Paris: Delagrave, 1868).

Brown, Stuart. "The Leibniz-Foucher Alliance and Its Philosophical Bases." In Paul Lodge, ed., *Leibniz and His Correspondents* (Cambridge: Cambridge University Press, 2004), 74–96.

Carraud, Vincent. "Arnauld: A Cartesian Theologian? Omnipotence, Freedom of In-difference, and the Creation of the Eternal Truths." In Elmar Kremer, ed., *Interpreting Arnauld* (Toronto: University of Toronto Press, 1996), 91–110.

Courtenay, William. *Covenant and Causality in Medieval Thought* (London: Variorum Reprints, 1984).

Cousin, Victor. *Oeuvres*. 3 vols. (Brussels, 1841).

Dibon, Paul, ed. *Pierre Bayle: Le Philosophe de Rotterdam* (Amsterdam: Elsevier, 1959).

Divers actes, lettres, et relations des religieuses de Port-Royal du Saint-Sacrament touchant au sujet de la signature du formulaire. 3 vols. (Utrecht, 1735).

Duns Scotus, Johannes. *Philosophical Writings*. Ed. Allan Wolter. (Indianapolis: Hackett, 1987).

Endres, J. A. "Die Dialektiker und ihre Gegner im 11. Jahrhundert." *Philosophisches Jahrbuch* 19 (1906): 20–33.

Fakhry, Majid. *Islamic Occasionalism and Its Critique by Averroës and Avicenna* (London: Allen and Unwin, 1958).

Fallon, Stephen M. " 'To Act or Not': Milton's Conception of Divine Freedom." *Journal of the History of Ideas* 49 (1988): 425–49.

Faye, Emmanuel. "The Cartesianism of Desgabets and Arnauld and the Problem of the Eternal Truths." *Oxford Studies in Early Modern Philosophy* 2 (2005): 193–209.

Fontaine, Nicolas. *Mémoires pour servir à l'histoire de Port-Royal*. 2 vols. (Utrecht, 1736); republished as *Mémoires ou histoire des Solitaires de Port-Royal* (Paris: Honoré Champion, 2001).

Frankfurt, Harry. "Descartes on the Creation of the Eternal Truths." *The Philosophical Review* 86 (1977): 36–57.

Freudenthal, Jacob, ed. *Die Lebensgeschichte Spinoza's* (Leipzig: Verlag Von Veit, 1899).

Friedmann, Georges. *Leibniz et Spinoza*. 2nd ed. (Paris: Gallimard, 1964).

Funkenstein, Amos. "Descartes, Eternal Truths, and the Divine Omnipotence." In Stephen Gaukroger, ed., *Descartes: Philosophy, Mathematics and Physics* (Sussex: Harvester Press, 1980), 181–95.

Garber, Daniel. "Leibniz and the Foundations of Physics: The Middle Years." In Kathleen Okruhlik and Gregory Brown, eds., *The Natural Philosophy of Leibniz* (Dordrecht: Reidel, 1985), 27–129.

———. *Descartes's Metaphysical Physics* (Chicago: University of Chicago Press, 1990).

Garber, Daniel, and Michael Ayers, eds. *The Cambridge History of Seventeenth-Century Philosophy*. 2 vols. (Cambridge: Cambridge University Press, 1998).

Gouhier, Henri. *Cartésianisme et Augustinisme au XVIIième siècle* (Paris: J. Vrin, 1978).

Huet, Pierre-Daniel. *Against Cartesian Philosophy*. Ed. and trans. Thomas M. Lennon (Amherst, N.Y.: Humanity Books, 2005).

Israel, Jonathan. *Radical Enlightenment: Philosophy and the Making of Modernity, 1650–1750* (Oxford: Oxford University Press, 2001).

Jacques, Emile. *Les Années d'exil d'Antoine Arnauld* (Louvain: Publications Universitaires de Louvain, 1976).

Jones, Colin. *Paris: The Biography of a City* (New York: Viking, 2005).

Jurieu, Pierre. *La Politique du clergé de France*, 2nd ed. (Cologne: Pierre Martean, 1681).

Kremer, Elmar. "Grace and Free Will in Arnauld." In Elmar Kremer, ed., *The Great Arnauld and Some of His Philosophical Correspondents* (Toronto: University of Toronto Press, 1994), 219–39.

Labrousse, Elisabeth. *Pierre Bayle*. 2 vols. (The Hague: Martinus Nijhoff, 1963–64).

Laporte, Jean. *La Doctrine de Port-Royal*. Vol. 2, part I: *Les Vérités de la grace* (Paris: Presses Universitaires de France, 1923).

Larmore, Charles. *Modernité et morale* (Paris: Presses Universitaires de France, 1993).

Leibniz, Gottfried Wilhelm. *Essais de Théodicée*. Ed. Jacques Brunschwig. (Paris: Garnier-Flammarion, 1969).

———. *Lettres de Leibniz à Arnauld*. Ed. Geneviève Rodis-Lewis (Paris: Presses Universitaires de France, 1952).

Lennon, Thomas M. "Occasionalism, Jansenism, and Skepticism: Divine Providence and the Order of Grace." *Irish Theological Quarterly* 45 (1978): 185–90.

Maimonides. *Guide of the Perplexed*. 2 vols. Trans. Shlomo Pines. (Chicago: University of Chicago Press, 1963).

Malebranche, Nicolas. *Correspondance avec J.-J. Dortous de Mairan*. Ed. Joseph Moreau (Paris: J. Vrin, 1947).

Marion, Jean-Luc. *Sur la théologie blanche de Descartes* (Paris: Presses Universitaires de France, 1981).

———. "De la creation des vérités éternelles au principe de la raison. Remarques sur l'anti-cartésianisme de Spinoza, Malebranche, Leibniz." *XVIIe siècle* 37 (1985): 143–64.

Mémoires sur la destruction de l'abbaye de Port-Royal des Champs. 2 vols. (Utrecht, 1759).

Mercer, Christia. *Leibniz's Metaphysics: Its Origins and Development* (Cambridge and New York: Cambridge University Press, 2001).

Moreau, Denis. *Deux Cartésiens: La Polémique Arnauld-Malebranche* (Paris: J. Vrin, 1999).

———. "Malebranche on Disorder and Physical Evil: Manicheanism or Philosophical Courage?" In Elmar Kremer and Michael Latzer, eds. *The Problem of Evil in Early Modern Philosophy* (Toronto: University of Toronto Press, 2001), 81–100.

Nadler, Steven. "Arnauld, Descartes, and Transubstantiation: Reconciling Cartesian Metaphysics and Real Presence." *Journal of the History of Ideas* 49 (1988): 229–46.

———. "Cartesianism and Port-Royal." *The Monist* 71 (1988): 573–84.

———. *Arnauld and the Cartesian Philosophy of Ideas* (Princeton, N.J.: Princeton University Press, 1989).

———. *Malebranche and Ideas* (Oxford: Oxford University Press, 1992).

———. "Occasionalism and General Will in Malebranche." *Journal of the History of Philosophy* 31 (1993): 31–47.

———. "Occasionalism and the Question of Arnauld's Cartesianism." In Roger Ariew and Marjorie Grene, eds., *Descartes and His Contemporaries* (Chicago: University of Chicago Press, 1995), 129–44.

———. *Spinoza: A Life* (Cambridge and New York: Cambridge University Press, 1999).

———. "Malebranche on Causation." In Steven Nadler, ed., *The Cambridge Companion to Malebranche* (Cambridge and New York: Cambridge University Press, 2000), 112–38.

———. *Spinoza's Heresy: Immortality and the Jewish Mind* (Oxford: Oxford University Press, 2002).

———. "Arnauld's God." *Journal of the History of Philosophy* (forthcoming).

Ndiaye, Aloyse-Raymond. *La Philosophie d'Antoine Arnauld* (Paris: J. Vrin, 1991).

———. "Le Statut des vérités éternelles dans la philosophie d'Antoine Arnauld: Cartésianisme ou Augustinisme?" In *Antoine Arnauld (1612–1694): Philosophe, écrivain, théologien, Chroniques de Port-Royal* 44 (Paris: Bibliothèque Mazarine, 1995), 283–96.

Oakley, Francis. *Omnipotence, Covenant, and Order: An Excursion in the History of Ideas from Abelard to Leibniz* (Ithaca, N.Y.: Cornell University Press, 1984).

Olivo, Gilles. *Descartes et l'essence de la vérité* (Paris: Presses Universitaires de France, 2005).

Pascal, Blaise. *The Provincial Letters* (Harmondsworth: Penguin, 1967).

Pellegrin, Marie-Frédérique. *Le Système de la loi de Nicolas Malebranche* (Paris: J. Vrin, 2006).

Redondi, Pietro. *Galileo Heretic* (Princeton, N.J.: Princeton University Press, 1989).

Remnant, Peter. "Peter Damian: Could God Change the Past?" *Canadian Journal of Philosophy* 8 (1978): 259–68.

Rescher, Nicholas. *Leibniz: An Introduction to His Philosophy* (Lanham, Md.: University Press of America, 1979).

Riley, Patrick. *The General Will Before Rousseau: The Transformation of the Divine into the Civic* (Princeton, N.J.: Princeton University Press, 1986).

Robinet, André. "L'aphilosophie de P. Bayle devant les philosophies de Malebranche et Leibniz." In Paul Dibon, ed., *Pierre Bayle: Le Philosophe de Rotterdam* (Amsterdam: Elsevier, 1959), 48–61.

———. *Système et existence dans l'oeuvre de Malebranche* (Paris: J. Vrin, 1965).

Robinson, Howard. *Bayle the Skeptic* (New York: Columbia University Press, 1931).

Robinson, J. H., ed. *Readings in European History*. 2 vols. (Boston: Ginn, 1906).

Ross, George MacDonald. "Leibniz and the Nuremberg Alchemical Society." *Studia Leibnitiana* 6 (1974): 222–48.

———. "Leibniz and the Concept of Metaphysical Perfection." *Studia Leibnitiana*, Sonderheft 21 (1992): 143–52.

Russell, Bertrand. *A Critical Exposition of the Philosophy of Leibniz*. 2nd ed. (London: George Allen and Unwin, 1937).

Rutherford, Donald. "Natures, Laws and Miracles: The Roots of Leibniz's Critique of Occasionalism." In Steven Nadler, ed., *Causation in Early Modern Philosophy: Cartesianism, Occasionalism and Preestablished Harmony* (University Park: Penn State Press, 1993), 135–58.

————. *Leibniz and the Rational Order of Nature* (Cambridge: Cambridge University Press, 1995).

————. "Malebranche's Theodicy." In Steven Nadler, ed., *The Cambridge Companion to Malebranche* (Cambridge: Cambridge University Press, 2000), 165–89.

Saint-Beuve, Charles Augustin. *Port-Royal*. 7 vols. (Paris: La Connaissance, 1928).

Schmaltz, Tad. *Radical Cartesianism: The French Reception of Descartes* (Cambridge: Cambridge University Press, 2002).

Scribano, Emanuela. "False Enemies: Malebranche, Leibniz, and the Best of All Possible Worlds." *Oxford Studies in Early Modern Philosophy* 1 (2003): 165–82.

Sedgwick, Alexander. *Jansenism in Seventeenth-Century France: Voices from the Wilderness* (Charlottesville: University Press of Virginia, 1977).

————. *The Travails of Conscience: The Arnauld Family and the Ancien Régime* (Cambridge, Mass.: Harvard University Press, 1998).

Sleigh, Jr., Robert C. *Leibniz and Arnauld: A Commentary on Their Correspondence* (New Haven, Conn.: Yale University Press, 1990).

————. "Arnauld on Efficacious Grace and Free Choice." In Elmar Kremer, ed., *Interpreting Arnauld* (Toronto: University of Toronto Press, 1996), 164–75.

Stein, Ludwig. *Leibniz und Spinoza: Ein Beitrag zur Entwicklungsgeschichte der Leibnizischen Philosophie* (Berlin: Georg Reimer, 1890).

Stewart, Matthew. *The Courtier and the Heretic: Leibniz, Spinoza, and the Fate of God in the Modern World* (New York: W. W. Norton and Co., 2006).

Watson, Richard A. *The Downfall of Cartesianism* (The Hague: Martinus Nijhoff, 1966).

William of Ockham. *Opera Theologica*. Ed. Gerard Etzkorn and Francis Kelley (New York: St. Bonaventure University Press, 1979).

————. *Philosophical Writings*. Ed. Philotheus Bohner (Indianapolis: Hackett, 1990).

Wilson, Catherine. "Leibnizian Optimism." *Journal of Philosophy* 80 (1983): 765–83.

————. *Leibniz's Metaphysics: A Historical and Comparative Study* (Princeton, N.J.: Princeton University Press, 1989).

Acknowledgments

I am extremely grateful to Donald Rutherford, Elliott Sober, and Red Watson for generously taking the time to read and comment on the manuscript of this book in its various stages. Their help on philosophical issues, historical detail, and literary style was invaluable. For their critical and insightful discussion of some of the book's themes, I would also like to thank Denis Moreau, Elmar Kremer, Tad Schmaltz, Daniel Garber, and audiences at the University of Wisconsin–Madison Center for Renaissance and Early Modern Studies, the Leibniz-Spinoza Conference at Princeton University in the fall of 2007, the Philosophy Faculty Seminar at the University of Amsterdam, the Montreal Interuniversity Workshop in the History of Philosophy, and the Philosophy Department at McGill University.

Research for this book was supported by much-appreciated funding from the University of Wisconsin–Madison: the Graduate School, the College of Letters and Science, and the Mosse/Weinstein Center for Jewish Studies, with additional support coming from the Max and Frieda Weinstein/Bascom Professorship of Jewish Studies, of which I have been honored to be the holder, and a Kellett Mid-Career Award.

Finally, I wish to extend my heartfelt thanks to Andrew Stuart, of the Stuart Agency, for his impressive efforts on behalf of this project; and especially to Eric Chinski, at Farrar, Straus and Giroux, not only for his great sympathy for a philosophical study but also for his devotion to helping make this book as good as it could be.

In the past, I have dedicated books to my wife, Jane Bernstein, and to our children, Rose and Ben. They all know they have my unconditional love and absolute devotion. But this book is for Richard A. ("Red") Watson, who, in my first semester of college, inspired in me a passion for the joys of philosophy. He continues to be my teacher and mentor, but now I am pleased also to be able to call him my friend.

Index

A

Abelard, Peter, 24

absolutism, royal, 213, 214

"Abstract Theory of Motion," 9, 13

Académie des Inscriptions et Belles-Lettres, 15

Académie des Sciences, 9, 13, 17, 48, 49; Cartesianism and, 34–35; founding of, 15, 18; Leibniz's election to, 19, 54–55, 248; Malebranche's election to, 247

Académie Française, 15

Académie Royale d'Architecture, 15

Académie Royale de Peinture et de Sculpture, 15

Acta Eruditorum, 168

Adam and Eve, 124, 156, 177

Adam of Balsham (Adam Parvipontanus, or Adam du Petit Pont), 24

André, Father Yves, 43, 114, 143, 144, 247–48

anthropomorphization of nature of God: Arnauld's objection to, xi, 162–63, 181–82, 211; Descartes's objection to, xi; Spinoza's criticism of, 221–22, 227–28, 229

Apology for M. Jansenius, Bishop of Ypres (Arnauld), 62

Aquinas, Thomas, 25, 162, 186; on best of all possible worlds, 95; on omnipotence of God, 186–87, 189; problem of evil, 85, 87, 98, 152; rationality of God, 182

Aristotelian philosophy, 24–25; Cartesianism as challenge to, 27, 30; Leibniz on, 37; as mandated curriculum in seventeenth-century France, 25–26, 27; matter and form in, 27–28; natural science and, 24–25, 28–29

Arnauld, Antoine ("Le Grand Arnauld"), x, xi, 33, 53–77, 141–83, 196, 241; *Apology for M. Jansenius, Bishop of Ypres*, 62; birth of, 53;

Arnauld, Antoine (*cont.*)
  Cartesianism and, xi, 67–69, 148,
  207; death of, 247; *Defense of Monsieur
  Arnauld, Doctor of the Sorbonne, Against
  the Response to the Book on True and
  False Ideas*, 164–65; *Dissertation of
  Monsieur Arnauld, Doctor of the Sorbonne, on the Manner in Which God
  Performed Frequent Miracles of the
  Ancient Law Through the Ministry of
  Angels*, 165; on divine freedom, 161–
  62, 163, 167, 174, 177, 179, 180–81;
  eternal truths and, 208–11, 213, 214;
  in exile, 53, 62, 64, 108–109, 141–
  42, 144–45, 169, 246; final years of,
  246–47; on freedom of the will, 65–
  67; on grace, 62, 65, 113–14, 150–
  51, 163–64; *Great Perpetuity of Faith
  on the Eucharist*, 71; on inscrutability
  of God, 158–60, 244; as Jansenist,
  58–65, 72, 113, 214; -Leibniz correspondence, *see* Leibniz-Arnauld correspondence; -Malebranche debate,
  142–67, 168–69, 182, 239, 240,
  246–47; -Malebranche friendship,
  75–76, 147, 169; *On Frequent Communion*, 61–62; *On True and False
  Ideas*, 149, 164, 169; *Philosophical and
  Theological Reflections on the New System of Nature and Grace*, 150–51, 154,
  158–59, 160, 164, 166–67, 168, 179,
  239–40; "Philosophical Conclusions,"
  206; "predestination without prescience," 56; on problem of evil, 211–
  12; *Second Apology for Jansenius*, 168;
  Spinoza and, 238–40; as teacher of
  philosophy, 205–206, 207; temperament of, 59, 60–61, 146, 148, 207,
  242; youth of, 58
Arnauld, Antoine (father), 53, 58
Arnauld, Antoine (grandfather), 53–54
Arnauld, Catherine Marion
  (mother), 53

Arnauld, Henri (brother), 246
Arnauld, Jacqueline (sister) (Mère
  Angélique), 54, 58, 60, 64
Arnauld, Jeanne (sister), 54, 58
Arnauld d'Andilly, Robert (brother), 53,
  59, 246
Arnauld de Pomponne, Simon, 14, 16,
  20, 52, 65, 71, 73
Arnauld family, 53–54, 59
Aubert de Versé, Noel, 237
Augustine, St., 42, 56, 148; Jansenists
  and Augustinianism, 54–55; *Pensées*,
  159; problem of evil, 85, 86–87;
  theory of divine illumination, 44
Augustinus (Jansen), 54, 60, 63, 64, 65
Averroës, 85

B

Bayle, Pierre (*le philosophe de Rotterdam*),
  80–85, 110, 112–13; Arnauld-
  Malebranche debate and, 166–67,
  169; background of, 80; death of, 92;
  Diverse Thoughts on the Comet, 81; on
  God's freedom, 135; *Historical and
  Critical Dictionary*, 80–82, 89–90,
  167; -Leibniz dialogue, 90–92, 102;
  Response to a Provincial's Questions,
  91–92
Benedictines, 34
Berlin Society of Sciences, 249
Bernard, Jacques, 91
Berrand, Pierre, 164
Bérulle, Cardinal Pierre de, 42–43
best of all possible worlds, 231–32;
  Aquinas on, 95; Malebranche and,
  114–15, 129–31
best of all possible worlds (Leibniz's
  theodicy), 18, 22, 75, 94–96, 98–
  107, 129, 130, 131, 171, 233–35,
  244; bad elements accentuating the
  good, 100–101, 116, 131–32, 180;

Bayle's challenge to, 102; *Candide* as
satire of, 96–98; Cartesian position
on eternal truths and, 199–200, 211;
God as rational being, xi, 133–36,
139–40, 181, 182, 198, 204, 213,
214, 215, 235; happiness in, 105, 106;
"harmony" and, 104–105; Leibniz-
Arnauld correspondence and, 178–
82; as metaphysically superior, 103;
simplicity of law and, 103–104, 106
Boineberg, Baron Johann Christian von,
7, 8, 10, 14, 16, 20–21, 70–71,
72, 73
Boineberg, Philipp Wilhelm, 20, 21
Bossuet, Bishop Jacques-Bénigne, 127–
28, 213
Bouillier, Francisque, 34
Boxel, Hugo, 229
Boyle, Robert, 19, 30
Brunswick-Lüneburg, House of, 196–
97, 250

C

calculus, invention of, 18, 19, 249
Calvinism, 57, 141–42, 164; religious
wars and, 4, 5–6
Candide, 96–98
Caroline, Princess (later queen of
England), 250
Cartesian circle, problem of the, 68
Cartesianism, 30–36; *see also* Descartes,
René; Arnauld and, xi, 67–69, 148,
207; causation and, 46, 79; as challenge to Aristotelian philosophy, 27,
30; dualist principle of mind and
body, 31, 32, 69; Leibniz and, 36–42,
109–10; Malebranche and, 42, 43,
44, 108, 109, 111, 148, 237; mechanistic explanation of natural world,
31–32; Spinoza and, 218–19; as
threat to Catholic Church, 27,

32–33, 34; transubstantiation and,
32–33, 34, 69
Cassini, Giovanni, 17
Catholic Church, *see* Roman Catholic
Church
Catholic Demonstrations (Leibniz), 12
causation: Aristotelian teachings, 24;
Cartesian theory, 46, 79; Leibniz on,
79–80; "occasionalism," 45–48, 49,
79, 81, 82, 110, 111, 117, 178, 197,
236–37; Spinoza on, 222
Censure of Cartesian Philosophy (Huet), 35
Christ, in Malebranche's theodicy, 116,
127
Christian Conversations (Malebranche),
109, 111, 113, 136, 169
Christina, Queen of Sweden, 26
circular reasoning, 68
Clarke, Samuel, 249–50
Clement IX, Pope, 65
Clerselier, Claude, 26, 35
Colbert, Jean-Baptiste, 14, 15, 18, 78
color: Aristotelian explanation of, 28;
Cartesian explanation of, 30–31
"Concrete Theory of Motion," 9
"Confession of a Philosopher, The," 75,
139, 171, 178
Confessions of Augsburg of 1530, 11
Congregation of the Oratory, 34,
42–43; Malebranche as member of,
see Malebranche, Nicolas
"consider the whole" approach, to
problem of evil, 87–89, 91, 100–101,
152–53, 244
constitutional monarchies, 213–14
continuum, problem of the, 9–10, 18
"Conversations of Philarète and Ariste,"
110
Corneille, Pierre, 17
Council of Trent, 11, 12, 72
Counter-Reformation, 5, 72
Critique of the Search After Truth
(Foucher), 36

D

Damian, Peter, 189
Defense of Monsieur Arnauld, Doctor of the Sorbonne, Against the Response to the Book on True and False Ideas (Arnauld), 164–65
de la Barde, Léonor, 205–206, 207
de Mansveld, Régnier, 219
Denmark, 4, 5
De Roucy, Marquis, 142–47, 144, 146
de Sallo, Denis, 78
Descartes, René, xi, 9, 29, 30, 42; *see also* Cartesianism; death and interment of, 25–26; *Discourse on Method,* 27; on divine freedom, 195–96, 235–36; divine voluntarism, 190–96, 204, 215; doctrine of equivocity, 207; *Meditations, see Meditations on First Philosophy* (Descartes); *Principles of Philosophy,* 27
de Sévigné, Madame, 34, 141
Dialogue Between a Christian Philosopher and a Chinese Philosopher (Malebranche), 249
Dialogues on Death (Malebranche), 248
Dialogues on Metaphysics and on Religion (Malebranche), 110–11, 114–15, 123, 132, 201–202
Discourse on Metaphysics (Leibniz), 132, 170–82, 214; Arnauld and, 170–82
Discourse on Method (Descartes), 27
Dissertation of Monsieur Arnauld, Doctor of the Sorbonne, on the Manner in Which God Performed Frequent Miracles of the Ancient Law Through the Ministry of Angels (Arnauld), 165
Diverse Thoughts on the Comet (Bayle), 81
divine illumination, Augustine's theory of, 44
divine voluntarism, 190–96, 204, 214–16; Descartes's, 190–96, 204, 215;

religious moral fundamentalism and, 244–45; Spinoza on, 231
Dutch Republic: Arnauld in exile in, 141–42, 144, 218; French invasion of, 6–7, 13, 20; *see also* Netherlands
du Vaucel, Louis-Paul, 170, 238, 246

E

Edict of Nantes of 1598, 4
Egyptian plan, Leibniz's, 13, 20, 52, 71
Elzevier, Daniel, 142, 144, 145
England: European warfare and, 4, 5; Leibniz in, 217–18
Enlightenment, 243
Epicurus, 85
equivocity, doctrine of, 205, 208
Essay Concerning Human Understanding (Locke), 92
Essays on Theodicy, on the Goodness of God, the Freedom of Man and the Origin of Evil (Theodicy) (Leibniz), 92–96, 98–107, 128, 171, 236; Malebranche and, 110–12; public response to, 110
eternal truths, 188–216; Arnauld and, 208–11, 213, 214, 215, 241; divine voluntarism, 190–96, 204, 214–16; laws of logic, 189–90, 192–93, 195, 203; Leibniz on, 198–200; Malebranche on, 200–204; mathematical principles, 188, 189, 191–92, 200–201, 202, 203; noncontradiction, principle of, 84, 189, 193, 203
Ethics (Spinoza), 221–22; anthropomorphism of God, criticism of, 227–28, 229; debunking of divine providence, 220–21; God as Nature, 222, 227–28, 230–31, 236; Leibniz and, 224–25, 227, 233, 236; Malebranche's

reaction to, 237–38; posthumous publication of, 219; sectarian religion, attack on, 228–29, 230

ethics, legacy of seventeenth-century philosophers for, 244–46

Eucharist, 12, 70, 71; Cartesianism and, 32–33, 34, 69

Euthyphro Problem, 184–86, 187–88; Descartes's views of God's omnipotence, 190–96; Leibniz's position, 199, 242; Malebranche's position on, 242; religious moral fundamentalism and, 244

evil, problem of (theodicy), 83–107; Aquinas and, 85, 87, 98, 152; Arnauld's approach to, 211–12; Augustine and, 85, 86–87; Bayle on, 90; best of possible worlds, see best of all possible worlds; Book of Job, 83–84, 212; conceptual and empirical ingredients of, 84; "consider the whole" approach, 87–89, 91, 100–101, 152–53, 244; continuing struggle with, 243–44; grace and, 86; Greek philosophers and, 85; legacy of seventeenth-century philosophers, 243–44; Leibniz-Arnauld correspondence and, 178–82; Leibniz's theodicy, see best of all possible worlds (Leibniz's theodicy); Malebranche on, see Malebranche's theodicy; Manicheanism and, 87

F

faith, Bayle on, 81, 90, 91

Fall, the, 124; Jansenists' beliefs, 55

Ferrand, Louis, 17, 71, 72, 73

Fontaine, Nicolas, 59, 61, 65

Foucher, Simon, 36, 49, 50, 79, 108, 168–69

France: European warfare and, 4, 5;

Fronde period, 62; invasion of Dutch Republic, 6–7, 13, 20

freedom, divine: Arnauld on, 161–62, 163, 167, 174, 177, 179, 180–81; Bayle on, 167; Descartes on, 195–96, 235–36; Leibniz on, 135–36, 140, 177, 180, 235; Malebranche on, 138, 161, 167, 180; Spinoza on, 231, 236

freedom of the will (human), 74, 86; Arnauld on, 65–67; Spinoza on, 222

fundamentalism, religious moral, 244–45

G

Galileo, 9, 29, 30

Gallois, Jean, 226

Gassendi, Pierre, 30

George I, King of England, 249

German states, European warfare and, 4–5, 13

God: absolute power or will of, 187; anthropomorphization of nature of, see anthropomorphization of nature of God; creation, relationship to, 47, 222, 233; divine voluntarism, see divine voluntarism; doctrine of equivocity, 207; doctrine of univocity, 204–205, 206–207; eternal truths, see eternal truths; Euthyphro Problem, see Euthyphro Problem; good works and, 55, 56, 93; freedom of, see freedom, divine; inscrutability of judgments of, 158–60, 244; as Nature, see Spinoza, Baruch de, God as Nature; omnipotence, see omnipotence of God; as omniscient, 84; ordained power of, 187; as rational being, see rationality of God; as ubiquitous, 45; volitions in, see Malebranche's theodicy: general volitions; Malebranche's theodicy: particular volitions

grace, divine, 55–57, 86, 93; Arnauld's
    and Jansenist beliefs, 55–57, 62, 65,
    113–14, 150–52, 156–58, 163–64;
    Catholic Church and, 11, 55–57, 86;
    efficacious, 57, 150, 151; Lutheran
    beliefs, 11; Malebranche on, 113–14,
    124–27, 150, 151–52, 156–57; Pela-
    gianism and, 56, 127, 150; Protestant
    view of, 55–56, 86
Graevius, Johann Georg, 223
gravity: Aristotelian explanation of, 28;
    Cartesian explanation of, 31
Great Perpetuity of Faith on the Eucharist
    (Arnauld), 71
Guelphe, Léonard, 142, 145
Guericke, Otto de, 17
Guide to the Perplexed (Maimonides), 88

H

Harlay, François de, 25
Histoire critique de la république des lettres,
    L', 83, 90
Histoire des ouvages des sçavans, L', 82
Historical and Critical Dictionary (Bayle),
    80–82, 89–90, 167
Hobbes, Thomas, 70, 77
Holy Roman Empire, 4–5; dissolution
    of, 5; religious factions in, 4–5
Hooke, Robert, 19
Huet, Pierre-Daniel, 17, 35–36, 108
Huguenots, French, 4; Arnauld family
    and, 53–54; St. Bartholomew's Day
    massacre, 53
Hume, David, 243
Huygens, Christiaan, 9, 18

I

immortality of the soul, 10, 12, 69;
    Spinoza on, 222

Incarnation, 116
indiscernibles, Leibniz's law of identity
    of, 134–35
Innocent X, Pope, 63

J

Jansen, Cornelius, 54–55, 56–57;
    Augustinus, 54, 60, 63, 64, 65
Jansenists, 34, 54–65; Arnauld's
    defense of Cartesianism and, 69;
    belief in essential corruption of
    human nature after the Fall, 55;
    French Church's relationship
    with, 59–65, 72; grace and salvation,
    beliefs about, 55–57; Peace of the
    Church, 65; the sacraments and,
    55, 57
Jerome, St., 188
Jesuits, 55, 110; Arnauld family and,
    53, 59; expulsion from France,
    53; On Frequent Communion
    and, 61, 62; Jansenists and, 54,
    57
Job, Book of, 83–84, 212
Johann Casmir, King of Poland, 8
Johann Friedrich, duke of Hanover, see
    von Braunschweig-Lüneburg, Johann
    Friedrich, duke of Hanover
Johann Philipp, Elector of Mainz, see
    von Schönborn, Johann Philipp, the
    Elector of Mainz
Journal des sçavans, 78–79, 165
Jurieu, Pierre, 80

K

Kant, Immanuel, 245
Kantian ethics, 245
Kepler, Johannes, 29
King, William, 91

L

L'Allemant, Father, 26
Latin Mass, 11
law of the identity of indiscernibles,
    Leibniz's, 134–35
laws: of grace, 125–27, 151, 155–56; of
    nature, 103–106, 115–24, 129–30
Le Bouvier de Fontenelle, Bernard,
    138
Le Brun, Charles, 15
Leeuwenhoek, Antonij van, 218
Leibniz, Catharina Schmuck (mother), 7
Leibniz, Friedrich (father), 7
Leibniz, Gottfried Wilhelm, x, xi, 7–22,
    168–82, 241–42; Arnauld-
    Malebranche debate and, 168–69;
    -Bayle dialogue, 90–92, 102; best of
    all possible worlds, see best of all pos-
    sible worlds (Leibniz's theodicy); birth
    of, 7; calculus, invention of, 18, 19,
    249; Cartesianism and, 36–42, 109–
    10; Catholic Demonstrations, 12; the
    continuum, problem of, 9–10, 18;
    "Conversations of Philarète and
    Ariste," 110–11; death of, 250–51;
    diplomatic mission to Paris and
    Egyptian plan, 3–4, 7, 13–14, 16, 20,
    52, 71; Discourse on Metaphysics, see
    Discourse on Metaphysics (Leibniz); on
    divine freedom, 135–36, 140, 177,
    180, 235; ecumenical mission of, 10–
    12, 13, 71–72, 74, 131, 169, 249; ed-
    ucation of, 7–8, 17; on eternal truths,
    198–200; final years of, 248–50; law
    of the identity of indiscernibles, 134–
    35; "Meditations on Knowledge,
    Truth and Ideas," 168; A Metaphysical
    Disputation on the Principle of Individua-
    tion (dissertation), 7; "monadology,"
    22, 42, 176–77; on moral necessity,
    136, 180, 181, 234, 235; The Most

Christian Man, 10; New Essays on Hu-
    man Understanding, 92; New Physical
    Hypothesis, 9; "New System of the
    Nature and Communication of Sub-
    stances, as well as the Union Between
    the Soul and the Body," 79–80; "A
    Note on Advanced Optics," 70, 223;
    on occasionalism, 48, 79, 82, 111,
    178; Paris period, 13–22, 33–36, 72–
    77, 108, 217; "permissive will," 102;
    "preestablished harmony," 22, 41, 79–
    80, 81–82, 90–91, 110, 178, 179,
    197; religious beliefs, 11, 93; "Reply
    to the Thoughts on the System of
    Preestablished Harmony Contained in
    the Second Edition of M. Bayle's
    Critical Dictionary, Article 'Rorar-
    ius,'" 90–91; Spinoza and, 218, 223–
    27, 232–36; spontaneity of sub-
    stances, 41, 79–80, 81–82, 90–91,
    170; start of relationship with Male-
    branche, 49–51; "The Confession of
    a Philosopher," 75, 139, 171, 178;
    theodicy, see best of all possible worlds
    (Leibniz's theodicy); Theodicy, see
    Essays on Theodicy, on the Goodness of
    God, the Freedom of Man and the Origin
    of Evil (Theodicy); theory of truth,
    170; "universal symbolism," 9, 74
Leibniz-Arnauld correspondence, 75,
    108, 168–82, 208–10, 239; letter of
    introduction to Arnauld of Novem-
    ber 1671, 69–72, 223
Leibniz-Malebranche correspondence,
    108–10, 111–12, 128–30, 133
Le Maistre de Sacy, Isaac Louis, 65
Le Vassor, Michel, 142–43
Liancourt, Duc de, 35
Locke, John, 77, 92; Arnauld-
    Malebranche debate and, 166
logic, laws of, 189–90, 192–93, 195,
    203
Longueville, Duchesse de, 64

Louis IX, King of France, 20; Descartes and, 26–27

Louis XIII, King of France, 62

Louis XIV, King of France, 62, 65, 128; Leibniz's diplomatic mission, 3–4, 7, 13–14, 20; Leibniz's satire on, 10; war with Dutch Republic in 1672, 6–7, 13, 20

Louvre, 14

Low Countries (Belgium, Luxembourg, Netherlands): Hapsburgs and, 5–6, 141; Louis XIV and, 6–7

Lutherans, 11, 93; Leibniz's ecumenical efforts and, 11; religious wars and, 5

M

magnetism, Aristotelian explanation of, 28

Maimonides, 85, 87–88; *Guide to the Perplexed*, 88

Malade imaginaire, Le, 29

Malebranche, Catherine de Lauzon, 42

Malebranche, Nicolas, x, xi, 108–109, 241–42; -Arnauld debate, 142–67, 168–69, 182, 239, 240, 246–47; -Arnauld friendship, 75–76, 147, 169; birth of, 42; Cartesianism and, 42, 43, 44, 108, 111, 148, 237; *Christian Conversations*, 109, 111, 113, 136, 169; death of, 248; *Dialogue Between a Christian Philosopher and a Chinese Philosopher*, 249; *Dialogues on Death*, 248; *Dialogues on Metaphysics and Religion*, 110–11, 114–15, 123, 201–202; education of, 42; health of, 247–48; -Leibniz correspondence, *see* Leibniz-Malebranche correspondence; "occasionalism," 45–48, 49, 79, 81, 82, 110, 111, 117, 178, 197, 236–37; personality of, 111, 148, 241; physics,

work on, 48; *Response by the Author of the Search After Truth to the Book of Monsieur Arnauld*, 164–65; *Response to a Dissertation by Monsieur Arnauld*, 165; *The Search After Truth, see Search After Truth, The* (Malebranche); Spinozism, accused of, 236–38; start of relationship with Leibniz, 49–51; theodicy of, *see* Malebranche's theodicy; *Treatise on Nature and Grace, see Treatise on Nature and Grace* (Malebranche); Vision in God, 44, 45, 111, 149, 158, 166, 203–204, 236

Malebranche, Nicolas, Sr., 42

Malebranche's theodicy, 113–28; Arnauld-Malebranche debate and, 152–58, 239; "disorder" in, 122, 123, 125; divine freedom, 138, 161, 167, 180; general volitions, 120, 122, 125, 143, 153, 154, 155, 180, 239; God as rational being, xi, 133, 136–39, 160, 182, 198, 204, 213, 214, 215; grace in, 124–27, 150, 151–52, 156–57; the Incarnation as reason for creation, 116; justice in, 118, 119; key to, 115; maximum simplicity of laws governing the universe and, 116–19, 121–22, 123–24, 125–26, 131, 132–33, 157–58, 180, 202; Order in, 137–38, 202; particular volitions, 120–21, 122–23, 124, 125, 143, 153, 154, 156, 166, 167, 239; simple volitions, 126–27, 181

Manicheanism, 87, 89–90

mathematical principles, eternal truths and, 188, 189, 191–92, 200–201, 202, 203

matter, 178; in Aristotelian philosophy, 27–28; Leibniz-Malebranche disagreement over nature of, 50

Mazarin, Cardinal, 62

mechanistic model, *see* Cartesianism

Meditations on First Philosophy

(Descartes), 27, 33, 44, 190, 207;
  Arnauld's comments on, 67–68
"Meditations on Knowledge, Truth
  and Ideas" (Leibniz), 168
*Memoirs to Serve as the History of Port-
  Royal* (Fontaine), 59
Mersenne, Marin, 33, 67, 191, 194,
  195, 196, 207
*Metaphysical Disputation on the Principle
  of Individuation, A* (Leibniz disserta-
  tion), 7
Metternich, Lothar Friedrich von, 21
Milton, John, 214
miracles, 187; for Leibniz, 82, 110; for
  Malebranche, 45, 110, 120, 122–23,
  155, 156, 166; Spinoza on, 219, 222
Molanus, Gerhard Wolter, 235
Molière, 15, 28–29
Molina, Luis de, 55
moral fundamentalism, religious, 244–45
moral rationalism, 245–46
More, Henry, 215
Most Christian Man, The (Leibniz), 10

N

necessitarianism: Leibniz and, 135–36,
  232–36, 239, 240; Malebranche and,
  238; Spinoza's, 231–32, 233, 234,
  238
Netherlands, European warfare and, 4,
  5, 6–7, 14
New Essays on Human Understanding
  (Leibniz), 92
New Physical Hypothesis (Leibniz), 9, 49
"New System of the Nature and Com-
  munication of Substances, as well as
  the Union Between the Soul and the
  Body" (Leibniz), 79–80
Newton, Isaac, 29, 77, 217; Arnauld-
  Malebranche debate and, 166; calcu-
  lus, invention of, 19, 249; *Opticks*, 166

Nicole, Pierre, 73, 165, 246
Nixon, Richard, 213
noncontradiction, principle of, 84, 189,
  193, 203
"Note on Advanced Optics, A" (Leibniz), 70, 223
Nôtre Dame, Cathedral of, 23, 24, 42
Nouvelles de la république des lettres, 80,
  81, 112, 165, 166, 169

O

"occasionalism," Malebranche's, 45–48,
  49, 79, 81, 82, 110, 111, 117, 178,
  197, 236–37
Ockham, William of, 182–83, 189
Oldenburg, Henry, 19, 38, 49, 217
omnipotence of God, 84; Aquinas on,
  186–87, 189; causation and, 46–47;
  Descartes's views on, 190–96; eternal
  truths and, *see* eternal truths; Euthyphro Problem, *see* Euthyphro Problem; problem of evil and, *see* evil,
  problem of (theodicy)
On Divine Omnipotence (Damian), 189
On Frequent Communion (Arnauld),
  61–62
On True and False Ideas (Arnauld), 149,
  164, 169
Opticks (Newton), 166
Oratorians, 34, 42–43; Malebranche as,
  see Malebranche, Nicolas
ordained power of God, 187
original sin, 93

P

Paris, Archbishop of, 60
Paris, France: as intellectual capital of
  Europe, 12–13, 15–16; Leibniz in,
  13–22, 33–36, 72–77, 108, 217;

Paris, France (*cont.*)
Louis XIV's and Colbert's remaking
of, 14–16; philosophy's development
in, 23–51
Paris Opera House, 15
Pascal, Blaise, 18, 57, 64
Peace of Westphalia of 1648, 5, 6
Pelagianism, 56, 127, 150
Pensées (Augustine), 159
Perrault, Claude, 17
*Philosophical and Theological Reflections on
the New System of Nature and Grace*
(Arnauld), 150–51, 154, 158–59,
160, 164, 166–67, 168, 179, 239–40
"Philosophical Conclusions" (Arnauld),
206
Plato, 184–85, 243
Port-Royal de Paris, 34, 54, 58, 59, 62,
64–65, 69; *solitaires* of, 59, 60, 64
Port-Royal des Champs, 54, 60
Port-Royal des Granges, 54
"Port-Royal Logic," 74
predestination, grace and, 55–56, 86,
113, 114
"preestablished harmony," 22, 41, 79–
80, 81–82, 90–91, 110, 178, 179,
197
Principles of Philosophy (Descartes), 27
Protestant Reformation, 3, 11, 83, 243;
European wars and, 4
Provincial Letters (Pascal), 57

Q

Quesnel, Pasquier, 144, 247

R

Racine, 15
rationality of God, 133–40, 158,
160, 181, 240, 241; inscrutability of

God's judgments, 158–60, 244;
legacy for moral rationalists, 245–46;
Leibniz's theodicy, xi, 133–36, 139–
40, 181, 182, 198, 204, 213, 214,
215, 235; Malebranche's theodicy,
xi, 133, 136–39, 160, 182, 198,
204, 213, 214, 215; Spinoza on,
231
reason, human: Bayle on limits of, 81,
90, 91; Leibniz's theodicy and, 91,
92–93, 94
Régis, Pierre Sylvain, 34
Rémond, Nicolas, 250
"Reply to the Thoughts on the System
of Preestablished Harmony Contained
in the Second Edition of M. Bayle's
Critical Dictionary, Article 'Rorarius' " (Leibniz), 90–91
*Response by the Author of the Search After
Truth to the Book of Monsieur Arnauld*
(Malebranche), 164–65
*Response to a Dissertation by Monsieur Ar-
nauld* (Malebranche), 165
Response to a Provincial's Questions
(Bayle), 91–92
resurrection of the body, 10
Richelieu, Cardinal, 15, 59, 60
Roberval, Gilles Personne de, 34–35
Roemer, Olaus, 17
Rohault, Jacques, 34, 36
Roman Catholic Church: Cartesianism
as challenge to, 27, 32–33, 34; Coun-
cil of Trent, 11, 12, 72; *Cum occasione*
encyclical, 63, 64; French Church and
the Vatican, 63, 64, 65; grace and
personal salvation, 11, 55–57, 86;
Leibniz's ecumenical efforts, 10–12,
13, 71–72, 74, 131, 169, 249; List of
Prohibited Books, 33, 69, 167–68,
247; religious wars and, 4–6; transubstantiation, 12, 32
Royal Society, London, 9, 19, 49,
249

S

Sablé, Marquis de, 34
sacraments: Arnauld on communion, 61; Jansenists' beliefs, 55, 57
Saint-Cyran, abbot of (Jean du Vergier de Hauranne), 54–55, 57, 58, 60
salvation, doctrine of: Council of Trent and, 11; good works and, 55, 56, 93; grace and, see grace, divine; Jansenists' beliefs, 55, 113–14
Satan, problem of evil and, 87
Schuller, Georg Hermann, 224–25
Scientific Revolution, 29–30, 243; hypotheses, verification of, 29–30
Search After Truth, The (Malebranche), 43–49, 113, 136; Arnauld's reaction to, 142; Foucher's critique of, 49, 50
Second Anglo-Dutch War of 1665, 6
Second Apology for Jansenius (Arnauld), 168
"Several Reasons for Preventing the Censure or Condemnation of Descartes's Philosophy" (Arnauld), 69
sin and evil, problem of, see evil, problem of (theodicy)
Sophie Charlotte, Queen of Prussia, 90
Sorbonne, 42, 59, 63, 64, 204, 205, 206
soul, nature of the, 18; Cartesianism and, 32; immortality of, see immortality of the soul
Spain, 141; European warfare and, 4, 5–6
Spinoza, Baruch de, 35, 70, 218–40; Arnauld and, 238–40; Cartesianism and, 218–19; childhood of, 219–20; death of, 218, 226; Ethics, see Ethics (Spinoza); God as Nature, 222, 226, 230–31, 236, 241; on immortality of the soul, 222; Leibniz and, 218, 223–27, 232–36; Malebranche accused of Spinozism, 236–38; necessitarianism

of, 231–32, 233, 234, 238; on origins of the Bible, 70, 219; ostracism from Sephardic community of Amsterdam, 220–21; sectarian religion, attack on, 219, 222, 228–29, 230; Theological-Political Treatise, see Theological-Political Treatise (Spinoza)
Spinoza, Gabriel, 220
spontaneity of substances, Leibniz's, 41, 79–80, 81–82, 90–91, 170
Sweden, European warfare and, 4, 5

T

Terence, 9
theodicy, see evil, problem of (theodicy)
Theodicy (Leibniz), see Essays on Theodicy, on the Goodness of God, the Freedom of Man and the Origin of Evil (Theodicy) (Leibniz)
Theological-Political Treatise (Spinoza), 70, 219, 223–24; Arnauld's criticism of, 238–39; condemnation of, 219, 223; on origins of the Bible, 70, 219; publication of, 219
Thirty Years War, 4
Thomasius, Jacob, 37, 223
transubstantiation, 70, 71; Cartesianism and, 32–33, 34, 69; Catholic dogma, 12, 32; Leibniz on, 12
Treatise of Man (Descartes), 43, 136
Treatise on Nature and Grace (Malebranche), 81, 112–14, 116–28, 132; see also Malebranche's theodicy; Arnauld-Malebranche debate and, 142–47, 150–58; Bayle's review of, 166; Bossuet's criticism of, 127–28; Leibniz's views and, 128–33; on Vatican's List of Prohibited Books, 167
Treaty of Münster, 6
Tschirnhaus, Ehrenfried Walther von, 224, 225, 233, 236

U

University of Altdorf, 8
University of Jena, 7
University of Leipzig, 7–8
University of Nuremburg, 8
University of Paris, 24, 34
univocity, doctrine of, 204–205, 206–207

V

van Blijenburgh, Willem, 229
van den Enden, Frans, 35
van Neercassel, Johann, 238
Vatican, see Roman Catholic Church
Vaugelade, 111
Versailles, 14, 15
Vision in God: Arnauld's criticism of, 149–50, 158; Malebranche's doctrine, 44, 45, 111, 149, 158, 166, 203–204, 236

Voltaire: Candide, 96–98; deism of, 243
voluntarism, divine, see divine voluntarism
von Braunschweig-Lüneburg, Johann Friedrich, duke of Hanover, 10–11, 21–22, 71, 73, 108
von der Pfalz, Prince Ruprecht, 218
von Greiffencranz, Joachim Nicolai, 110
von Hessen-Rheinfels, Count Ernst, 11, 73, 168, 169–70, 172, 175, 196, 249
von Schönborn, Johann Philipp, the Elector of Mainz, 7, 8, 10, 13, 21
von Tschirnhaus, Walther von, 168–69

W

Wallon de Beaupuis, Charles, 204, 205, 206, 207
Wedderkopf, Magnus, 139, 232
will: antecedent, 105–106, 107, 181; consequent, 106–107, 181